AGINCOURT

AGINCOURT

HENRY V, THE MAN-AT-ARMS & THE ARCHER

W. B. BARTLETT

AMBERLEY

Dedicated to the memory of Private Joseph Thomas Bartlett, 14782, of the 1st Battalion Dorsetshire Regiment, who lost his life on 20 August 1915, a day's march from the battlefield of Agincourt

First published 2015

Amberley Publishing
The Hill, Stroud
Gloucestershire, GL5 4EP

www.amberley-books.com

Copyright © W. B. Bartlett, 2015

The right of W. B. Bartlett to be identified as the Author of this work has been asserted in accordance with the Copyrights, Designs and Patents Act 1988.

ISBN 978 1 4456 3949 9 (hardback)
ISBN 978 1 4456 3960 4 (ebook)

British Library Cataloguing in Publication Data. A catalogue record for this book is available from the British Library.

Typesetting and Origination by Amberley Publishing
Map redrawing by Thomas Bohm, User Design Illustration
Printed in the UK.

CONTENTS

MAPS

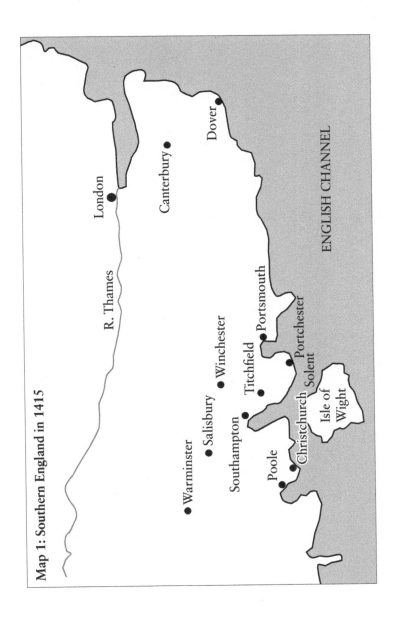

Map 1: Southern England in 1415

Warminster
Salisbury
Winchester
Southampton
Titchfield
Portsmouth
Portchester
Poole
Christchurch
Solent
Isle of Wight
Canterbury
Dover
London
R. Thames
ENGLISH CHANNEL

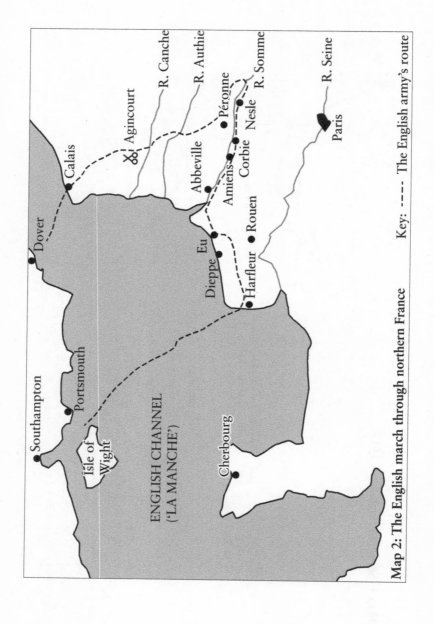

Map 2: The English march through northern France   Key: - - - - The English army's route

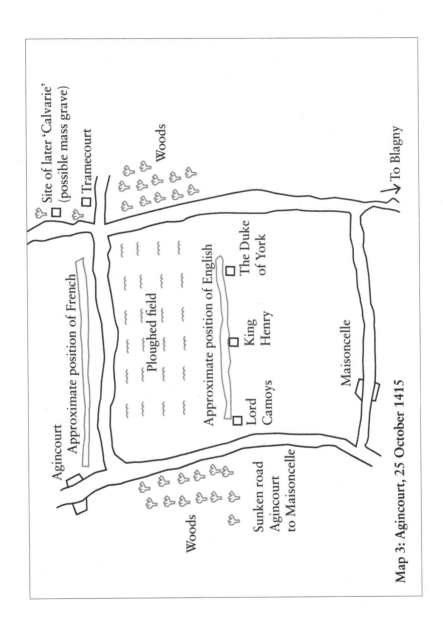

Site of later 'Calvarie'
(possible mass grave)

Tramecourt

Woods

Agincourt
Approximate position of French

Ploughed field

Approximate position of English

King
Henry

The Duke
of York

Lord
Camoys

Maisoncelle

To Blagny

Woods

Sunken road
Agincourt
to Maisoncelle

Map 3: Agincourt, 25 October 1415

INTRODUCTION

What follows is not so much a history as an interpretation. There are a number of chroniclers who wrote about the Battle of Agincourt both at the time and in the years, decades and centuries that followed. It might be thought that this makes us more certain of our facts, but this is not so. The chroniclers wrote with specific audiences in mind, to make a point either for or against a certain cause, and in the process they were not above making up a fact or two; such at least we can assume from our general knowledge of human nature, not to mention the contradictions that appear in the various accounts.

It is impossible to write the definitive story of the Battle of Agincourt; not only has the story become varnished with layer after layer of myth, but the original sources often contradict each other in key details. As a result, anyone who writes of Agincourt is forced to paint their own personal picture of events. Not everyone will agree with the end result, but this is what makes the study of history interesting.

But there is one thing that nearly all the chroniclers, both English and French, agree about, and that is the remarkable nature of Henry V's triumph. If there is a consistency to be found among most of the chroniclers it is in the conclusion that the English were significantly outnumbered by their French foe and that their victory represented a triumph over great adversity. This is how the battle has been remembered, partly of course thanks to a truly remarkable Englishman by the name of William Shakespeare.

Much has been done in recent years to interpret the battle properly and some outstanding historical research, in particular by Professor Anne Curry of the University of Southampton, has painstakingly recreated precious information such as the Muster Rolls of all those who embarked for France from England in August 1415. This has enabled others to understand much more about the campaign than would ever have been the case in the past, and all those who wish to understand the Battle of Agincourt are forever in the debt of such experts for their insight and talent as well as their hard work.

Walking the ground in southern England and north-western France has been a rewarding exercise in itself, and many an interesting site remains from those days. The site of the battlefield still remains atmospheric (if one ignores the painted cardboard figures of archers and knights now present in the hedges that make a slightly surreal impression on modern visitors), informative up to a point and, on a soggy October day, truly muddy.

It is hard, though, to walk the ground in the area of Agincourt, a peaceful farming landscape through which most English visitors rush from the Channel Tunnel at Calais to points further south in France, without being reminded of another, much bloodier battle, or more accurately series of battles, which took place on a world stage almost exactly 500 years later nearby. The example of the later sacrifice of ordinary men and women in the First World War serves as a salutary reminder that war is very rarely glorious, whatever the Shakespeares of this world would have us believe.

Most English families were affected by that later conflict, and mine most certainly was. It was in part as a result of my research for this book that I knelt for the first time by the grave of my great-grandfather Joseph Thomas Bartlett, buried in Dartmoor Cemetery just outside Albert, past which Henry V and his army marched on their way to the field of Agincourt. Private Bartlett lost his life on 20 August 1915, exactly 500 years after Henry V was laying siege to Harfleur. He died during a supposedly 'quiet' time on the front, nearly a year before the famous Battle of the Somme began.

It was a humbling and emotional experience to remember the life of a twenty-nine-year-old from a working-class background who left behind him a widow and several young children, who would later face their own heroic struggle to survive during the terrible years of the Great Depression of the 1930s in particular, a struggle that helped create some of my own family's legends. Their ultimate victory too was, in its own way, a triumph against the odds. I could only find one simple phrase to enter in the visitor's book at the cemetery – 'thank you'.

Life goes full circle. We will see in what follows that life could be as hard for a 'war hero' in 1415 as it was in 1915, particularly in the remarkable story of Thomas Hostell. Agincourt told different tales for different people. For the king, Henry V, it was the day that shaped his legacy in history. For men-at-arms, such as Edward, Duke of York, it would also be a remarkable occasion. And for English archers such as Thomas Pokkeswell it would be a day that made legends of a class known simply as 'the English yeoman', to whom the triumph of Agincourt more than any others belongs.

I

PROLOGUE

I am afeard there are few die well that die in a battle.
William Shakespeare, *Henry V*, Act 4, Scene 1

Henry V, by the Grace of God King of England, Ireland and France. So at least Henry would have it, although there were some even in England who would dispute his right to be king of anywhere at all. But as he looked across the muddy, ordinary field in front of him, even the undemonstrative Henry would have allowed himself to feel a degree of self-satisfaction. For he had just struck a blow (or more to the point his army had) that would surely prove, in this age when might equated to right and the judgement of battle was equivalent to the judgement of God, that there was now no doubting his claim to rule on anyone's part.

Yet for many round about him there was little to celebrate, for there, thrown up in heaps across the mud-choked ground, were pile after pile of the dead (mainly French but not exclusively so). There they lay; in the main still, bloodied, lifeless, a thick hedge of corpses (though wounded and dying there still were in plenty).

As they had breathed out their last, their bodies pierced by arrows or their heads smashed in with poleaxes, they formed as effective a barrier against further French attacks as any wall made of stone would have done. The thousands of French soldiers behind them, whether or not they wished to make their way past them into the killing zone, were unable to do so. The English were protected from further French attacks by the cadavers of those they had already slain.

In the minutes and hours before, waves of tightly packed French warriors had sought to charge across the narrow wedge of land, that unexceptional field on either side of which stood woodland that had channelled them into a squeezed and overcrowded space which quickly became filled with desperate men and frantic, panicking horses, funnelling them into a trap from which there was no escape. Those ensnared in the killing zone were unable to move back because of those behind pushing forward, and unable to move forward because of that unbreakable phalanx of Englishmen (and of course Welshmen too) that stood defiantly before them, immovable behind their barrier of sharpened wooden stakes. Unable to move in either direction, all that remained for those Frenchmen in the killing zone to do was stay where they were and die.

If this was a day of exultation for the English, it was in contrast one of despair for their adversaries. France prided herself on being the representation of all that was chivalric in the world. Battles were fought according to a code, with rules to be followed and etiquette to be respected. Even the French, of course, knew that away from the field of battle the rules were rather different if indeed they existed at all. Civilians, even French civilians, were there to be exploited, to have their possessions seized for the greater good with no recompense for the peasants and defenceless villagers and townsfolk from whom they were taken, to be robbed of all their valuables, to stand obligingly by while their women were violated by French soldiers as much as English ones, and in the current campaign much more so.

But what happened away from the field did not matter. In the paradoxical mores of the time, a different standard of behaviour was expected when two armies came to blows. Rules were there to be followed, important ones especially if one happened to be a member of a high social class. Of course, the rules did not apply to the common folk who made up the bulk of the armies. Everyone knew that the most likely outcome for a commoner unable to flee the battle and subsequently captured was a quick flash of the knife across the windpipe and an unremarked (and hopefully rapid) death, unmourned and not noticed by anyone save the few unimportant family and friends he had.

It was different for the rich, the nobles and the knightly class. They had a value, literally. Taken in battle they could expect to live – to be held for ransom, quite possibly at exorbitant cost, but alive nevertheless. Such were the rules. But in many cases on that day at Agincourt the rules had not been followed, something that had come to the French as the greatest of shocks, although earlier defeats against the pragmatic English at Crécy and Poitiers had set a clear precedent, not to mention subsequent decades of raiding across France by brutal men driven on by an all-consuming lust for blood and plunder. Here on the nondescript field of Agincourt, the cream of French society lay dead, a huge loss for an already fragmented kingdom.

For the victors the emotions were completely the opposite. They had written themselves into history. For the rest of their lives, the feast day of St Crispin and St Crispinian would be remembered (though it was also the feast day of St John of Beverley, a personal favourite of the English king and far more important to him at the time), both in their hearts and also by their fellows in England who would glory in the fantastic triumph.

They would tell tales of victory against impossible odds, of a huge host that outnumbered them enormously being overcome in a triumph so stunning that it was only possible through the beneficence of God Himself. They would regale their friends and their families with stories of brave and chivalric deeds, of a battle fiercely but honourably fought. It is likely that the chests of the veterans of Agincourt, like those of soldiers in many other times, would swell with pride when mention of the great victory was made and they were able to say, 'I was there'; or as one particular writer so much more eloquently put it, that 'gentlemen in England now abed shall think themselves accursed they were not here'.

There were men from many different social classes who had fought at Henry's side and witnessed the events of that incredible day up close. There were, naturally enough, those from the highest echelons of society, men-at-arms such as Edward of Langley, Duke of York, one of the greatest men in England and himself a relative of the king through the complicated dynastic intertwining that characterised the family tree of the royal family at this time and indeed would lead to so much trouble and chaos in England. Here was a man with something to prove, and he had done so in unmistakable fashion. This would be a seminal day in his life, for it would be his last.

For others, the outcome would be rather different. John Holland, soon to be the Earl of Huntingdon, was a young man at the time, and he had already done Henry good service in the campaign even before the battle. It had proved to be a great opportunity to demonstrate his good qualities to the king, who was himself yet young in the job and was hoping to find men whom he could trust, who could grow with him throughout his reign. For Holland, the campaign as a whole was a seminal moment too but in a rather different way, for at the end of it he would be a man whose career was definitely on the up. He too would become a great man in England, in the process restoring family fortunes that had plummeted in recent decades.

Both these men were in the highest ranks of English society, the nobility. In a time before parliamentary democracy as we would understand it, these individuals were in the king's inner circle and in a position to influence his policy, though as an autocratic monarch to a significant (though not complete) extent he was still in many ways the ultimate decision maker. Below them in the social pyramid in this very class-conscious society were humbler men-at-arms with importance in their own locality but of limited significance beyond it.

But they had an important part to play in this victory too. The army included many minor men of this station, who individually brought relatively small numbers of soldiers to the campaign when compared to the large numbers in the retinues of the great lords but, when the numbers of their men were added together, proved fundamental to the composition of the victorious English army. By 1415, rather than providing feudal service as they had done in the past, such men were indentured, effectively hired for pay, and this applied not just to the great and the good but a number of less significant men-at-arms too. This undoubtedly added to the potential quality of the forces raised, as instead of a feudal host which was often largely untrained, men could now be picked to a greater extent based on merit and their skills than had been the case in former times.

The greatest of them would have been knighted. Below the knights in the pecking order were the esquires, 'apprentice knights' they could be called, who also fought hard in the battle. They were seeking to prove their worth and in the process to set out on adventures whereby their chances in life could be improved. A battle, more than any other event, gave them the opportunity to do so, not only by fighting bravely in defence of their lord and ensuring that they were at his beck and call during the fight but also in more immediately lucrative ways too. Many of them hoped to be in a position to capture some great lord of the enemy and hold him for ransom, though this would rarely be the case in practice. However, as far as one man, an esquire named William Wolf, was concerned, today was the day that he hit the jackpot.

At the bottom of the social pyramid were the faceless masses, the archers, the poor bloody infantry; in this age, as in too many others, the expendables. Yet today had been their day; it was they who had above all others won the battle. Agincourt was a clash between two styles of warfare. The French had relied on their dismounted men-at-arms to a significant extent, among whom were their great nobles, their chivalric elite. Their crossbowmen and other bowmen were there in fewer numbers than the English archers and their already potentially inferior influence was even more diminished because they were placed at the rear.

On the other hand, the English relied heavily on their archers, not just for their undoubted archery skills but also for their efficacy as auxiliary infantry. Arrows, like bullets in more recent times, can run out, especially if the enemy is not obliging by shooting them back at you. An archer therefore had to be adaptable, able to use his knife or his falchion (a cleaver-like sword) or capable of smashing an axe or even a mallet into the skull of his enemy. The archers came from the lower (though not the bottom) ranks of society, the opposite of the great knights they were facing. Not for the first nor the last time in warfare during the late medieval period, it was the lower ranks, the *hoi polloi* of society, who came out on top.

As the autumnal daylight started to retreat and the shadows of twilight heralded the coming of night, Henry V, a devout and pious man, gave thanks to God for the victory. He had an Old Testament view of such matters; if the Lord awarded success in battle in such a spectacular fashion as He had done today, it meant that Henry's cause was undoubtedly just. It would be rank arrogance, against the will of the Almighty Himself, if the king of France and his lords were to ignore the decisive outcome of the battle and continue to refuse to accede to Henry's just demands.

If Henry had realised then that this was not the end of the battle for France, and was rather merely the end of the beginning, perhaps he would have wondered if the huge effort had been worth it, though his subsequent perseverance suggests otherwise. Perhaps if he had been able to foresee that, despite herculean exertions, the throne of France would never be his, then he might have pondered even more.

Yet such thoughts might have been banished by another, quite different, consideration; the Battle of Agincourt had secured Henry's position both in his country and in history in a process that would raise him to the pantheon of great English kings, capable of inspiring future generations of Englishmen right down into modern times. In many ways the results of the battle were not decisive, far from it. Yet Agincourt deserves its place as one of the greatest set-piece battles of the medieval era as it was, first, last and foremost, pivotal to the making of the legend of Henry V, one of England's most renowned warrior-kings.

2

ENGLAND AND FRANCE: THE ROAD TO AGINCOURT (TO JULY 1415)

Victory does not depend on a multitude of people but ... on the power of God.

Letter by Henry, Prince of Wales (later Henry V),
after a victory on campaign

Our understanding of history is shaped far more by perception which mutates into legend than it is by fact. What really happened in the past is very often obscured by what is believed to have happened, or in an idealised way what should have happened. The Battle of Agincourt is a prime example of this. Chroniclers including those who were actually present at the battle wrote with an audience in mind and in so doing helped to shape our perceptions; for English writers this audience included especially the king, Henry V, and his supporters and successors. So although we have a number of surviving chronicles as potential sources of information we should not assume that they are unbiased and a hard and fast indicator of the truth.

One such chronicle, the *Gesta Henrici Quinti* (*The Deeds of Henry the Fifth*), was written by a man, now sadly unidentifiable but probably a priest (according to some he is John Stevens, a canon of Exeter Cathedral), who said he was present at the great battle. It is his detailed account of the Agincourt campaign that has helped shape perceptions more than any other. He wrote within a year of the battle that he described, and within a few years other English writers, such as the monk Thomas of Walsingham of St Albans Abbey, were almost certainly accessing his version of events for their own works (while in some respects adding further details of their own). So legends, quickly put in place after the battle, started to embed themselves permanently in the collective English consciousness. Once there, they would be very hard to shift.

The Hundred Years War, which broke out anew with the Agincourt campaign, was presented by the English chroniclers of the time as a divinely inspired just cause. So it seems it was especially presented by Henry V himself, and given his character he may well have believed this to be true. But a more cynical interpretation would see this extended and bloody conflict as little more than a dynastic squabble attended by horrific violence and motivated mainly by the rather more mundane inspiration of a land- and power-grab.

When Henry V led his invasion force to France, he had only been king of England for two years. The war that he was involved in, though, had been going on for seven decades, a long-running dynastic dispute about who exactly was the rightful King of France, if one that was frequently interrupted by periods of inaction. There had been several notable English triumphs in this conflict during the fourteenth century, at Crécy and Poitiers as well as the sea fight at Sluys and the now less remembered triumph of the Black Prince at Nájera in northern Spain in 1367.

For a time, the war had appeared to come to a halt with the Treaty of Brétigny in 1360 (which became known as 'the Great Peace'). Under its terms English-held lands in France, which had been almost entirely lost during the disastrous reign of King John a century and a half earlier, would be significantly restored (though some regions previously held by English kings, particularly Normandy, were excluded from the agreement).

However, the terms of the treaty were not subsequently honoured and England and France were therefore practically still at war. In practice, internal turmoil in both countries meant that regular truces were renewed on a yearly basis, though it should be noted that France took significant chunks of Guienne (Gascony) from the English in the 1360s and 1370s. The truces meant little in reality at a local level and France was exposed to a horrific period of raiding by robber bands of English and rogue French troops that brutally exploited the land and its people. The so-called 'free companies' (free, that is, of any real control by any government) spread chaos and devastation in their wake.

It was a time of terror and neither was England exempt from the turmoil. The French also regularly raided the English coasts and raiders from across the Scottish border frequently crossed the frontier and attacked the north. To a nation that, like France, had also been exposed to the horrors of the Black Death and where there were frequent internecine civil conflicts to cope with, these were harrowing times indeed. A so-called Little Ice Age during the fourteenth century had not helped either. No wonder the twentieth-century American historian Barbara W. Tuchman wrote of 'the calamitous fourteenth century'.

Only the debatable concept of 'chivalry' made sense of these violent times. If there was an end point to this concept – and some have suggested that Agincourt marked the moment at which it died – the path towards it started long before 1415. Of course, an idea rarely if ever reaches its final moments as the result of one event and usually it dies a long and extended death (so long that it is possible not to notice that it is expiring at the time) and such was the case with that of 'chivalry'.

But one historian who has studied the general picture extensively has concluded that 'it is not surprising that the knights as a class fell into disrepute during the fifteenth century', suggesting that the decline of ordered government in France as a result of the Hundred Years War, and especially during the period at the end of the fourteenth and beginning of the fifteenth centuries, allowed 'the old instincts for plunder and rapine' to reappear among them. Chivalry was on its way out some time before Agincourt was fought.[1] It was really only the temporary imposition of a code – never fully accepted by everyone anyway – in a determined but ultimately unsuccessful attempt to keep the warrior classes in some sort of check.

It is easy, though, to get hyperbolic about Agincourt. A recent television documentary called *The Battle of Agincourt: The Bloodiest Battle of the Medieval Age*[2] was in many ways well made, informative and interesting. Yet, perhaps in the interests of good viewing, it makes some sweeping statements that do not survive careful scrutiny. The programme begins with the lines, 'On 25 October 1415, the age of chivalry died. This was the moment when one hundred years of war came to its bloody climax.'

There are question marks arising from several perspectives about such sweeping statements. Firstly, to say that Agincourt was the day on which chivalry died is the most simplifying of simplifications. That does not mean that some of the French nobles who fought in that memorable battle, particularly the younger hotheads, were not inspired by dreams of chivalric glory, but that approach was one that was not glorious; it was plain foolish and, even at the time, an anachronism. Both the English and the French nobility had already suffered terrible reverses fighting against opponents who did not sign up to the debatable concepts of chivalry, the English at Bannockburn in 1314 and the French at several confrontations such as Courtrai (1302), Nicopolis (1396) and other battles against the English earlier in the Hundred Years War. The evidence of Agincourt was that the English had learned their lessons rather better, though even the French had improved their position against the English in recent decades by carefully avoiding battle with them, hardly a strategy that can claim to be based on the pursuit of chivalric glory.

Secondly, Agincourt most definitely did not mark the bloody climax of the Hundred Years War, which still had nearly four decades left to run. The real climax came at Castillon in 1453 and Agincourt did not even mark the end of Henry V's war with France; in fact it was more or less the beginning of it. Neither was it the bloodiest battle of the medieval age, not even for the English. At the Battle of Towton during the Wars of the Roses in 1461, 28,000 men were said to have died, losses that would outnumber those at Agincourt by possibly five to one and maybe more. But these are the background perceptions of Agincourt that cement its place in history.

What became known as the Hundred Years War[3] had its roots much further back in history than the fourteenth century when it officially began. When William, Duke of Normandy, triumphed at

Hastings in 1066 he was soon after crowned King of England but in France he was still a vassal of the French monarch. Normandy was only his in theory, on the say-so of the French king. Subsequent English rulers were in the same position, which frequently led to problems, peaking in the times of the Angevin kings (suzerains of more French territory than the King of France was), Henry II, Richard I and John. This period saw frequent flare-ups in France and at the end of it all a large proportion of the French lands formerly held by the English monarchs were lost by the time that John's reign ended in 1216. That, however, was a long way from being the end of the matter.

In 1337 war broke out between England and France, largely at the instigation of the latter, and French incursions into Guienne, the sole remaining English-held territory in the country, and raids on the English coast were launched as a result. After previously swearing homage for his lands in Guienne in France to King Philip VI – and thereby recognising him as the legitimate ruler of the country – Edward III later retracted it. Edward's argument was simple. When a previous French king, Charles IV, died in 1328 Edward was his closest surviving male relative. However, under what was known as Salic Law, a claim inherited through the female line was invalid and so Edward, whose title derived from such a situation (his mother Isabella was Charles' sister), did not succeed as King of France.

The applicability of the Salic Law was contested by Edward and his supporters; restrictions prohibiting female succession allegedly (the French side argued) dated back to the time of Clovis, King of the Franks, who lived in the sixth century, but the legal interpretation of the matter was murky and not accepted by the English king or indeed most of his successors. But in fairness to the French, the rules also debarred potential claimants from their own country from the crown. For example, when Charles IV died his wife, Jeanne d'Évreux, was pregnant. No decision was therefore made on who should succeed the late king until the pregnancy went to its full term to see if a male heir would be born. In the event, it was a girl (Jeanne had already produced another daughter with Charles while the king was still alive) and only after this did the widening of the search for a male heir take place.

So Edward was debarred from the succession to his late uncle's throne by these conventions. Instead the throne went to Philip. Edward later retrospectively refused to accept this situation and insisted that he was the rightful King of France (though as part of the terms of the Treaty of Brétigny, which temporarily ended the war in 1360, Edward would drop his claim to the country in return for holding the territories he had won free of homage to the French king). It was nevertheless a claim that would be picked up vigorously by his great-grandson, King Henry V.[4]

The future Henry V was born at Monmouth in the Marcher borders between England and Wales in either 1386 or 1387 (it is not clear which). As the son of a prominent noble, a grandson of John of Gaunt and a great-grandson of Edward III, his birth was an important moment but, as he was not an immediate heir to the crown, not necessarily a momentous national event. This perhaps helps to explain the uncertainty over his exact date of birth, as might the fact that high rates of infant mortality meant that there was a risk that he would not survive childhood.

But his position would change, enabling him to eventually become king. As a result, by 1415 Henry was a man with something to prove. His right to rule England, let alone France, was not incontestable. His father, the late Henry IV, who was previously Henry Bolingbroke, Earl of Derby, had been exiled from England by King Richard II in 1399. But he returned at the head of an army when his lands in the Duchy of Lancaster were unwisely and illegally confiscated from him when his father, the famous John of Gaunt, died. Richard II had a limited power base of support and was unable to resist the invasion that duly followed on from this unwise act on his part.

Taken as a whole, the reign of Richard II had not been a happy time for the people of England. Coming so soon after the horrors of the Black Death, during which between a third and a half of the population had died, this was a period of great social upheaval in the country. In the aftermath of the terrible plague that had decimated the realm during these awful times, the common folk of England had ironically seen their position strengthened. They had previously been tied to the land within a short circumference of where they were born before the arrival on English shores of the pestilence. After it blew like a vicious storm across the country, leaving untold devastation in its wake, there was a shortage of labour, a situation that allowed the working masses a chance to demand greater rights.

Of course, this was not something that the ruling classes took kindly to; few enjoy giving up their rights, however arbitrary they may be. This was the time of Wat Tyler, of the great revolt of the common man, which ended with many expectations totally frustrated. Ironically, it was during those days, when little more than a youth, that Richard II enjoyed his finest hour. He faced up to Tyler even while some of the greatest men of the realm were slaughtered around him. He promised Tyler's supporters various improvements if he brought his revolt to an end – promises that were not kept. The striving for social justice led to no sustainable change, for the time being at least.

The exiled Henry Bolingbroke had made his play for England while Richard II was out of the country, campaigning in Ireland. Leaving England while he was very unpopular transpired to be a terminal mistake for Richard, for when Bolingbroke landed in the east of the country he proved unstoppable. At first, Henry had claimed that he was only interested in regaining the rights that were due him from being the heir to the Duchy of Lancaster, which had been arbitrarily removed from him by Richard shortly before. However, he did not maintain this pretence for long. He too had a strong claim to be King of England; both he and Richard shared Edward III as a grandfather. Richard's claim was, by right of inheritance, undoubtedly stronger, but that proved no obstacle to Henry.

Richard was quickly persuaded to abdicate towards the end of 1399. A year later he was dead, murdered in Pontefract Castle (probably starved to death). To kill a king, even a largely ineffective one, was in those times an especially terrible act. It set a dangerous precedent for future monarchs. It was an offence not just against the victim but also against God. When a king was anointed with the sacred oil it was an act that was more than just symbolic. It was nothing less than the blessing of the Heavenly Father, His confirmation that this man was now transformed into something greater, a king, sanctioned by the Almighty to rule. To fight against God's anointed was to fight against the will of God Himself.

Ironically, Bolingbroke's removal of Richard and his installation as King Henry IV set a dangerous precedent that he was always fighting against, for if one monarch had been removed, so could another. This was to be no smooth transition of power. Henry IV was forced to fight to secure his right to the throne, which was for him both physically and emotionally tiring and financially debilitating. The new king was to experience a difficult reign. Between 1400 and 1408 he was forced to put down four baronial revolts, though some were more threatening to his position than others.[5] These revolts were tiring, exhausting and expensive. Henry had the potential to be a very good king despite his shaky claim to the crown. But he would die before his time, worn out, his promise largely unfulfilled.

Perhaps the most serious of the uprisings against him took place in 1403. The Percys were large landowners in the north of England. During the early part of Henry IV's reign they were strong supporters of his both in England and in resisting the rebellion in Wales led by Owen Glendower. However, at the end of it all they were not given the rewards that they wished or which they felt they had been promised. They therefore instigated an uprising against Henry.

The earls of Northumberland and Worcester, both prominent members of the Percy faction, led this uprising. They accused Henry IV of seizing the throne, of murdering God's anointed king and of ignoring the rights of Parliament. Henry Percy (Northumberland) marched from his lands on the borders with Scotland with a small force. He was joined in the Midlands by more men, led by the Earl of Worcester and some Welshmen. Others were recruited too, including a number of archers from Cheshire, an area that was hostile to Henry IV. Henry was an experienced warrior – he had even participated in crusades in Lithuania – and duly assembled an army to meet the threat which included his young son, then Prince of Wales, later King Henry V.

The two armies met just outside Shrewsbury on 21 July 1403.

There was no fighting at first. The morning passed in negotiation, an opening formality that would be followed in many medieval battles, including Agincourt. This failed. Just around noon the two forces moved on each other. Henry IV ordered the battle to begin with a massive archery barrage. However, the archers from Cheshire on the other side proved superior. Soon the king's men were dropping 'like apples fallen in the autumn', as one chronicler described it.[6]

Among those struck was the king's son, the future Henry V. He received an arrow full in the face, though he stoically refused to leave the field even though the missile had allegedly penetrated six inches into his skull. His wound was serious and when examined later it proved very difficult to extract the arrowhead. But he survived a harrowing, excruciating and anaesthetic-free session of surgery that followed. He recovered through the attentions of a physician who treated his wound with a compound of honey and alcohol. It is interesting that the surgery took place at Kenilworth, many miles away from Shrewsbury and therefore some time after the wound had been received.[7] This was an early indication that, whatever else could be said about the future king, there was no reason to doubt his stoicism or personal courage.

In the battle at Shrewsbury Henry IV's forces eventually came out on top. Henry Percy, the famous 'Hotspur', was killed. The rebels started to retreat, though for a while the battle could have gone the other way. Hotspur was struck down in a heroic but desperate charge to eliminate the king. For a short time the king's standard was overrun. Hotspur died in the fight; some accounts say that he was struck down when he opened the visor of his helmet to grab some air and was shot in the face with an arrow. After the battle a bloodletting against the captured aristocracy followed. In scenes that presaged the later dynastic bitterness seen in the Wars of the Roses, some of the rebel lords were publicly executed.

The losses suffered by both sides on the field of battle were substantial. One chronicler noted that 200 knights and esquires from Cheshire fell, along with an untold number of servants and foot soldiers.[8] It was ironic that here they died fighting against the Lancastrian cause, for just a dozen years later some of them would risk their lives for it at Agincourt.

This was a painful lesson for the Prince of Wales. He had learned first-hand just how devastating the longbow could be and what damage it could do to an opponent. He would also see in these dangerous times just how difficult it was to trust anybody. The prince's next years were ones of personal development, especially in a military sense as he fought a hard campaign against those forces in Wales that wished to expel the English from their country.

This was a school of hard knocks, not always marked with success. At the end of it young Henry would be an efficient and hardened warrior. This would stand him in good stead during his subsequent kingship. But the scar on his face did not go away and he would have a visible reminder for the rest of his life of just what an arrow could do to a man. However, suggestions that this is why his famous portrait shows him in profile are not supported by the evidence of John Bradmore, his surgeon, who wrote that he 'was struck by an arrow next to his nose on the left side', the very side that can be seen in the profile portrait.[9]

Prince Henry would have discovered much, too, about the skill and stopping power of the archers, especially those from Cheshire. Men from that county had formed the backbone of the archer bodyguard of the late Richard II.[10] They also provided the most significant portion of the army of the Percy rebels who took the field at Shrewsbury. After the war both the county of Cheshire and the principal city, Chester, were fined.[11] Henry may well have marked these men for future reference.

In 1405 there was another uprising, which was to have distant echoes in 1415, right on the eve of Henry V's departure for France. It involved Richard Scrope, Archbishop of York. He led an army of around 8,000 men against Henry IV, a most un-archbishoplike function superficially perhaps, but warrior bishops were far from unique in the annals of medieval history. Composed mainly of peasants and poorly-armed men, it was ill matched against a force led by the Earl of Westmorland and Henry IV's third son, John of Lancaster (who would later become the Duke of Bedford).

There was no battle as Scrope agreed, over a drink of wine with the Earl of Westmorland (the commander of the king's army in his absence), to disband his men. Scrope had no real wish for a fight and allowed himself to be convinced that the king would be willing to talk about a negotiated settlement. It was a fatal error of judgement on Scrope's part. Henry IV was enraged at the rebellion and Scrope was executed for his part in it soon after, following a travesty of a trial. Scrope was the only senior ecclesiastic to be judicially killed before the time of Henry VIII and the Reformation for which it set a precedent. Scrope also became in the eyes of some a martyr, a perception that was only added to when he reportedly asked the executioner to strike him five times with his axe to commemorate the five wounds of Christ. All things considered, his execution was a massive error of judgement on Henry IV's part.

Within a very short time following Scrope's execution, the king – previously seeming to be in good health – was taken seriously ill (possibly with leprosy, which seemed to some like a punishment from God). The rest of his reign was punctuated with long bouts of illness. Towards the end of it, he was forced for a time to hand over the reins of power to his son, Prince Henry, the Prince of Wales, Duke of Lancaster and Cornwall and the formally designated heir to the crown of England. There was frequent talk then that the king might be forced to abdicate, though for a time he recovered well enough to put the future Henry V firmly in his place. Young Henry was marked out by these events as an ambitious individual who cared far more for the trappings of power than he did for his father. Although he denied this, the latter part of Henry IV's life was marked by barely concealed tension between father and son.

Before that, the wars against the Welsh rebels were a proving ground for Henry. The Battle of Shrewsbury was a brutal set-piece affair which left him with a permanent reminder of the dangers of such a confrontation. But it was not symptomatic of the wider war, which lasted for years and required much of what would now be called 'grunt work', slogging and yomping through the harsh terrain of Wales, searching for an elusive enemy in the mists and the rain, before the conflict was brought to a close.

Nor were these years marked solely by triumph. Henry had been outwitted by Glendower at the siege of Aberystwyth, as a result of which its eventual capture was delayed for a year. He had allowed the self-appointed rival Prince of Wales to come to the relief of the town by stating that if he did not arrive there with an army by a certain date then it would capitulate to him. Glendower had called his bluff, catching the young Prince of Wales by surprise when he came up with troops, causing him enormous embarrassment. It was a lesson about complacency that Henry was unlikely to forget.

These were defining times then for the young Henry; by the time he was twenty he already had 'considerable experience of war and decision-making' behind him.[12] The nature of the war in France would be very different from that fought in the rugged fastnesses of Wales, but these were still invaluable lessons being learned. These included how to organise an army and keep it in the field (and the difficulties of paying for it) and the importance of effective leadership in particular. The reverses he suffered also no doubt played their part in his education and made him determined not to suffer a repeat in the future. But there were triumphs too, and after one, in a battle in Wales where he fought against a numerically superior force, he gave an insight into his views of warfare with his pronouncement that 'victory does not depend on a multitude of people but, as was well demonstrated in that place, on the power of God'.[13] It was an appropriate precursor to the later situation at Agincourt.

Such were the formative years of Henry V. It had been a tough upbringing in which he had learned the arts of both politics and war through practical experience rather than merely theoretical knowledge. A contemporary chronicler described him as 'young in years but old in experience'.[14] When he came to the throne it appears that he had already decided that he needed to do something spectacular to cement his position as king. And it was quickly clear just what he meant to do to achieve this; nothing less than the conquest of France, an objective that would become an obsession for him. In some ways, the lingering death of his father, whom he may have thought would have died several years before he actually did, gave him a chance to think through his strategy for kingship long before he had an opportunity to put it into practice.

Even though there had not been a major battle in France for over three decades, there had been frequent raiding in the interim. Sometimes these raids were tit-for-tat. One of the most famous privateers of the time (the French would have called him a pirate) was Harry Paye, who regularly launched attacks on French and Spanish shipping and towns. His target area spread from Normandy to the north coast of Spain. The French and Spanish grew so tired of his depredations that in 1405 they raided his home port of Poole on the south coast of England, set fire to a number of buildings and killed several leading citizens, including Paye's brother.

Such raids were a regular occurrence both on the English and the French side of the Channel. But on the whole a degree of peace, and the absence at least of any major expeditions, had suited both England and France for their own good reasons. England's domestic problems have already been considered but France too had good reason to want to avoid war.

For in 1413, when Henry V at last came to the throne after the death of his father, France was in turmoil and he was therefore presented with a moment of opportunity. The French king, Charles VI, was for one thing mentally unstable. He flitted in and out of lucidity, and his grip on reality was unreliable. Charles VI has been given two nicknames by history, 'the Beloved' or 'the Mad'; the first suggested that as a man he was not without virtue, the latter that his maladies did not fit him to be a good king. He had come to the throne in 1380 when just eleven years of age. Eight years later he took the bold step of dismissing his uncles, who had been running France during his minority and had squandered much of the treasury in the process. This was widely applauded and earned him the epithet 'Beloved'.

But soon he earned the other, less complimentary, nickname. Without warning, he went berserk and killed four of his knights and almost slew his brother Louis of Orléans too. This outburst presaged increasingly frequent bouts of insanity, during which he would believe that he was made of glass and would deny that he had a wife or children. In fact, there were a number of offspring from his marriage to Isabeau of Bavaria, though many died in their infancy. However, the third of them, Isabella, became Richard II of England's queen (this was hardly a love match – she was seven and he was twenty-nine at the time). The fifth child, Charles, would be the eldest surviving son and would become the dauphin, Charles VI's heir.

The king's strange 'glass delusion' led him to refuse to allow people to touch him and to wear protective clothing in case he accidentally shattered. This strange phenomenon was not unique, although judging by medical treatises on the subject it would not peak until the seventeenth century, though in modern times the condition is largely unknown. It was hardly an ideal malady for a monarch to suffer from when his country was under imminent danger of attack.

The timing of all this was disastrous for France, for Charles's massive problems occurred at just the time that the country needed a strong king more than ever. Not only was there the danger of the English resurrecting their old claims to much of France, but the country was also hopelessly divided between two rival factions, a situation that in the years immediately before the accession of Henry V became a very serious problem. One faction, led by the Duke of Burgundy, John the Fearless, threatened to bring down the other, named the Armagnacs after one of their current leaders, Bernard, Count of Armagnac.

The atmosphere in France was poisonous. The most alarming demonstration of this had occurred a few years before in 1407 when the Duke of Orléans, the only brother of the king, was brutally cut down in the dark alleyways of Paris one night on the orders of John the Fearless, Duke of Burgundy, his cousin. The act understandably created a storm that threatened to blow the country apart. The Duke of Orléans was certainly not popular in Paris, where he had earned an unwelcome reputation both for hitting the citizens with heavy taxes and also for his uncontrolled womanising, which created great scandal. Nevertheless, to strike down someone so prominent in the French royal bloodline could only create enormous resentment in those connected to his party.

The problem was that the Duke of Burgundy was simply too powerful for his enemies to bring to book for his rash and violent actions; that he was well aware of this was evidenced by the lack of any real effort on his part to deny his involvement in the murder. He controlled not only the territory in the east of France that his dukedom was named after but also much of Flanders and the Low Countries, critical at the time for their wealth. They were particularly significant for the substantial trade in wool which was imported from England and from there into continental markets. England was an important continental economic power at the time and it was the humble sheep on which its fortunes were built.

The Armagnacs, powerless for a time, brooded and looked for the right moment to strike down the Burgundian John the Fearless in revenge. Charles VI's son, the dauphin, was particularly prominent in these designs but for some time a very uneasy peace was maintained. No one believed it could last. John himself was so wary of an assassination attempt in Paris, even though he was very popular there, that he had a raised room built in the city, lifted on thin stone supports some 60 feet off the ground, probably so that no one could set fire to it while he was in residence.

This was all deeply distressing for Charles VI. The competing factions were led by members of the royal family, so it was difficult for him to take sides even when he was stable enough to do so in his periods of relative lucidity. In reality, both factions tried their best to control him and to an extent his son the dauphin, as he was his designated heir. The king was forced to balance on an especially slippery tightrope and at various times found himself allied with either side. But by 1415 his sympathies were decidedly with the Armagnac rather than the Burgundian cause. One thing that must be emphasised, though, is that neither party ever sought to remove the king, which contrasted markedly with the situation in England.

While there was good reason to be cautious about inviting England to get involved in French affairs on any pretext, both Burgundians and Armagnacs saw great potential in the English as allies for their cause. Each party therefore made overtures to Henry IV while he was still alive. On the whole, the late English king was more partial to the Armagnac cause while his son, the then Prince of Wales, was inclined towards the Burgundians. Henry IV in particular was more than capable of attempting to negotiate with both parties. To complicate the situation still further, Henry IV's long-term illness meant that while his son was regent relations between Burgundy and England became closer, but when the king recovered a semblance of good health that situation was reversed.

In 1411, Burgundian negotiators had made their way to England, the situation of Flanders at the time in particular being uppermost in their mind. Later that year, 1,000 English archers proved their worth during a Burgundian victory against their Armagnac opponents at St Cloud near Paris. The French should have learned more from this experience than was apparently the case judging from their tactics at Agincourt in 1415. But there were men fighting alongside each other, English and French, in the Burgundian army who would end up as adversaries at Agincourt.

These closer relationships between England and Burgundy did not last. When Henry IV had recovered from his illness well enough to briefly resume his reign, his second and favourite son, Thomas, Duke of Clarence, was sent to France to agree a treaty with the Armagnacs. The result of this embassy, the Treaty of Bourges, entered into on 6 April 1412, saw the Armagnacs agreeing to help England secure sovereignty in Guienne, then as now famous and valued for its quality wine. This opportunistic positioning on the part of the Armagnacs was of very dubious benefit to France as a whole.

But soon after these events there was a complication. An English army was sent to France in August 1412 to support the Armagnacs, only to find when they arrived there that they were no longer needed. French internal politics had led to a reconciliation of sorts being negotiated between the competing French factions. The English army, some 4,000 strong, landed on the Cotentin Peninsula jutting out from Normandy into the English Channel. With his army's services no longer required, the Duke of Clarence marched south to English territory in Guienne. En route his force proved a serious threat to the stability of France although in the end the English were bought off without causing serious damage.

This gave some of the English army valuable geographical knowledge of France that would later prove useful in 1415. Among the senior commanders in Clarence's army were Edward, the Duke of York, Thomas Beaufort, Earl of Dorset (the future Henry V's uncle), and Sir John Cornwall, a renowned knight who would play a key role in Henry V's Agincourt campaign.

By April 1413 the Armagnacs were definitely in the ascendancy in France against the Duke of Burgundy, though by this time the English had a different king. The new man on the throne had recently been crowned Henry V and he was inclined towards the Burgundians. He had disagreed with his late father over support for the Armagnacs, something that had led, allied to other matters, to a very serious falling out. This had only subsequently been ended by a very public and emotional reconciliation. Whether this would have brought an end to the family squabbles once and for all will never be known, for soon after this touching reunion Henry IV fell seriously ill again. This time there would be no recovery. On 20 March 1413, he died.

Henry V was crowned at Westminster Abbey on 9 April, Passion Sunday. The day was unusually cold and there was a heavy fall of snow, a sombre, almost wintry start to the new reign. Some of his subjects took this as a sign that 'he would be a man of cold deeds and severe in his management of the kingdom'. Others, though, saw it as a sign that the winter was over and the snowfall marked its conclusion and the coming of spring. Thomas of Walsingham wrote that Henry was a different man once he became king, suggesting that perhaps he was not a paragon of virtue before this time.[15] This may allude to the early roots of Shakespeare's later portrayal of Henry being somewhat wild in his youth, though frivolity certainly did not accord with his later character.[16]

So the young prince became King Henry V, having completed a demanding and not always easy apprenticeship. This would perhaps be an opportune point at which to perform a stocktake of the man's character. First and foremost, as we have seen, he was already an experienced warrior even though his record was not unblemished. The scar on his cheek, a permanent reminder of the devastating power of the longbow, bore very obvious witness to the fighting in which he had already been involved. Such martial qualities would be much needed given the plans he had already started to formulate, and they would form the basis for much of his future reputation.

But what of his policies? It was clear almost from the start of his reign that France was to figure prominently in his plans. Within a very short space, an arms build-up had already started. It soon became apparent that Henry's ambitions in France were virtually unlimited. Certainly he looked back with sharp interest to the reign of Edward III, who had shown that, in the words of one modern historian, 'through successful overseas campaigning, a king could guarantee his kingdom domestic peace, national unity, strong government and foreign glory'.[17]

This all contrasted rather markedly with the late Henry IV's reign, of which the same historian said that it 'had become a period of domestic unrest, national disunity, financial insecurity and foreign antipathy', in other words the complete antithesis of Edward III's time on the throne. Certainly Henry V was quick to see the potential that a war in France brought. He would be right in his analysis that a successful foreign venture would do much to bring stability to England, though he would not live to see the reverse of this, that failure would in contrast lead to domestic chaos.

These observations on motivations for war have some high-pedigree indirect support from an unlikely direction. In September 1932, two of the greatest figures of the twentieth century, Albert Einstein and Sigmund Freud, exchanged correspondence on the question of why wars start. In the opinion of the latter, the potential for domestic violence from a disunited group of subjects and the threat of revolution can be overcome by 'the transference of power to a larger unity, which is held together by emotional ties between its members', and a war was a way of doing such a thing.[18] This is exactly what Henry was seeking to do now, with the emotional tie a patriotic one in the shape of England. The hope was that its potentially fragmented segments could be stuck together by the glue of an overseas adventure against one of England's old enemies. The national nature of the army that Henry planned to take to France would help to solidify these ties.

While there were fewer signs of domestic dissent when he first inherited the throne than there had been during the early years of his father's reign, Henry V did not have far to seek for problems. Wales had been in a state of war for the best part of a decade. Although the conflict had at long last turned in England's favour, this problematic region (since the days of the harsh Edward I it had no longer been treated as a separate kingdom) was still not completely subdued. There was always tension too from the direction of Scotland, where cross-border raids were frequent. French pirate attacks were another regular occurrence, particularly those launched from the key port of Harfleur in Normandy. In short, this was hardly a picture of stability and tranquillity.

Then there were significant social tensions in England to contend with too. In the aftermath of the Black Death, a number of the king's subjects were starting to question long-accepted conventions more and more. This was most apparent in the fraught question of religion. The Catholic Church had come under intense scrutiny in recent times, which was hardly surprising as by this time there were no less than three popes claiming to lead it.

England indeed had been a wellspring of this discontent. One man, John Wycliffe (who died in 1384 but whose influence continued to mark the country and Europe more widely even after his death), had called certain key tenets of the Church into question. For example, he denied that the bread and wine were literally turned into the body and blood of Christ during the celebration of the Eucharist. He also argued that the Church should, like Christ, be poor; a most dangerous suggestion in the eyes of the leaders of this still largely omnipotent institution, who benefited from its great material holdings and the associated trappings of power.

Wycliffe also argued that the Church should not claim ownership of men's minds; individuals should be free to think for themselves. To assist them in this process, the Bible should, he claimed, be available in the native language of the people rather than Latin. The use of Latin made spiritual knowledge a virtual monopoly of Churchmen, though a bible in the vernacular would in the main have an impact on the higher classes, with many people still largely illiterate. He duly proceeded to translate it into English himself. The Catholic Church was violently opposed to all of this, for the simple and obvious reason that it reduced its importance and power.

For a time this new thinking was tolerated in England and its essential seditiousness ignored. However, a fightback had later started which Henry V would be at the heart of. For Henry was, even by the standards of that time – so different from our secular age – a devout and pious man. In this context it is notable that in 1415, the year of Agincourt, the Council of Constance declared that Wycliffe's corpse should be exhumed and burned.

The king had a virtual army of saints whom he especially venerated: Edward the Confessor, Saint George, the Virgin Mary and two Saint Johns (of Beverley and Bridlington). He was also especially devoted to the Holy Trinity of the Father, Son and Holy

Ghost. He always endeavoured to hear Mass three times a day and could not abide immorality. In short, he was severe and stern, and supremely orthodox in his religious beliefs and affiliations. In many ways, he was rather like the Defender of the Faith that another King Henry, three further down the line, would become a century later, at least during the opening years of that future monarch's reign.

John of Bridlington, one of Henry V's most revered saints, has been described as 'the saintly patron of the House of Lancaster'. He was the last Englishman to be canonised before the Reformation changed the world of religion in the country forever. He had been first adopted by Henry IV, perhaps on the grounds of regional affiliation; Bolingbroke in Lincolnshire was not far away from Bridlington. It has even been suggested that support for John was a way of offering 'a kind of resistance, or better, a kind of positive rivalry to the rising cult of Archbishop Scrope at York', a man whom the late king had been responsible for the death of.[19]

There would also prove to be another similarity between Henry V and Henry VIII. By the time that the former was crowned, a number of monastic foundations had been set up in England with French mother houses. They were known as 'alien priories'. In a time when church and politics, including those at the international level, were irrevocably mixed, the king was not prepared to have such foundations with French sympathies operating freely in his realm. It was not long before he started a programme to dissolve these alien establishments.[20]

The French, aware that the new King of England was raising the unwelcome prospect of a war if his claimed rights were not restored, sought to forestall him by negotiation. A delegation of

French envoys made their way to Henry during the parliament that was held at Leicester in April 1414. So too did another party representing the Duke of Burgundy. They were after quite different things. The Armagnacs wished to delay or even better stop any plans that Henry might have to enforce a serious claim for the throne of France. The Burgundians, on the other hand, wished for help in the ongoing infighting with their domestic enemies in France. Hedging his bets, Henry decided to send delegations in return to both parties.

It did not take long for Henry V to despatch his demands across the Channel to France in response to these approaches. The first delegation he sent was led by bishops Langley and Courtenay in April and the last of them reached Paris in August 1414. Their demands were so extreme that they can only be seen either as an opening negotiation gambit or a clear statement of intent that Henry was not planning a negotiation at all and that his heart was already set on war. His subsequent actions suggest that the latter was probably the case. But in the interests of appearances he needed to go through the motions. War could not be declared without at least the appearance of an attempt to achieve his objectives by diplomacy first of all.

The English king's claims were extreme. He demanded that all the territories due from the Treaty of Brétigny should be handed over. He also required the sovereignty of Aquitaine, Normandy, Flanders, Touraine, Anjou and half of Provence. This equated to a massive proportion of France. It was unthinkable that Charles VI would meekly acquiesce.

In addition Henry wanted 1.6 million crowns (about £267,000) to be paid to him as the amount of ransom that had been unpaid when the late King of France, Jean II, had died nearly half a century ago in 1364 when he was an English captive. He also demanded the hand of the French king's daughter, Catherine of Valois, and a dowry of 2 million crowns. Contrary to Shakespeare's portrayal of this wooing as a love match, Catherine was a very young teenager who was unlikely to have been romantically besotted by this older and very serious monarch. The French in response took the most obvious approach and responded diplomatically but in a non-committal fashion, hoping to play for time.

The discussions were not seriously conducted in earnest, at least on the English side. It was clear from early on that the king was building up for a fight. As one chronicler said, 'more than once these envoys were sent to France and the French envoys were sent to England, and both sides spent vast amounts of money, while hopes of peace were completely put to sleep'.[21]

With the Armagnacs now at this time in the ascendancy in France, the Duke of Burgundy saw that for the time being the game was up, so he beat a hasty retreat from Paris. That was not the end of the Armagnac–Burgundian friction – far from it – but John the Fearless saw that he must bide his time, though negotiations with Henry led to no obvious end result. The duke would certainly have proved to be a potentially dangerous ally to have should these discussions ever lead to anything definitive. Behind Henry's back he was also negotiating with the Scots, to whom he planned to send troops to help in their fight against the English.

Henry would make his future plans clear enough back in England. When Parliament was opened in November 1414, his Chancellor, Henry Beaufort, the Bishop of Winchester (another of the king's uncles), told his listeners that 'the king desires especially that good and wise action should be taken against his enemies outside the realm, and furthermore he will strive for the recovery and the inheritance and right of his crown outside the realm, which has been a long time held and wrongfully retained'.[22] It did not take much to work out what the Chancellor was driving at, or which 'wrongfully retained' lands he meant.[23]

But not everyone in England was convinced that war with France was the right option. It would be very expensive and there were no guarantees of success. Edward III's campaigns had brought glory to England initially but this was only a temporary triumph. Even the great Edward had been unable to make many permanent gains in France, the important port of Calais excepted.

The Speaker of Parliament in 1415, Thomas Chaucer (son of the famous poet Geoffrey), had great difficulty in persuading those present that they should back the king, though in the end they did so. But the drive for war was certainly not unanimously supported and Chaucer suggested to the king that he should send another delegation to the French and not give up yet on diplomacy.[24] There were two groups in particular that Henry needed to convince: Parliament and the Church.

Parliament's primary function as far as the king was concerned was to approve and finance his activities, especially wartime ones. Parliament was far from a representative assembly in the modern sense of the word but that did not mean that it lacked power. It was composed of some of the leading men of the land and their support was a barometer of sentiment as well as a practical source of financing.

The Church too was important for practical as well as spiritual reasons. Given its position as a major land and property owner, it was also the potential source of large amounts of funding. The institution had often been a primary provider of money for Crusades but if they could be persuaded of the rightness of the king's plans to reclaim France for the English crown then they could also be invaluable on this occasion too.

On 10 January 1415, a convocation of the Church in the north of England at York duly voted subsidies to the king. The negotiations were successfully steered through by Archbishop Henry Bowet of York, a determined if ageing supporter of the House of Lancaster.

This was still largely a stage of phoney war. However threatening the language might get, Henry was as yet not ready for conflict and the French did not want it at all. So on 24 January 1415, the truce between England and France was extended once more for a few months. It is doubtful if anyone was fooled by this; Henry still spoke of Charles VI as 'our adversary of France', a compliment that was reciprocated in kind by the French king. But for the time being a peace of sorts was maintained.

Over the next few months, embassies would pass to and from France and also to Burgundy, the latter still a potential ally given the duke's current position in France. One of the key participants in the negotiations with John the Fearless was Henry, Lord Scrope of Masham. Henry V seems to have put a lot of confidence in Scrope at the time.

Born in around 1370, Scrope had gone on a brief crusade in 1390 with John Beaufort, the half-brother of Henry IV and the current King Henry's uncle. He had been recognised with an annuity by Richard II but then found himself in the good graces of Henry IV and fought alongside him at Shrewsbury. In December 1414 Henry V had forgiven all Scrope's debts to him, and for a monarch who currently needed every penny that he could get, that was not something to be taken lightly. He had also made a grant of £46 15s to Scrope annually, not a massive sum but a sign nevertheless of some kind of favour. The evidence suggests that the king did indeed place a good deal of trust in Scrope and would have regarded him as one of his more reliable supporters. This would soon have important repercussions.

In France, there was an increasing acceptance that war would come sooner or later despite the best efforts of the ruling council to avoid it. The King of England was taking very obvious measures to build up his forces. The French hoped that if they managed to stall for enough time the sense of momentum in England would be lost and the forces that Henry planned to assemble would dissipate of their own accord. But the Armagnacs knew that war would likely come, whether they wanted it or not. Their spies would have kept them well supplied with details of the large-scale preparations that were taking place across the English Channel.

The French recognised that there was a real risk that war might not be avoided as a result of the negotiations. Therefore they took defensive measures to protect themselves just in case. Some of these were political. There was an urgent need to bring the Duke of Burgundy into line and restore some form of equilibrium to France. At the beginning of February 1415 Charles VI commanded that no one – including and perhaps especially the Duke of Burgundy – was to make a separate peace with King Henry of England. He sought to bring an end to the infernal squabbling that was blighting his lands. He also looked for help and support from wider afield on the Continent.

But Henry won a major battle with the French before he ever left English shores. He was far more successful in his diplomatic overtures to potential foreign friends than Charles VI was. It was not that the French did not try, merely that they failed to find much in the way of meaningful support from abroad. For example, on 22 February 1415 a delegation from the rebel Welshman Owen

Glendower was granted a gift by Charles of £200 with which to aid his efforts to disrupt the English in Wales. But it was a meaningless gesture; the rebellion was already long past its peak and Glendower would die a disappointed man before the year was out.

In contrast Henry was playing a magnificent game in winning support from abroad, or at least the abstention of those who could otherwise have created a good deal of trouble for him. A truce with the Spanish kingdom of Castile and Léon was extended and orders sent out to maritime counties in England that they were not to interfere with ships from these lands.

Henry would need a vast number of ships to transport his army, and his own resources with respect to what we might now call a 'Royal Navy' were tiny. Something needed to be done to bridge the massive gap that existed between what was needed and what was initially available. On 27 February 1415 orders were sent by Henry that ambassadors should make their way to the lands of Zeeland and Holland and hire all the ships they could from there to become part of the planned English armada. The region had significant numbers of vessels that could help Henry greatly. The cost was significant by the standards of the time – £2,000 – but the shipping duly arrived.

With the kingdoms of Scandinavia being ruled by his brother-in-law and with his approaches to the Holy Roman Emperor, Sigismund, being well received, Henry was completely outmanoeuvring his French opponent in terms of international support. It was a magnificent performance by a man who was still new to the job of being king. The French on the other hand were performing ineptly. A delegation at the crucial church council at Constance taking place at around the same time had only succeeded in offending Sigismund, making him more likely to take England's part.

This church council was to be a crucial one. At the time there were no less than three popes competing against each other. There was an increasing realisation that this situation was nonsensical and the council was to sort the issue out definitively, though the only one of the three rivals who was present, John XXIII, would do all that he could to hang on to power. The English delegation that was sent to Constance worked hard on their king's orders to improve England's position with some success. Previously the English delegates had formed part of a composite 'German' block, but they now succeeded in getting England recognised as a separate nation in voting terms.

At around the same time, King Henry was making his own arrangements for who was to govern England while he was absent. The crusades of Richard I had demonstrated what could happen when an English monarch was away for any length of time. Richard had been captured by an opponent (ironically one who superficially was on the same side as him) and then imprisoned for several years. He had then been required to raise an enormous ransom for his freedom and was in the meantime faced with the threat of losing his throne to his brother John; not happy precedents.

Henry chose to proceed with his plans regardless of French attempts to stall him. The port of embarkation for the English army was to be Southampton and the surrounding area of the Solent. Royal ships would be making their way there such as the *Trinity Royal* (which had been completed not long before at Greenwich and would have as her master Stephen Thomas), to be manned by 200 men along with literally hundreds of other vessels.[25]

The *Trinity Royal* was to be decked out with some impressive symbolic insignia, such as a swan and an antelope. At 760 tons she was four times bigger than the 195-ton ship that was the largest in Edward I's fleet, ferrying soldiers from Ireland to Scotland just over a century before; a reflection of the rapid rate of evolution that shipbuilding was currently going through. However, this small royal armada would not be anything like enough even with the help of those vessels contracted from Holland and Zeeland and hundreds of other ships were to be 'arrested' or impounded into Henry's service, along with the men to man them.

The final size of the fleet, supposedly around 1,500 ships, dwarfed previous expeditions during the medieval period. Edward I had led an army to Flanders in 1297 transported by a fleet of 300 vessels. Edward III needed about 750 to take his army to France in 1346–7.[26] Such numbers were way beyond the scope of any royal ships the king might have; even Henry V, who built up the navy, would only have thirty-eight in his royal fleet by 1418. The widespread requisitioning of other ships from their owners was understandably widely resented as there was no compensation for loss of earnings from trade. Any ships that were subsequently lost were rarely compensated for either.

The requisitioned ships normally needed to be converted for their new purpose. Fighting castles needed to be added to the superstructure, making already cumbersome vessels even less manoeuvrable. In an age of sail, ships were also at the mercy of the wind and journeys could be painfully slow; records show that the voyage of the *Nicholas* in 1301 took eight days to travel the short distance from Newcastle to Berwick, an average speed of less than a third of a knot per hour.[27]

As 1415 advanced Southampton became the royal dockyard.

The king's master shipbuilders, men like William Catton and William Soper, were frantically busy trying to get everything ready for the time that the king set sail. Catton masterminded the assembly of the royal fleet, which was kept busy looking out for pirate activity from French, Breton and Spanish vessels or ferrying supplies. The king's navy had declined under recent monarchs after a high point during the reign of Edward III. Henry was determined to build it back up again and set about the task with typical driven efficiency. This asked much of himself and even more of those who worked for him.

Provisions for the large army he planned to assemble were also frenetically pursued. On 20 April 1415, the king gave orders to Nicholas Frost, his bowyer, to get together as many arrows as he could. Large quantities of lance staves were also requisitioned.[28] The king's guns, based at the Tower of London, were got ready to be shipped over to France when the time was right. Instructions were also sent to Robert Hunt, the sergeant of the wagons, and to Stephen Ferrour (the surname probably being a play on his craft), the sergeant of the king's farriers who was to assemble horseshoes. Simon Lewys and John Benet, the king's masons, were also later ordered to assemble one hundred of their fellows for the expedition.

And so it went on; John Southemede to provide sixty two-wheeled carts, Thomas Mathew and William Gill to supply one hundred and twenty carpenters and turners, William Mersh and Nicholas Thokyngton to provide forty smiths. Then there was the king's physician, his surgeons, his minstrels.[29] This is evidence of a massive logistical undertaking.

Despite this intense activity, English delegations continued to make their way to France, going through the pretence that their king still desired peace. It helped enormously no doubt when one made its way across the Channel in February, passing through Harfleur en route to Paris; the French port would be the first stop on Henry's invasion later that year. This was a wonderful way to obtain intelligence about its state of preparedness. Although the English made some concessions in their demands, at the end of the mission there were still enormous differences between the two sides. War was ever more probable.

England had not long before been a feudal society, but that had changed. The troops in Henry's army were now contracted. That said, in return for the lands that they held as grantees of the king, a number of England's most prominent nobles were pressured to provide men to fight. Henry drew on well-established procedures of raising an army, which had been effectively used for example by his own father and before him by Edward III. But the origins of these not so new ways of raising an army went even further back and were used in the reign of another great warrior king, Edward I, a century and more before. During the course of the fourteenth century the use of feudal service declined – for one thing, the time limits of forty days that normally attached to such service made it of little practical use especially for a protracted campaign in France. Although last used in 1385 in a campaign in Scotland launched by Richard II (even by then it was an anachronism), it had effectively gone by now.[30]

Of course, men to fight and support the army were one of the most crucial requirements. On 22 February 1415, the sheriffs of London were instructed to summon all lords who held lands as gifts from Edward III, the Black Prince, Richard II, John of Gaunt, Henry IV or Henry V to assemble in London by 24 April at the latest. There would then be discussions about how many men each of them should contribute towards the expedition. They were to march from there to Southampton with their men and be ready to sail by 8 May.[31] Henry was effectively calling in debts from men who owed their lands to the beneficence of the monarchy, though he would have to pay them for this help in return.

The French in the meantime continued to try and persuade the English king to change his plans, with very limited success. Shakespeare famously later made reference in *Henry V* to an incident where the dauphin, the son and heir of the French king, sent a box of tennis balls to England. This was to mock the king's youthful impetuousness and inexperience when Henry sent his imperious demands to France. It is a story that does not altogether ring true.

For one thing Henry was a good ten years older than the dauphin, who was therefore much the more youthful of the two. For another it was a singularly undiplomatic action on the part of France if those governing her wished to avoid war, which all other evidence suggests was the case. Also, as the nineteenth-century historian Sir Nicholas Harris Nicolas said, Henry later issued a challenge to single combat to the dauphin when he invaded France and it is unlikely that he would not have mentioned the tennis ball incident in his letter laying out his challenge if it had actually happened.[32]

Yet intriguingly there are near-contemporary allusions to this story, almost two centuries before Shakespeare's time. Thomas Elmham wrote of the story in his *Liber Metricus*, probably before 1418. Another man, John Strecche, also recorded it in 1422.[33] Therefore it cannot easily be dismissed and it is certainly not a much later fabrication. What is certainly true is that Henry was new and 'raw' to the arts of kingship though not to those of warfare, for of the latter he already had a good ten years' worth of experience. That being so, he would show himself to be a very quick learner as a monarch.

One early account of the 'tennis ball incident' was to be found in the *Chronicle of London*, which appeared in the fifteenth century, and it is worth quoting from as it gives a firm basis for Shakespeare's later usage:

And his lords gave him council to send ambassadors unto the King of France and his council, and that he should give up to him his right heritage, that is to say Normandy, Gascony and Guienne, the which his predecessors had held before him, or else he would it win with dint of sword, in short time, with the help of Almighty God.

And then the Dolphin [*sic*] of France answered to our ambassadors, and said in this manner that the king was over-young and too tender of age to make any war against him, and was not like yet to be no good warrior to do and to make such a conquest there upon him; and somewhat in scorn and dispute he sent to him a tun [a large cask] full of tennis balls because he would have somewhat for to play with for all him and his lords, and that became him better than to maintain any war; and then anon our lords that was ambassadors took their leave and came into England anon and told the king and his council of the ungoodly answer that they had of the Dolphin and of the present the which he had sent unto the King; and when the King heard his words, and the answer of the Dolphin, he was wonderfully sore aggrieved and right evil felt towards the Frenchmen, and towards the king and the Dolphin, and thought to avenge himself upon him as soon as God would send him grace and might, and anon let make tennis balls for the Dolphin, in all the haste they might be made; and they were great gunstones for the Dolphin to play withal.[34]

Whatever the truth of the 'tennis ball incident', which seems inherently unlikely in its details, the French came to realise that their efforts to forestall Henry and prevent the looming spectre of war from becoming a terrible reality were doomed to fail. By March 1415, they had started to superficially get their internal affairs in order in preparation for any conflict. The ratification of the Treaty of Arras on 13 March brought an end to the confrontation between Armagnacs and Burgundians for the time being. Soon after, the French were starting to put together their plans for defending the country against an invasion from England.

However, this only disguised various fundamental problems within France that remained as real as ever. For one thing the agreement between the two opposing factions in the country could only paper over the cracks; even when Henry finally landed there, Armagnacs and Burgundians were still fighting each other. Neither side trusted the other and cooperation between them would remain difficult. And in terms of the looming war, the English had the advantage of dictating where they would launch their attack. Given the limited communications capabilities at the time and the slow pace of a large French army in response to any attack from the English, it was difficult for the French to work out where the English would land and to respond quickly when they did so. The northern coast of France is not the easiest to defend, as other more modern armies have found out.

As the momentum towards war increased, Henry took further actions to cover off all options while he was away from England. A particular concern was what the Scots would do while an

English army was in France. Orders were sent to the great lords of the north to take all possible precautions against raids from that direction. No knight, squire or yeoman in the north of England was to leave his lands because of the threat from the Scots 'as the king has information that his said enemies are minded shortly to invade the realm with no small power'.[35]

France and Scotland were long-term allies. This was a situation that dated back to 1295 when the Scots were beginning their struggle for independence from their powerful neighbour in England. Since then there had been an understanding that if England invaded France then Scotland would intervene on the side of the latter, and vice-versa should the English invade Scotland. Therefore an invasion of either France or Scotland would very likely lead to England fighting a war on two fronts and Henry had to take precautions to guard against this.

By the spring of 1415, Henry's delegation to France had returned home, as the king probably suspected they would, with their demands unmet. Public relations also needed to be considered by the English king. He would now be able to paint a picture that he was first and foremost desirous of peace but that the unwillingness of the French to accept the justness of his cause meant that he had no option but to fight for what was his. He summoned his great council to join him in London. When they were duly assembled on 15 April, Chancellor Henry Beaufort described an English king who had been the picture of magnanimity and reasonableness but who had been rebuffed by the duplicitous French.

An acceptance that war was now inevitable also followed in England but the difficult question of how to pay for it was then raised at the council that was held soon after. The lords present were given some time to see if they could agree with the king's 'requests' for funding via loans. They responded that they were happy to do so. However, they would be expected to commit considerable amounts of their own money up front and reclaim them later from the king. As kings of England had often proved far from obliging debtors in the past when it came to the knotty problem of repayment, they then enquired as tactfully as they could as to what security they would be given for their investment.

That same day Henry wrote to the King of France with a letter that laid out his case. France and England were always stronger united, he said (an interesting claim as the two nations had never actually been formally or properly united in the past so there was no precedent). He reminded them that Europe was divided and even the Church was going through a state of unprecedented schism. The unwritten subscript was that it was time for the kings of England and France to set an example by acting in a responsible way – and that of course meant that the latter should obligingly acquiesce to the rightful claims of the former.

In case of any doubts that Henry's patience was wearing thin the letter also made another point. It stated that a message recently received from the Duke of Berry, which spoke of a forthcoming French delegation to England, wanted too much time for further negotiations when they arrived. The king had therefore unilaterally decided to shorten it by removing some of the 'useless days' that were built in to the timescale.[36] Not only was this a possible sign of anxiety but Henry was now putting his pieces into place on the chessboard to launch an invasion of France in the near future. Any further delays were unconscionable as they would compromise the timetable for war.

The letter to Charles of 15 April followed another of 7 April which is very significant. 'Most serene prince and very dear cousin,'

Henry began with insincere politeness, 'we have endeavoured from our accession to our crown, by the ardent passion that we have had for the love of him who is the author of peace, to reconcile the difference between us and our people; to chase and banish forever that sad division, mother of so many misfortunes, cause of the misery of so many men, and of the loss of so many souls which have been shipwrecked in the slaughter of war.' Henry desired nothing more than peace, the letter claimed, but he also wanted justice.[37]

When looking at medieval history, sources of information are always important. The colour and texture of great events is normally found in the accounts written by the chroniclers of the time. Yet these need to be treated with great caution. Chroniclers wrote with a particular audience in mind and this affected the way that they presented the 'facts' and the picture that they painted. As such they are far from disinterested observers and there is every reason to be suspect of the details of their accounts.

On the other hand, the clerks who wrote up the books of account, the 'ledgers' or 'cashbooks' as we might call them today, had no such hidden agenda. Their audience was the king and his officials who would audit their books. The information included in them needed to be precise and accurate; any attempt at repainting the picture on their part could have serious personal consequences. This was true especially when the king had exhibited tendencies towards 'micro-management' of the situation and would be looking over their shoulders with a piercing, inquisitive mind.

As such, occasionally a gem of detail emerges almost by accident from the account books of the time. One such jewel was recorded by a clerk in the Issue Rolls for 16 April 1415. The entry in question noted that John Bower, a turner, was to receive payment for the provision of axes and mattocks for the king's works on his voyage to Harfleur in Normandy.[38] This was enormously significant; there had been no announcement publicly about the king's future plans and it shows that Henry had already decided on his invasion route even though he had not let his great council in on the secret.

He wanted to keep his planned destination as secret as possible. It is not difficult to work out why. In modern times, the Allied invasion of Normandy in 1944 was preceded by enormous efforts to provide disinformation to confuse the enemy (ironically there had even been an English raid on a town near Dieppe in 1413, in the same region that the Allied forces would launch a disastrous raid in 1942). Henry was playing the same game as his fellow countrymen played half a millennium later.

With a last-ditch French embassy planning to come to England to try and forestall the war, and every chance that they would pick up the details of any invasion plans that had been announced while they were there, secrecy was crucial. Henry planned to let as few people as possible know what his plans were so that the French were forced to cover several options at once when they started to think about defensive measures.

There were certainly challenges even with an attack on Harfleur. It would be much easier logistically to send the invasion force across to Calais, which had recently (in 1413) had its fortifications strengthened.[39] Calais was safely in English hands and was a relatively short crossing from England at just over 20 miles. Normandy conversely was 70 miles away and there was always the danger that bad weather could disrupt the plans (another echo of 1944). Furthermore, Harfleur was decidedly in enemy hands and would potentially be a tough nut to crack.

Some historians suggest that Henry wanted to emulate the

glorious actions of his predecessor Edward III and bring his enemy to a decisive battle.[40] There are good reasons to think that this would appeal to the proud king. A successful battle would certainly build his reputation and further strengthen his position on the throne of England, but thinking that this was his sole reason for leading his army across the Channel understates the strategic importance of the port of Harfleur (a position that has been inherited in more recent times by nearby Le Havre, where the harbour is not so prone to silting up).

From here at Harfleur pirate raids had frequently been launched against English ships for many years and capturing it would remove a significant thorn in English flesh. But there was another factor, perhaps even more important in terms of strategic significance, that was also enticing; this was the fact that possession of Harfleur gave access to the hinterland of France. The town sat on the banks of the Seine, which flowed down through Rouen, past the great castle of Chateau Gaillard and from there on to Paris. It was therefore in some ways the key to the outer gate to the capital of France itself.

There was also the need for Henry to be able to show a permanent benefit as a result of the campaign and not just a one-off battle. Victories in battle were rarely decisive; medieval examples such as Hastings and Bannockburn were the exception to the more general rule. Edward I had spent immense sums trying to conquer Scotland but despite victories such as that at Falkirk in 1298 left only an empty exchequer as a long-term result. Edward III too had won great triumphs at Sluys and Crécy, and his son the Black Prince at Poitiers, but France had not been secured as a consequence of these set-piece battles.

Did that mean that there were no long-term results to show

from the efforts of Edward I and Edward III? The answer was a very clear 'no'. Edward I had invested massive sums in building castles in Wales. Two centuries later the mighty fortresses that he had built as a constricting ring around the country were still a core part of making sure that the English king kept control of it. Edward III had won Calais by his efforts and now, half a century and more on, it remained a crucial strategic English possession in France and would be so for another century and more beyond Henry's reign. Battles were important in building reputation and securing glory but their long-term impact was something of a lottery. Any legacy from military campaigning was often to be found in the possession of what we would now call 'bricks and mortar'. In this respect, adding to England's little foothold in northern France was of critical long-term consequence.

In the second half of April 1415, further details for the defence of the realm were discussed in London. Some 200 men-at-arms and 400 archers were to be sent to the March in Scotland to guard against trouble there. A further 150 men-at-arms and 300 archers were sent to Wales for the same reason (the one-to-two ratio of men-at-arms to archers shows where Henry saw his priorities in terms of military tactics).[41] These forces, while not huge in number, would have been useful in France and show that the king was understandably and rightly concerned for what would happen when his back was turned.

Then there was the question of who should be in charge in England while the king was in France. This responsibility was given to John, Duke of Bedford, the king's brother (born in 1389, he would later be married to the daughter of John the Fearless). He was to be given a salary of 5,000 marks per year while he was regent (a mark was equivalent to two-thirds of £1). He would be supported in his government of the realm in Henry's absence by a council of nine men including the Archbishop of Canterbury, several bishops and a number of lords.

More detailed points were also addressed at this stage. Pay for the army was one important issue, both to the men themselves as individuals and also in aggregate for the exchequer. A duke was to receive one mark per day, an earl half a mark, a baron 4 shillings (a shilling being 5p in modern British parlance), a knight two shillings, an esquire one shilling and an archer sixpence.[42] These payments were one thing in theory, but finding the money to pay them in practice was quite another.

A key event took place in London on 29 April when the lords of the land signed their indentures with the king confirming how many men they were going to provide. Top of the list was Thomas, Duke of Clarence, who was to provide 240 men-at-arms and 720 archers, followed by others with lesser amounts of men but all with a 3:1 archers to men-at-arms ratio.[43]

The terms laid out stipulated that the men were to serve for a year, suggesting a lengthy campaign was in prospect. A quarter of the amount to be paid would be delivered up front to the leaders of each retinue, the other three payments being made at the end of each subsequent quarter. Given the high level of implied credit involved, with men serving for much of the time in advance of their wages being paid in arrears, the king would hand over much of the royal jewel collection as a form of security.

These indentures were essentially a contract between the king and other men who were responsible for providing a certain number of specified troops in the stated ratios. The same information was written on the indenture document twice. It was then cut in two with jagged lines. One half stayed with the officials of the Crown, the other with the man responsible for delivering the required number of men on the indenture. In case of dispute the two halves could be compared. If the jagged lines on each half did not neatly meet or if the text on the two halves was not the same then fraud was afoot – a simple but effective procedure.

It also meant that the troops provided could be to a certain extent hand-picked. In its way then this was a professional force, not a feudal host as had been the case earlier in the medieval period. This had been the normal way in which such men had been provided for several decades. What made the Agincourt campaign unique, though, was the large numbers of indentures issued, with 250 such agreements identified to date.

This was an extraordinary number; the next highest number of indentures on record is less than half this amount. It meant that as well as the largest indentured groups, with men like the Duke of Clarence and the Duke of York, and the medium-sized groups such as those with Sir Thomas Erpingham, there were literally dozens of smaller companies. This may have made coordination a bit more difficult but may also, some suggest, have helped make this enterprise more of a national one than it might otherwise have been.[44]

This made it clear once more what Henry's tactics in France were going to be. There was an even higher concentration of archers than he was to deploy in Scotland and Wales while he was away. This probably reflected the different type of warfare that was expected. Archers would be particularly effective against massed ranks of cavalry and men-at-arms, as might be expected in France. It may well have been a consideration that archers were cheaper than men-at-arms too. With a cash-strapped treasury that needed to hire thousands of soldiers, that was a very practical argument in favour of using more archers than men-at-arms.

But it was not just troops that were considered. Other important support staff such as surgeons and even minstrels were also indentured. It was a massive undertaking to organise this in a relatively short time. As the date for departure grew near there was much to do; too much. The departure date was pushed back to 1 July.

However, it was still unclear to most just where the blow on France would fall. Even as he discussed the indentures with his captains, Henry included two different rates of pay. One would apply if the men were to serve in Guienne and another, lower rate if they served elsewhere in the country. The differing rates represented historical variations that had previously been the practice. But their adoption had several potential benefits for the English king. Firstly, it acted as a lure for men to enlist, tempted by the prospect of higher pay if they went to Guienne. Secondly, it potentially confused the French as to the intended destination of the English army (the French would almost certainly have found out about the different possibilities being discussed through their spy network).

Many of these indentures survive. One of them was with Thomas Tunstall, who was required to provide six men-at-arms (himself included) and eighteen archers. The different rates of pay (twenty marks for each archer for a year in Guienne or sixpence a day if the army went to other parts of France) were specifically mentioned. Payment was to be made each quarter. For the first quarter's payment, half was to be paid upfront and half when the men duly arrived at the muster. There they would be inspected to confirm that all the men contracted for had actually turned up. For the second quarter, payment was to be secured by handing over certain of the king's jewels to the required value. These were to be redeemed by the king 'the hour that he can redeem them within a year and a half and one month next after the receipt of the same jewels'.

If the jewels were not duly redeemed in the required timescale, then Thomas could sell them. For the third quarter's wages, payment was to be made within six months of the start of that quarter. If adequate security was not given by the king for the last quarter, then Thomas was to be relieved of all obligation to serve further.[45] This was in every sense of the word a contract with security. It also required that if Thomas were to make any gains in the war then one-third of the value (including from any ransom of prisoners) was to be passed to the king. Any particularly prominent captives such as members of the French royal blood were to be handed over to the king in return for adequate compensation. The arrangement was witnessed by Gilbert Umfraville, Robert Stanley and Thomas Strickland, the king's standard-bearer.

The records that survive bear fascinating witness to the objects that the king was forced to part with to finance his expedition. They included the crown of the late Richard II, which was given to the Abbot of Westminster and not redeemed until the subsequent reign of Henry VI. There was also a great circle of gold garnished with fifty balays (a peach-coloured ruby), forty sapphires, eight diamonds and seven pearls to the mayor, sheriffs and 'commonalty' of Norwich and a host of other items to a wide range of people. They ranged from the exotic and the extravagant to the relatively commonplace, but collectively put a great strain on the Crown's resources. Henry was in hock up to his eyeballs because of the imminent expedition and failure was unthinkable.[46] He had used every trick in the book to raise money, including imprisoning representatives of the Italian city-states of Lucca, Venice and Florence, demanding sums of £200, £1,000 and £1,200 respectively before he would release them.[47]

There were also what we would think of as subcontracts in place for his army. One that survives is between the Earl of Salisbury and William Bedyk, one of his retinue. Bedyk was to supply himself and two archers on payment terms that mirrored those in the main contract, an example of which has been shown above. In the case of any war gains, a third was to go to the earl and a third of a third to the king. The earl was obliged to provide *bouche of court* to Bedyk, that is to say provide provisions for him, though these might be as simple as bread, beer and wine. Bedyk was to be 'ready at the sea' at the due date (stated as 1 July) with his archers 'well mounted and equipped, suitably to their condition'. The earl should 'provide proper shipping for him, his archers, and horses, going and returning'.[48]

There was no going back now. On 18 June Henry V left London, heading for the coast. Before doing so, he made his way to St Paul's in the company of the mayor and a number of the leading citizens. He took leave of his stepmother and made an offering to St George, then he headed off towards Southampton.

The rest of his army duly started to form and the momentum for war gathered an unstoppable pace. During June the French, still desperate to avoid a conflict, sent a large delegation to England to stay Henry's hand. They landed at Dover on the seventeenth of the month and then moved through Canterbury to London, only to find that Henry was no longer there. They caught up with the king at Winchester and met him at Wolvesey Castle in the city but further days had been lost in the process. When they at last met, on the surface all was sweetness and light. Henry greeted the French king's envoys with polite cordiality. It was very unlikely indeed that anyone was fooled by this charade.

On 1 July – the day for departure of the fleet from Southampton having again been pushed back – events began well enough, with Mass celebrated by the English and French together in a completely false display of Christian unity. This was followed by a well-scripted sermon delivered by the Archbishop of Bourges, Guillaume Boisratier, the leader of the French delegation. Its theme was the virtues of peace. The negotiations were under way, even though by this time the delegations still could not agree what language negotiations should be in, the English wanting Latin, the visiting party of course desiring French.[49]

They lasted until 6 July and, predictably enough, achieved nothing. The chroniclers give two different accounts of how they ended. One version is that Henry said that the French had omitted to provide any practical details of how their latest offers would be turned into reality. He implied that the discussions were nothing more than an attempt at further prevarication. The other version is that the Archbishop of Bourges, speaking remarkably frankly, told Henry that he was not the rightful King of England, let alone France. Henry told the delegation to leave and return home, telling them ominously that he would soon follow them. This latter version seems to imply, if true, that the archbishop was a very impolitic man whose attitude would do nothing to reduce the prospects of war.[50] But in any event, war had now moved another decisive step closer.

By this stage Henry had no real interest in peace. He had gone too far for that and had already staked too much to backtrack. His fleet was contracted and starting to assemble; so too was his army of well over 10,000 men. The negotiations dragged on for several days. Although Henry conceded as much as he dared so that he could look reasonable in the eyes of the rest of the world, there was still a gulf between the two sides when they finally fizzled out. The French departed and made their way gloomily back towards France. Henry steeled himself for the battle that at last lay just ahead.

Henry had mortgaged himself to the hilt to pay for the invasion. In return for the large debts that he had taken on to finance it, as we have seen, he had broken up most of the crown jewels. He had also distributed most other things of value that were in his hands as security (the value of the security being calculated by the weight of the precious metals involved). One of those involved was the Duke of York, who was given a magnificent gold alms dish (called the 'Tygre') in the form of a ship on top of a bear in return for the loans he had advanced to the king. This was valued at a princely £332 but the Crown would not be in a position to redeem it until 1430.[51]

So great was the need for funds that some items, such as the jewel-bedecked 'Harry Crown', were broken into pieces and used as security for several different individuals. The cost was potentially ruinous and, if the military campaign in France were to fail, then who knew what the repercussions might be? There was even a chance that Henry's position in England might come under close scrutiny, just as his father's had so often. The stakes had been laid and they were as high as they could have been. It was now time to roll the dice. Henry committed himself and his venture to the hands of God and prepared himself mentally and spiritually for the immense challenge that loomed before him. It would potentially make or break his kingship, not to mention his place in history.

3

SOUTHAMPTON: THE COUP ATTEMPT
(JULY – AUGUST 1415)

... friend, give us what we are owed.
Letter from Henry V to Charles VI of France in 1415

Large bodies of men had by now made their way from all across England and parts of south Wales. It is important to remember that this was not really a conscripted army (even though pressure had been put on a number of the country's leading magnates to provide men) but a paid force. Even the archers stood to make more from their efforts than they would from their everyday activities. There had not been a major Continental expedition for half a century but that only told part of the story. There had been plenty of fighting within the troubled southern part of the British Isles in recent times. There had also been expeditions to Scotland and several significant forays to France more recently.

Large-scale English raids in France had been given a special name, *chevauchées* (literally 'rides'), a source of terror to any community unfortunate enough to be in their way as they brought death and devastation in their wake. During the second half of the fourteenth century in particular they were certainly a source of loot and plunder but they also had a political purpose. They served as a powerful reminder that England had not given up her rights in France, even though there might be a regular sequence of truces in place. They also demonstrated that the King of France was powerless to protect his subjects, undermining his position in the process. Some of the participants would have had a chance to significantly increase their wealth; an example, albeit an extreme one, was that of James Audley who, after the Battle of Poitiers, received a promise of £400 a year for life in recognition of his services in the fighting, which must have been exceptional given the sum of money involved.[1]

Plenty of men no doubt had a sense of adventure as well as apprehension in their stomachs as they trudged or rode along the lanes of England and Wales headed for the port of Southampton and its environs. There were no doubt a mix of motivations in place. For the nobles of the land, there was a chance to show their worth to the king and place themselves higher in his good graces; the war might be a financial risk in the short term but the possibility of gains from the fighting and preferment afterwards was a tantalising enough bait.

For the captains at a lower level, they too could win favour but also make themselves some money so the prospect of a major campaign was alluring. For the archers there was a financial incentive too, as well as a chance to widen their horizons, which would not come along too often. And for some patriotism would be a motive, for the king had tried to sell his expedition as an opportunity to put right national wrongs. Some no doubt were driven by loyalty to the king in person though the regular national mood-swings in the past three decades cannot have helped in this respect.

The great armada assembled at Southampton and in the Solent in preparation for the departure for France. At last, the talking was over and the time for action drew near. It was said that 1,500 vessels were anchored waiting to sail. The whole of the area around the Solent was a hive of activity. There were not just thousands of men to ship but immense amounts of supplies too. Again accounts records are revealing, such as the instruction sent to the sheriffs of Kent, Oxfordshire, Wiltshire and Hampshire at the end of April to each send 200 oxen to Titchfield, Southwick, Beaulieu and Southampton.[2] There were thousands of horses to be shipped too. Now these teeming masses of humans and animals were crowded together waiting to cross the Channel and the time for departure was at hand. It was a moment that the king probably savoured, as he had worked very hard to get to this stage.

By 12 July, the king was at Southampton having spent a few days at the Premonstratensian foundation of Titchfield Abbey on the way down from Winchester. Perhaps appropriately given the king's uncomplicated attitude to religion, the Order was renowned for its austerity and the solemnity of their rituals. At Titchfield Henry got together copies of documents from his father's reign that had been sent to the French making certain agreements, which were subsequently not honoured by the latter. He would send these on to the Council of Constance and the Emperor Sigismund in particular, as a way of further reinforcing the perceived justice of his claim.[3] He was now mentally looking south towards France and the great campaign that was imminent. But he would have done better at this moment to have looked behind him as, even as the army assembled, a plot was brewing close at hand that could scupper the expedition before it even set sail.

Henry's claim to the throne was inherited from his father's seizure of it in 1399. It was a claim that was to an extent sullied by the way in which that change of power had been achieved and certainly from the fact that Richard II had been in all probability deliberately killed not long after.

Both the King Henrys, father and son, were conscious of the fact that such a precedent was unhealthy for them personally, though it was the latter who appeared to be most troubled in his conscience about it. He was so affected by it indeed that one of his first acts after coming to the throne was to have the late King Richard reburied in Westminster Abbey, in what has been interpreted as 'an attempt ... to lay the ghost of his father's ill-fated predecessor'.[4] Henry's attitude towards Richard was certainly a complex one, unsurprising as he had been made a knight by the late king during the latter days of his reign.

It was perhaps providential for the House of Lancaster that Richard left no son to stake a claim to the crown after his death. However, that would not completely stop others attempting to do so instead. Even in 1415, there were hardly believable claims in some quarters that Richard II was not dead at all and was alive in Scotland. Henry IV had stated some time before that the individual in question was an impostor, who was really the much humbler Thomas Warde of Trumpington, Cambridgeshire.[5] This man had been found wandering around on the Scottish island of Islay, a very remote spot for a former King of England to be. Nevertheless the rumours, though unlikely to be true, were persistent and not at all welcome to the Lancastrian kings who came in Richard's wake.

A more substantial threat to the House of Lancaster, because there was no doubting that he had a strong claim to the throne, was to be found in the shape of Edmund, 5th Earl of March, who was in the line of succession due to his Mortimer antecedents. As such, he was directly descended from Philippa, the daughter of Edward III's second son. He was therefore in some ways more senior in the succession bloodline than the Lancastrian kings. Indeed, during Richard II's lifetime March was formally the heir apparent as the late king and his wife had not had any children.

This privileged position all changed with Henry Bolingbroke's deposition of Richard II. The Earl of March was in no real position to resist his loss of opportunity as a result, not least because he was only eight years old at the time. Nevertheless as he grew up it was no surprise that March was unhappy at his reduced status. Fortunately for the Lancastrian kings he was not particularly astute, otherwise he could have posed a greater threat than he did. Unfortunately for Henry V in particular, he did not handle March's situation very well and it would come back to haunt him just when he could least afford it – right on the eve of the armada's departure for France.

Early on in 1415, the Earl of March had found himself in deep water with Henry. It would have been wise to have avoided the king's displeasure; the earl had spent much of his adolescence as a hostage, pampered maybe but no doubt a prisoner, in various castles around England and Wales, his strong claim to the throne a complication that the Lancastrians could well do without. In the context of the times, he could perhaps consider himself fortunate to have survived at all. It was unwise in such circumstances to attract attention to himself.

But because, in the words of one historian, 'he was regarded as too mediocre in his abilities to be a hazard to the Lancastrian dynasty',[6] he had eventually been set free. However, he still harboured ambitions, best evidenced when in 1415 he married Anne, sister and heir-presumptress of the Earl of Stafford and herself descended from that same Philippa of Clarence whose blood ran in the veins of her husband. It was a complicated match for several reasons. Their closeness as cousins required papal dispensation from Pope John XXIII, whose agreement was sought and duly given. It also was not welcomed by the king as it strengthened still further the royal ties of the Earl of March, something that Henry V would have been most anxious to avoid.

The king could not actually stop the marriage but he could insist on the payment of a fine for going ahead with it. This action was of dubious legality but March was powerless to resist. Henry duly imposed a fine, and the price – 10,000 marks or £6,667 – was enormous. The Earl of March was understandably enraged at this act, into which several things can be read about the king himself. One is Henry's ruthlessness; he was quick to remind March where the real power lay by hitting him in the pocket, a sharp reminder of March's own reduced position in the hierarchy.

Another is a suggestion of Henry's opportunistic rapaciousness and in particular his desire to tap every source to fund his grandiose overseas ambitions, something that his royal ancestor, Richard I, had also demonstrated on many occasions. But it sent a strong message to March to stay in line, one which he would have done well to take to heart.

However, it was far from ideal that there was a discontented rival claimant to the throne in England just at the moment that Henry needed stability at home more than ever. Certainly the fact that all these issues with March took place just months before the campaign to France was due to start did not speak well for Henry's approach to risk management.

Perhaps Henry was encouraged to take these steps because he had a low opinion of the earl and his abilities. March was certainly something of a contradiction. He was in terms of his landholdings one of the foremost men in England, wealthier than any of his illustrious Mortimer predecessors. His lofty position in the hierarchy of the country, closely connected to the royal bloodline of the realm, appeared to make him important.

Yet he was not closely connected to the political scene and lacked much in the way of influence, though that did not mean he could be ignored. He was after all a human being and if he lacked charisma, that did not mean he completely lacked a sense of his own importance. It would be wise to treat him carefully. But there was little evidence of any great qualities lying dormant in the earl and this probably encouraged Henry in his harshness.

There was another potential complicating political factor in 1415, to be found in the shape of the young Henry Percy, Earl of Northumberland, who was currently in Scotland where he had been for some years. Henry V was well aware of Percy's potential to cause difficulties. Percy's family had officially been deprived of their lands due to the death in battle of his father in 1408 while involved in rebellion against Henry IV; not the first time that he had been so implicated. His son was taken to Scotland as a child for his safety following the failed revolt, but had successfully applied to have his lands restored by Henry V in 1414 and therefore now intended to return to England.

His appeal for the restoration of his lands was granted, probably because, given his huge power base in the north of England, right on the border with Scotland, he was better to have as a friend than an enemy especially given the looming war with France and the need to protect the borders against an invasion from the north. However, whoever had control of Percy held a significant bargaining chip in their possession and in early 1415 he was still effectively in the custody of the Duke of Albany, the regent of Scotland. Negotiations for Percy's release were well advanced and as the time to depart Southampton drew near, the young lord was due to make his way back to England where Henry had clearly decided to restore the family fortunes as a way of buying his loyalty and securing an important part of the north of England in his absence.

Each one of these three men, Thomas of Trumpington (the supposed Richard II), the Earl of March and Henry Percy, were about to be involved in a plot that threatened to abort the expedition to France before it even began, not least because its goal was to depose Henry V. Two of these individuals, Trumpington – the man that academics love to call the 'pseudo-Richard II' – and Percy, would be, as far as we can gather, unwilling participants while the third, March, would in contrast find himself hopelessly entangled in the spider's web of intrigue that was about to be woven.

None of these men, however, were directly responsible for hatching the plot that now developed which aimed at nothing less than the removal of Henry V. That dubious honour belonged to Richard, Earl of Cambridge. He was also a part of the royal bloodline of England (a Yorkist and a grandson of Edward III) but he was, despite his grandiose title and antecedents, a man without much real power and even less in the way of wealth, a situation that owed much to the king. Despite being given the earldom of Cambridge in 1414, he had little reason to be grateful to Henry V for very unusually he received no gift of money-bearing lands with it which meant that he was, from an aristocratic perspective, decidedly disadvantaged. It was unprecedented for a man to be made an earl without being given an income to match.

Perhaps it reflected the impoverished state of royal finances at the time that the earldom was granted without supporting revenues, but it made a potential enemy of an ostensibly powerful man with little good reason to do so. An earl could normally expect an income of £1,000 a year; Cambridge had received just £285 of annuities in the previous two.[7] While the king had many competing financial demands to manage at a time of extraordinary pressures on expenditure given the looming expensive war, it would be fully understandable if the newly made earl had felt insulted and aggrieved.

Possibly Henry V believed that Cambridge could never be much of a threat, as not only was he short of money, he possessed few other qualities either. However, as the current heir to the large landholdings of his childless elder brother, the Duke of York, he was certainly far from insignificant. In addition, Cambridge had married Anne Mortimer, sister of the Earl of March, and was as a consequence connected closely to the alternative royal bloodline in England. In summary, he was a man who had been shabbily treated by the king, to the point of humiliation given the uniqueness of his position of being an earl without an income, but he was also well connected to a possible rival. He was therefore potentially a source of threat to Henry, though up until 1415 he had been careful to not step out of line and attract attention to himself.

But at the time there appeared to be few real threats to the king internally, at least from the ranks of the high aristocracy, though there were regular stories of possible Lollard uprisings to worry about. After the instability of much of Henry IV's reign, it seemed that there was now no real desire to rock the boat from the upper echelons of society. The Earl of March was too insignificant a character to set himself up as any kind of alternative to Henry V and, as Cambridge inwardly fumed, he found no one from the higher aristocracy to give him support in any plans he might have to improve his position. He therefore sought and found it lower down the social scale in the shape of Sir Thomas Grey of Heton in the northern border counties of England, the traditional heartlands of the Percy family who had proved so troublesome to the late king.

The Greys, though not 'top notch' in terms of aristocratic position, were far from unimportant either, having married into the powerful Nevill family. Ralph Nevill was currently Earl of Westmorland and a staunch supporter of the new king and Thomas Grey had married his daughter, Alice. Thomas had later entered the entourage of Henry V while he was still Prince of Wales. Yet Grey too had money worries and found it difficult to make his way in baronial circles as a result. Several times faced with insolvency, he had become the son-in-law of Richard, Earl of Cambridge. But this did little to improve his monetary situation.

As Cambridge started to develop a plan to replace Henry V with a king more to his liking, Grey became a willing ally, reckoning that he had nothing to gain by waiting for patronage from the king which was unlikely to be forthcoming. Ironically, his younger brother John became a staunch supporter of Henry V and would find himself well rewarded for his efforts, being later made a Knight of the Garter as well as the Count of Tancarville. It would eventually become clear that the king valued loyalty above most other things and would look after those who showed it; on the other hand, he would be absolutely ruthless with those who did not. Unfortunately these lessons were not apparent at the time of Grey's participation in the plot to remove the king.

Who to replace the king with was the key question. Frustrated by his financial difficulties, a frustration compounded by resentment against the king whom he blamed for his problems, Cambridge reasoned that he would be much better off if the Earl of March, to whom he was connected by marriage, were to take the throne. It was not an unreasonable supposition but making it come to pass would be problematic. Henry V would not meekly step aside to let it happen. And the Earl of March was no great enthusiast for the idea either. In fact, it was claimed that his confessors regularly berated him for his failure to take stronger action to assert what they saw as his rightful and superior claim to the throne.

As the time to leave for France drew near, Cambridge started to take measures to put his plans into place. Grey became an enthusiastic supporter. There was no great altruism cementing this particular alliance together, just grubby self-interest. But it would quickly become obvious that the Earl of Cambridge had ambitions that far exceeded his abilities.

Cambridge had at least initially realised that the Earl of March would not be too excited about the prospect of taking on Henry V. That is to Cambridge's credit; what was not was the hare-brained alternative that he came up with instead. He started to negotiate with the Scots for custody of that so-called 'pseudo-Richard II', Thomas Warde of Trumpington. If the impostor had been still alive it would have been a ridiculous long shot; as he was now dead, it was a non-starter.

Cambridge also had designs on the custody of the soon-to-return Henry Percy, hoping that he could be brought back to England to him rather than the king. Given his family's recent record of fighting against Henry IV, he wished to convince Percy to come in on his side and bring into play his considerable resources in the north.

This unlikely plot now starting to develop, Cambridge moved into action, out of sight of the king far away in London at first, with the initial manoeuvres taking place in Yorkshire and the north. On 17 June Cambridge was with Grey at Conisbrough castle in Yorkshire formulating his next steps. According to Grey's later confession, he had been informed by the Scots holding Thomas Warde that they were prepared to exchange him for a prominent Englishman. A list of eighteen such men had been helpfully provided; they included the Earl of Westmorland, one of the king's most loyal supporters, as well as the famous Dick Whittington, three times the Lord Mayor of London. Whittington was certainly a practical backer of the king, making him a loan of £2,000 in 1413.[8]

Cambridge was now committed to the scheme and Grey had allowed himself to be talked into it too. However this was not enough and more prominent men needed to be persuaded to come in. It appears that Cambridge approached Sir John Clifford, his brother-in-law, but received no response; Clifford was invited to a meeting at Conisbrough but failed to turn up.

The prospects for success were not good given the narrow base of support that the plot had attracted. The situation was made worse still for Cambridge by the attitude of Henry Percy, who it appears wanted nothing more than to return to England and rebuild his stock with Henry V and reclaim the lands that he had been away from for so long, something that he would soon succeed in doing. Henry himself was not always a great reader of men but in Percy's case he played the right part splendidly. Percy had petitioned for a return of his lands and the king had responded positively to the request. Percy had very little to gain and a great deal potentially to lose by becoming involved in Cambridge's poorly thought-out plotting.

There was about to be something of a twist which perhaps should have put the king on his guard. The Regent of Scotland, Robert Stewart, Duke of Albany, had no intention of letting Percy go without receiving something (or more pertinently someone) useful in return. Henry had therefore agreed that Albany's son and heir, Murdoch, Earl of Fife, who had been captured at the Battle of Homildon Hill over a decade earlier, should be exchanged.

This at least was the plan, but it was stalled when Murdoch was seized on his way north near Leeds, suspiciously close to the area where Cambridge was based. However, it was merely a temporary hiccup and the captured earl was retaken a week after. The most likely reason for grabbing Murdoch was, in hindsight, to use him as a negotiating point with the Scots for the return of the so-called Richard II and Henry Percy. However the king does not appear at the time to have suspected Cambridge's involvement.

Cambridge also hoped that his scheming would be supported by Sir Robert Umfraville, a prominent border warrior and connected to the Percys. The Umfraville family had originally come from Normandy with William the Conqueror and had a long-term interest in the Marcher lands between England and Scotland. They had for many years played a key role on the side of the English in the latter country in the reigns of the three King Edwards. Now Sir Robert was the commander of the crucial border fortress at Roxburgh but he had apparently decided that his fortunes were firmly entwined with those of the House of Lancaster. On 22 July 1415, less than a month after Cambridge's scheming began, he would show this in the best way possible by routing a Scottish raiding party that he intercepted. It made later accusations that he had been part of the plot difficult to credit.

There was little visible significant support for Cambridge's plans even as the various bodies of men that would make up the force for the invasion of France began to converge on Southampton during the latter part of July 1415. But with the reality dawning that the 'pseudo-Richard II' was not a viable candidate for the throne, there was one particularly important building-brick missing even at this late stage: an alternative to replace Henry.

It was clear that the strongest rival candidate to the current king was the Earl of March. However, as yet there had not been discussions with March as to whether or not he would go along with a scheme that offered him on the one hand a great prize but on the other the prospect of a premature death – the latter the more likely option. The plotters could possibly still have stepped back at this stage, although even this may have been difficult given the number of people that they had started to talk to. Instead they decided that now was the time to go for broke and so they raised the stakes in their dangerous game.

It was at Southampton, where the army that was supposed to head for France assembled during July, that the Earl of March was finally approached and asked if he was willing to take part in the plot. On the afternoon of Sunday 21 July, Thomas Grey made his way to the lodgings of March where the earl was staying prior to setting out for France with some of the contingent of men that he was required to lead during the invasion.

According to Grey's own account, the earl was reluctant to commit himself though he did not reject the idea out of hand. Certainly he must still have been livid at the heavy fine imposed on him by the king for his marriage. Against this he needed to set his own innate caution and limited ambition. It may also have been the case that he saw well enough just how formidable a foe Henry V would be and plain common sense would suggest to him that Cambridge and Grey were hardly the most convincing co-plotters. It is quite possible that he could see that the enterprise under discussion had a very uncertain outcome and that its chances of success were not high. And the price he would personally pay for failure would almost certainly be the ultimate one.

March nevertheless invited Grey and Cambridge to join him along with Lord Clifford the following day at his hunting lodge at Cranbury, just a few miles to the north of Southampton. They did so, though no firm decisions were arrived at as a result. March was still hedging his bets and there was still a chance for the plotters to abandon their plans.

In the midst of all these dangerous conversations, Henry was blithely oblivious to the danger that threatened. Yet he was enough of a pragmatist to realise that he may not come back alive from the expedition and he therefore took steps to ensure that his affairs were in order. On 22 July he made provision for what should happen to the Duchy of Lancaster, the source of much of the king's wealth, should he die. Among the sixteen trustees appointed was Henry, Lord Scrope, clearly a trusted confidante of the king.

The king's will was finally completed on 24 July. He directed that his body should be buried in Westminster Abbey, that great mausoleum of English monarchs (though his father Henry IV was not buried there but at Canterbury, near the shrine of the martyr bishop St Thomas à Becket). He gave orders that an enormous number of Masses should be said for his soul, symptomatic perhaps of both extreme piety and also maybe of a guilty conscience given the dubious death of Richard II, whom he had been close to during that late king's life, and the need for a large amount of praying to ease his way into Heaven as a result.

That said, Henry was very much a conventional man of his time. The concept of Purgatory was a relatively recent theological development which in the early fifteenth century reached its peak. A former Archbishop of Canterbury, William Courtenay, who died in 1396 had asked for 10,000 prayers to be said for his soul and King Henry VII would later instruct that 15,000 would be said for him. Purgatory, in the English view of it, was not a pleasant place and the saying of prayers for the soul could lessen the amount of time that a man spent there.[9]

In his will, Henry also made bequests to religious foundations in England. A number of items were left to his younger brother and earmarked successor, Thomas, Duke of Clarence. Among the designated other beneficiaries was Edmund, Earl of March, though Henry, Lord Scrope, was not on the list – both situations would soon assume added significance.

By now there was one other conspirator implicated in the plot to replace the king. To contemporaries the participation of Henry, Lord Scrope of Masham, was the hardest to explain. Shakespeare writes of Scrope as if he were Henry's closest friend, though more hard-nosed evidence suggests that this was not the case. It has been pointed out that Henry's will, made out on 24 July – bang in the middle of the period when the plot was being hatched – makes no mention of Scrope though the king did make provision in it for other close confidantes. This suggests that Scrope was not as close to Henry as the Bard would have us believe.[10]

On the other hand, Scrope did make his will on 23 June in preparation for his departure for France and he did include the king in his last testament.[11] And certainly contemporary chroniclers attest that Scrope was an important adviser, 'one who was almost second to none in the kingdom among those in the king's confidence'.[12]

However, there were other reasons to suspect that Scrope was not fully in Henry's inner circle. Scrope's uncle, Richard, Archbishop of York, had led an army that was faced down by the forces of Henry IV on Shipton Moor in 1405. Though everyone knew well enough what the punishment for rebellion would most probably be, the subsequent execution of a cleric was nevertheless a shock for many and proved to be one of the more controversial acts of the late king's reign. So Henry Scrope had some significant family reasons for not being too keen on Henry V.

He had other possible reasons, too. During the reign of Henry IV, he had been treasurer of England for a short time. He did a good job in this role but resigned. However, his performance maybe gave him hope that when Henry V ascended the throne he would receive some recognition of his qualities. Although he became one of Henry's council, the more lucrative rewards that would come from the higher offices of state were not forthcoming.

Scrope was nevertheless a wealthy man, his financial position secured by two lucrative marriages. But there were indications that all was not well. He had recently made his will and in it he asked for prayers to be said for the soul of his executed uncle, put to death a decade before by the king's father, giving some hint that the action still rankled.

The precise shape of Scrope's involvement in the plot to remove Henry V is shadowy to say the least and historians are still unsure of its exact nature. His own confession suggested that at some time in mid-July he visited Grey at his lodgings at the Greyfriars and in the discussions that followed details of the plot were laid out. After this meeting Scrope visited March and, according to Scrope's account, told him not to get involved in the scheme. Scrope was it seems not enthusiastic about the forthcoming invasion but could not, according to his own account, see any chances for success in the plot. According to him, he talked March out of any involvement in the plan but in the process he had unwittingly signed his own death warrant.

It is significant that Scrope was kept at arm's length as far as the inner details of the plot were concerned, suggesting that the plotters were not sure where his loyalties lay. That he knew of its existence at a high level, though, is not in dispute. He continued to urge March to stay clear of the plot and the earl in reply said that he would make sure that he did so, although he reserved the option of considering such a scheme at a later stage, perhaps after his return from France. Scrope certainly did not make Henry aware of the plot and this proved to be a terminal error of judgement.

There was a meeting between Cambridge, Grey and Scrope outside the walls of Southampton by the Itchen Ferry on 25 July. Cambridge planned to abort the planned invasion of France, so Grey later asserted, by burning the ships in the harbour, though if he really planned to destroy the hundreds of ships at anchor, spread out over a wide area, it merely served to show how hare-brained this plot was. The scheme seemed poorly thought-out and it would have been foolhardy to make it public when its chances of success were virtually nil.

The king, still in the dark about these plans, was now seriously worried about the state of the expedition. Money problems were increasing and he was desperately seeking around to find ways of adding to his revenues. He was still short of ships, too. Just as worrying was the fact that the expedition still had not left and the season for campaigning was rapidly running out. Winter campaigns were certainly not unheard of, but given the size of the army it was probably something that the king wanted to avoid. If there were many more delays, there might be no departure in 1415 and the chance might perhaps never come again.

Still the conspiracy continued to gestate out of the sight of the king. It would take an extra spark to bring about a decisive move by the as yet undiscovered plotters and unwittingly Henry V would be responsible for it. On Sunday 28 July the Earl of March had a difficult interview with the king. Henry was now so desperate for money that he did not particularly care how he raised it or who was upset in the process. He now demanded a rapid down-payment of £2,000 from March as the initial instalment of the fine levied for his unsanctioned marriage. March sought a delay but the king was in no mood to accommodate this, particularly given the need to finance his imminent invasion. The meeting between Henry and March saw the king unwilling to compromise and the latter left as a disappointed and angry man.

This was an important day for several reasons, for during it Henry also sent a last, majestic letter to 'our cousin and adversary' Charles VI. It was a powerful yet sanctimonious epistle, full of references to the Bible, the Almighty and Jesus Christ. It was underpinned by piety and indirect references to the divine sanction that Henry felt was his for his actions. In it, he wrote that

as we wish to be confident of a clear conscience, we now address you with a final request, at the moment of setting out to demand from you the reason for this denial of justice, and we repeat to you in the name of the entrails of Jesus Christ, following the example shown us by the perfection of evangelical doctrine; friend, give us what we are owed and by the will of the Almighty avoid a deluge of human blood, which has been created according to God; restore to us our inheritance and our rights that have been unjustly stolen, or at least those things that we have demanded earnestly and repeatedly by our various ambassadors and deputies, and with which we would be contented in respect of God and in the interests of peace.[13]

It was a superb letter, penned on the orders of a king who felt his finest hour was imminent. It was regal, dignified, eloquent and, as Henry almost certainly knew when it was sent, doomed to be completely futile.

All these moments of tension marked a fateful moment when the dice was decisively cast at last. In the meantime subterranean plotting was still afoot, simmering away and threatening to erupt in a sudden, violent, volcanic eruption at any moment. March left his meeting with the king on the 28th in a bitter mood. This was the moment that he decided to cross his own personal Rubicon. He sent a message to Cambridge and Grey telling of his frustration and this was enough to act as a catalyst to put the plot to replace the king into action. It was decided that March would be moved to Beaulieu in the nearby New Forest on 31 July and from here he would escape to Wales where the recent lengthy rebellion gave encouragement that he would find considerable support in his efforts to dethrone the king.

That fateful meeting between the earl and the king on 28 July had then precipitated a crisis. A fuming March had left the interview persuaded that he needed to take firm action to counteract Henry's harsh attitude and this convinced him to go along with Cambridge's scheming. It was an action fuelled by temper rather than any constructive plan. Nevertheless, driven on by a fit of ill-advised pique, March had written to both Cambridge and Grey expressing his bitterness. It was only later, when he had had time to think and consider what he had done and as he thought over the implications of these momentous events that their full import slowly dawned on him and a frightening dose of reality started to break in.

The next day Grey and Cambridge – significantly Scrope was not present – made their way to Hamble, a few miles distant from prying eyes and ears in Southampton, to discuss their next steps with the Earl of March. They agreed to meet again in two days' time to finalise the plan to whisk March off to Wales. They were to have supper together on 31 July before making their way to Beaulieu and formally launching their rebellion from there.

When the two men left, March pondered on what he was now committed to. Presumably he had given the impression at the meeting with them that he was still committed to the plan but as the time for action loomed his enthusiasm waned by the hour. What exactly went through his mind can only be speculated on but some informed guesses may be made. Henry had already proved himself a determined warrior in Wales and here he was with a strong army ready at hand. If March deserted on the eve of the invasion of France Henry already had a strong force that he could redirect at once to put down the rebellion. March was no great soldier and the outcome of any battle with the king was uncertain, to put it mildly.

There was also no sign of widespread support for the plan. The earl did not have a large retinue of followers to call on for assistance and neither did the plotters. It would be a very narrowly based uprising and its chances of success were small. In the cold light of day, logic started to take prominence over ambition. It was clear that disaster loomed and the point of no return was fast approaching and might even have been passed. Faced with the enormity of what would follow once the plot was made public, March panicked.

All of a sudden the terror of the likely outcome of the imminent revolt made itself crystal clear to the earl. He could see no alternative but catastrophic defeat, the loss of all his possessions and almost certainly his life too. With the plot now too far gone to stop it becoming public knowledge within hours, March could only see one way out. The decision he was about to take represented the biggest risk of his life: nothing less than to make his way to the king and tell him all that he knew in the hope of mercy in return. It was a move driven either by cold, calculating courage or downright panic; the latter seems by far the most probable motivation.

March accordingly made the short journey to the king and sought an audience with him. The scene that was then played out must have been a dramatic one as it seems that the king still had no idea that a rebellion loomed and March's news came as a bolt from the blue. The earl, who must have been terrified throughout, blurted out to Henry all the details of the plot of which he would have been the main beneficiary. The interview took place at Portchester Castle, whose massive keep towered over the Roman walls that still enclosed it in its prominent spot overlooking Portsmouth Harbour. It occurred on 31 July and showed all too clearly why March was so poorly suited to be king as he effectively gave Henry the information that would sentence his co-conspirators to death to save his own neck.

Even some of the conspirators had serious doubts over March's personal qualities – Grey had called him the 'hog' – and these were well founded as he took measures to save his own life at the expense of theirs. After listening with increasing disbelief to the earl's tale, Henry sent orders summoning Cambridge, Grey and Scrope to Portchester. Each of them must surely have been terrified at receiving these instructions, and as they made the short journey from Southampton to Portchester they had little time to prepare themselves for the most awful interview of their life.

Henry's portrait, almost monkish in its severity, suggests a stern, hard man and those meetings with the king must have been terrifying because of the inevitability of their outcome. There was no option but to plead for mercy and no likelihood at all that that would be forthcoming. Faced with the prospect of a traitor's death, the plotters were taken back to Southampton for trial after their harrowing discussions with Henry. It was an awful day in the life of the conspirators; so too probably in a different way for the king, who must have been shocked to the core at what he had learned.

We cannot be certain exactly where in the castle these interviews took place. Portchester had been used several times before as the launching point for expeditions to France. From here King John had sent forth expeditions to recover lost lands in France in both 1205 and 1213, both of which ended in failure. More successfully Edward III had led his army from here in the campaign that culminated in the triumph of Crécy.[14] In fact, the Hundred Years War had given Portchester a new lease of life. Its position was perfect for launching an invasion of France but before the outbreak of the war it had fallen on hard times and was in danger of becoming dilapidated.

The castle's position, embraced by the waters of Portsmouth Harbour but adjacent to the Solent, made it an ideal embarkation point for France. It had been a royal castle for the majority of its existence. Richard II had added a palace, of which little but the shell now remains but at its peak it would have been a luxurious contrast to the grim keep. It now became the backdrop to an extraordinary scene. Henry may have had his initial interview with the Earl of March in his private apartments in the palace but probably grilled the co-conspirators in public in the great hall of the keep. Such great treason needed to be exposed publicly.

News of the plot could not have come at a worse time. Henry had sent out orders to the sheriff of Hampshire that all the thousands and thousands of men who had now assembled around Southampton should be ready to sail on 1 August or risk his 'grievous wrath' (they were spread over a wide area within thirty miles and more of the town). It would be a brave or foolish man who refused to take these stern words literally. March's disclosure shattered that plan. To leave England without the plot completely crushed would be an unforgivable risk. It would have been a perplexed, frustrated and, most of all, furious king who was suddenly forced to turn his attention elsewhere.

And so, with the port overflowing with troops awaiting their departure and with a reputed 1,500 ships bobbing at anchor offshore, Southampton witnessed the drama of this misguided and doomed plot move towards its grim conclusion as the three guilty men were brought out to face judgement. Grey had sought to receive mercy by condemning his fellow conspirators; he told of the meeting at Conisbrough with Cambridge and also of a chance meeting with his cousin, Sir Walter Lucy, on 19 July near Guildford as they were on their way to the south coast to embark for France.

Lucy was a close confidante of the Earl of March and was

informed of the plot, significant as 'no one was more familiar with the Earl of March's affairs' than he was.[15] Given his awareness of what was going on, and his lack of proactivity in informing Henry of it, he was lucky to escape the fate of those on trial for their lives; so too was Lord Clifford, who was also well aware of the plot by all accounts. Grey also gave a great deal of detail on Cambridge's plans, in particular his attempts to stir up rebellion in the north of England and Wales, making the outcome of the forthcoming trial an inevitability.

Grey's most damning intervention, though, concerned Lord Scrope, who was placed firmly at the centre of the plot even though he had been kept away from some of the key conversations. Scrope had a strong vested interest in keeping the Earl of March alive, as he was a significant debtor of his – the earl was hugely in debt as a consequence of the vast borrowings he had been forced to make to pay his fine. If March had been tried and condemned for treason, then his goods would have been forfeit and all chance of repayment would be gone.

Scrope was a man who appears to have loved his money more than most if not all other things, and therefore it is plausible to argue that he did not inform Henry of the plot so that his financial interests would be protected. It was hardly glorious and with the benefit of hindsight his actions were reckless and foolhardy; that does not mean, though, that he actively sought to remove the king from his throne.

The three men were charged with plotting the death of the king, the most heinous crime imaginable. Its very seriousness meant that there was no possibility of reprieve. Although a trial must be held for form's sake, its findings were mere formalities. Nevertheless the motions must be gone through and the men were incarcerated in

Southampton Castle pending trial. They would not have long to wait; it seems that Henry was in a hurry for justice and wished to make an example of those who sought to stir up trouble even as he was about to sail across the water. The precedent of the removal of Richard II, who effectively lost his throne while campaigning in Ireland, was too recent to ignore. Examples must be made.

Most modern historians point out that there is no evidence that there was a plot against the king's life.[16] From a modern legal perspective this may be true, but it is a point of view that takes too little cognisance of how matters appeared back in the fifteenth century, the context of that time as opposed to ours being crucial. Plotting to depose a king at the time would inevitably pose an enormous risk to his life, either in battle or after the event, as indeed had happened with Richard II. But it followed that if Henry were indeed a usurper who had himself benefited from the murder of God's anointed then his own position was not sanctified in the way that would be the case if he were the rightful king. All things considered deposition likely meant death. To argue otherwise would feel like splitting hairs to a man in Henry V's position when judged by the mores of the time.

The men had been arrested at Portchester on 31 July. A commission had then been set up to investigate the case as rapidly as possible led by John Mowbray, Earl Marshal, supported by a panel of earls, barons and judges with twelve jurors selected to pass judgement. On 2 August, the trial duly went ahead in Southampton. Both Cambridge and Grey admitted their guilt but Scrope denied any part in plotting to kill the king. The latter then claimed his right by law to be judged by his peers, which was undeniably due to him and was therefore granted both to Scrope and Cambridge, who also qualified for the privilege. Such a right dated back to the reign of Edward III, a monarch much admired by Henry V and therefore somebody whose precedent he would be reluctant to ignore.

As Grey came from a position further down the social ladder, no such privilege was granted him. He was condemned and promptly executed by the North Gate of Southampton though he was allowed to walk to his fate rather than being dragged to it on a hurdle. He was at least relieved of some of the worst barbarities of the penalty prescribed for high treason and 'merely' deprived of his head, which was sent off to Newcastle-on-Tyne to serve as a public reminder of the penalties of treason if any wished to follow his example.

That left Cambridge and Scrope to be dealt with. A panel was set up for the trial led by Thomas, Duke of Clarence, the king's brother. There were plenty of peers close at hand given the imminent departure of a number of them in Henry's army. It was an impressive array on the panel indeed: two dukes, eight earls and nine barons.

There would be one noticeable absentee from the trial, though. Edward, Duke of York, was given permission not to take part in it as his brother, the Earl of Cambridge, was one of those on trial for his life and the Earl of Dorset was to stand in as his deputy. Extraordinarily, one of those sitting in judgement was none other than the Earl of March, whose part in the plot that he stood to benefit from the most had been far from glorious. It was the ultimate conflict of interest.

Also sitting in judgement were William Botreaux and a number of nobles including John Holland, the future Earl of Huntingdon, and the earls of Arundel, Salisbury, Suffolk and Oxford. Clarence was given clear instruction in advance that following judgement, the substance of which was in no doubt, he should move rapidly to execution of the expected sentence.

In his confession, in which he talked of the plans to unseat 'Harry of Lancaster, usurper of England', Cambridge admitted his part in planning to take the Earl of March to Wales and set him up as king. Rebels in Wales were to seize several castles in support. He made no real defence of his actions, throwing himself on the king's mercy: 'Have you compassion on me, your liege man.' In a second and final appeal to the king he wrote one last time for mercy: 'For the love of our Lady and of the blissful Holy Ghost, to whom I pray that they may your heart induce to all pity and grace for their high goodness.'[17] Such eloquence would have no impact.

Scrope, on the other hand, refused to admit any part in a plan to kill the king. To some extent, Cambridge's confession, which stated that Scrope had not been kept informed of all developments, supported him. Scrope maintained that rather than encouraging March to go through with the plan, he did everything he could to talk him out of it. However, Grey's confession took the opposite line, firmly putting Scrope at the heart of the plot. In it, he had written that Walter Lucy, March's right-hand man, told Grey that Scrope had been to the earl 'and bade him take on hand for his right of the crown', in other words to seize the throne which was rightfully his. The Earl of Arundel was also accused of being in on this scheme by the confession, but he was a close supporter of the king and no further action was taken against him. However, this was also effectively 'hearsay' evidence as Grey had not heard the discussions first-hand.

Grey's confession proved to be the more convincing, although the lords had certainly made up their mind on the guilt of the men anyway. A panel of nineteen peers sat in judgement and did not take long to reach a conclusion. They listened unmoved as letters written by Cambridge and Scrope were read out at the start of the hearings before proceeding to hear the evidence.

Both men were found guilty at the hearing on 5 August and condemned to death. Cambridge was shown mercy to the extent that he would be beheaded without any of the torturous disembowelling or the hanging that sometimes preceded this punishment, an act of mercy which was formally attributed to his place in the royal bloodline. Scrope would suffer the indignity of being drawn through the streets of Southampton on a hurdle before also being beheaded. Being dragged along through the streets in this way was an extra humiliation that was said to be due to the fact that his disgrace was all the greater as he was a Knight of the Garter, that most esteemed of all English chivalric orders.

It was right and proper according to a chronicler of the time anyway, as Scrope was 'the more culpable an enemy because the more intimate a friend'.[18] Another near-contemporary commentator vividly described Scrope as 'the cunning fox'.[19] Other writers assert that the harsher sentence on the Lord of Masham was to 'mark the perfidy and ingratitude of Scrope, who had enjoyed the king's utmost confidence and friendship and had even shared his bed'.[20]

Scrope therefore received the more severe penalty and the king's malice towards him continued after his death later that day, soon after the trial ended; perhaps the king's grief had turned to anger for at least one chronicler stated that he had been moved to tears when he heard the details of Scrope's alleged conspiracy.[21] Cambridge, the arch-plotter, would be buried in Southampton with a degree of dignity, along with his head. Scrope's head, on the other hand, was sent to York for public display. It was almost black humour; Scrope was a devout man and he had written in his will that he wished to be buried in York Minster. Instead a public display at the Micklegate entrance to the city was the closest he would get.

Once he was gone Henry ruthlessly hunted down all Scrope's possessions, effectively condemning future generations of the family to relative hardship compared to their peers. In so doing, he conspicuously ignored Scrope's final pleas regarding the disposition of his goods, written out by him in a last pleading missive on the very day of his execution. Instead, within twenty-four hours of his execution he was reallocating Scrope's properties to his own supporters and sending his bailiffs to London to track down his movable possessions.[22]

But on the other hand Scrope was a man who was much more in the confidences of the king than Cambridge or Grey were. Earlier in the year, for example, he had been party to the king's defence plans for the realm as one of his inner circle. Henry was a human being as well as a king. Further, he was one who valued loyalty and the sense of his own kingly position highly. Given this, if he believed that Scrope was seriously plotting to replace him – and despite Scrope's protestations to the contrary, he had certainly handled the sensitive information he was party to with surprising ineptitude – then his harsh treatment of Scrope becomes more understandable, especially as there were suggestions made that he was not really committed to Henry's French venture. At the heart of all of this was an ultimate sense of betrayal felt by the king.

No such vindictiveness was meted out to Cambridge's family, though in fairness he had few possessions to worry about and perhaps the king did not want to upset the Duke of York who would be an important asset in France either. However, history has a habit of indulging in bitter irony from time to time. Cambridge left a young son, who would later become Duke of York, ironically because of the death of Cambridge's older brother at Agincourt. It was he who led the Yorkist party in that later dynastic struggle known to subsequent generations with misleading romance as the Wars of the Roses.

In turn this later duke's son would become Edward IV, King of England. In a twist of fate, the incumbent king he replaced, Henry VI, would be deposed, just as Henry IV had turned out Richard II. And Henry V's son, the disinherited king, would later die, almost certainly murdered on the orders of the executed Earl of Cambridge's grandson. History would travel full circle and Cambridge in his way would have his revenge. Perhaps unsurprisingly given this later regime change, the sentences against the plotters were annulled in 1461, nearly half a century too late to be of any practical benefit, as they were the result of an 'erroneous judgement'.[23]

The plot could hardly have come at a worse time for Henry. With his attentions fully focussed on France, the last thing he needed was trouble behind his back in England. The only saving grace was that March had not had the courage or conviction to go through with it. If a rebellion had actually started then it is very difficult to see how the king could have left England until it had been fully suppressed. Then the expedition would need to be abandoned for the year and there would have been no Agincourt.

Shakespeare, picking up on accusations that appeared at the time of these great events in the chronicles that were written, suggests that the plotters were in the pay of France. He was merely repeating what chroniclers at the time said; one spoke of 'the stench of French promises or bribes'.[24] Modern historians however are unconvinced and suggest that the planned coup appears to have been inspired more by frustrated ambitions and a desire to improve their lot on the part of the plotters. It is certainly true to say that the plotters, who seem to have been remarkably frank in their confessions on most other fronts, say nothing of any French involvement though of course that may be a deliberate and calculated omission on their part. It was fortunate for Henry that March was not a stronger personality, as the results may otherwise have been far more serious for him.

Yet in its own way the narrow base of the planned revolt and its small chances of success – the plot smacks more of desperation than any other characteristic – did suggest that the king's position was relatively secure. It was a far cry from the situation a decade before when his father had been forced to fight vigorously – with the help of his son – to put down determined attempts to remove him.

That said it is almost as easy to understate the dangers as it is to overstate them. Henry's actions on hearing of the plot are revealing. On the very same day that it was uncovered, he wrote to the Mayor of London of the risk of a Lollard uprising. As it happened, when a Lollard threat emerged just a few days later it was not from London at all but from Wales, where that arch-heretic (in Henry's eyes) Sir John Oldcastle emerged from hiding to issue a threat to the Lord of Abergavenny, Richard Beauchamp.[25]

It is interesting to say the least that at this very moment, if the plot had gone ahead as planned, the Earl of March should also have been in Wales. Cambridge had certainly considered the prospect of Lollard support for the uprising, though the devoutly orthodox Catholic Lord Scrope was apparently aghast at the idea. But the timing of Oldcastle's emergence from hiding is suspicious to say the least and the possibility that he had been to some extent involved in the plotting cannot be discounted though it also cannot be proven.

There was also still the threat from Scotland to consider. The Scots and the French were allies with a common enemy (much of the time) in England. The alleged involvement of Sir Robert Umfraville in the plot did not go unnoticed and he was relieved of his command of Roxburgh Castle, though no more severe action against him was taken than this. Ironically, his nephew Gilbert would play an important role in the Agincourt campaign. On 3 August, writs were sent to the Scottish borders commanding the regional militias to assemble to hold back any subsequent invasion of England from the north.

The nerve of many of Henry's commanders was badly shaken by these events. With a serious plot uncovered, the re-emergence of the Lollard threat and the danger of an attack from Scotland, the entire expedition was now in doubt. The writer of the *Gesta* stated frankly that 'many of those most devoted to the king wanted him to abandon his resolve to make such a crossing, both in case there should be any similar acts of treason still undiscovered and also, and especially, on account of the madness of Sir John Oldcastle and those of his persuasion – rumours spreading of an insurrection by him after the king had sailed'.

Faced with all these challenges the sensible thing to do would have been to have stayed in England. To leave now would be to take a grave risk. This seems to have been the advice of a number of his advisers: 'Many of those most devoted to the king still wanted him to abandon his resolve to make such a crossing.' The pressure was on for the king to abandon his enterprise.[26]

Modern historians have sometimes been critical of Henry and have stated with some possible justification that his greatness as a king has been exaggerated. He was also a flawed human being, capable of severity and ruthlessness, a cold, calculating man. All true – but also ignoring his ability to take the greatest of gambles in a winner-takes-all situation, something of a contrast to what might superficially appear to be his innate conservatism.

Now was such a time. Henry stayed strong and decided that it was now or never; his moment might never come again, his great army had assembled possibly for the one and only time. The expedition would leave as planned. Henry was capable of enormous personal courage, as would be seen just a few months later on the field of Agincourt. Arguably, though, his most courageous decision was to leave England at all in the first place.

But even though the departure of the armada had been delayed for only a few days it was still unfortunate for Henry's plans as it was now very late in the season to be thinking about an invasion of France. A medieval army's Achilles' heel was its supply lines, and to be trudging through the north of France, forced to live off the land when the weather was deteriorating, was a worrying thought. It was a delay that Henry could well do without.

This had been a sobering experience for the king. The plot caught him completely off guard. His response had been immediate and ruthless, a reaction that tells us much about Henry. Nothing angered him more than disloyalty, even when to be frank he had done little to deserve loyalty in the first instance from both March and Cambridge. It cannot have put him in a very good frame of mind as at last the fleet prepared to depart.

At least he could keep an eye on some other potential troublemakers who would be with him in France. The Duke of York cannot have been happy at the execution of his younger brother, though on the other hand maybe he would be inspired to fight all the harder in an attempt to prove his own loyalty. The plotters had gone out of their way in their confessions to confirm that he had no knowledge of the plot but it would have been understandable if some question marks had nevertheless been raised in the king's mind. It was good at least that Henry could see first-hand in France how York would react to this great personal blow.

And then there was that very lucky man, Edmund, Earl of March, whose spineless actions had broken the plot that had been hatched to put him on the throne of England. He was fortunate indeed to have survived it all; given the ruthless streak that ran through Henry we can only conclude that historians are right when they say that March was altogether too mediocre to be a genuine threat. In any event, almost immediately – on 7 August in fact – the earl was pardoned of any part that he might have played in the planned rebellion. But at least he too would be close at hand in France and could be watched. He would also need to be on his best behaviour.

It was a chastened king who at last gave the order that the fleet was to set out. At least the time for talking was finally over. It was now time for action. The king had staked all on going ahead as planned in an attempt for two of the greatest prizes possible: nothing less than France and his own place in history.

4

SOUTHAMPTON AND FRANCE: THE INVASION BEGINS (AUGUST 1415)

Dio Faza el meiody Christianity. (God help Christianity!)
The Venetian contemporary commentator d'Antonio Morisini

The area around the Solent had been home to thousands of troops for several weeks now. In its own way this was a smaller-scale version of the situation in 1944 when hundreds of thousands of soldiers gathered to invade France in a similar part of England. The presence of all these men in 1415 stretched the ability of the local economy to supply them with provisions to the limit. This situation would not have been helped by the further delays that had occurred because of the failed plot. Supplies had been brought in to a number of places including Titchfield, Southwick, Southampton, Lymington, Romsey, Alresford and Fareham. Some accounts infer that troops may even have been stationed 30 miles to the west at Poole, Christchurch and Canford, showing that the men were widely dispersed in an effort not to overload the local population.[1]

It is worth remembering that then, as in any other time, assembling large numbers of young men together in such a situation inevitably posed problems regarding law and order, even when they were in England. Adrenaline was running high and a sense of excitement was in the air. They also had a long march in some cases with plenty of opportunities for trouble.

Those men who had made their way down from Lancashire, Cheshire and Wales for example had to march hundreds of miles to get to the embarkation zone, a long journey even for mounted men. It is not clear they would all have been paid upfront. Henry had given undertakings that he would pay some of the first quarter of all soldier's wages in advance and he appears to have delivered on them; but passing the money on to the men's captains was one thing, being confident that they would hand it all on to their men quite another.

Men short of money was one matter likely to cause a problem; they needed to eat, drink and have lodgings en route to the south coast, which all needed to be paid for. On the other hand, paying them in advance created different difficulties. Young men could quickly squander the money and excessive alcohol consumption would create its own disciplinary problems. This situation was made worse as the contingents on their way to the south coast were not under a unified command yet as they would be in France.

In this context, it is interesting to note that several breakdowns in law and order were recorded while the men were still in England. In one incident English and Welsh soldiers took goods without paying in Warminster and were subsequently required to reimburse those they had wronged; if they did not do so then the local sheriff could call out a posse to bring them to order. And, in another very serious incident, four inhabitants of Salisbury were killed by men from Lancashire from the group of James Harington, a man-at-arms in Humphrey, Duke of Gloucester's contingent.[2]

The fighting took place upon the Fisherton Bridge. The dead were John Baker, William Hoare, Henry his servant and John Tanner. Among the assailants were two archers by the name of William Thornton and John Leveridge. The archers were far from natural-born heroes; some of them were rough, tough individuals, on occasion with a criminal background. Patriotism may have motivated some but most probably had reasons that were not all altruistic. For most personal profit from the campaign was the main motivator.

Given his problems, both with the failed plot and the practical difficulties in assembling and paying this very large army, it was probably with a sense of relief that the king was at last ready to set off for France. At around the same time Sir John Tiptoft also sailed with a much smaller force from Plymouth bound for Guienne. On 7 August, Henry was taken out from Portchester on the royal barge to join the armada. It was not until 11 August, though, that Henry was finally ready to set sail for France aboard the pride of his fleet, *Trinity Royal*, which was moored between Southampton and Portsmouth. Along the surrounding coastline thousands of men made their way out to the ships, some through the substantial town walls of Southampton, which had ironically been built as a response to a French sacking of the city in 1338 when it had been virtually defenceless against the assault.

It took several days to get everything on board the ships. For a start there were over 12,000 horses to be loaded and probably many more, as many of the archers were mounted and many of the knights would have each had a number of mounts with them. Each horse had to be raised on a hoist and lifted to the vessels on which they were to sail, which must have been a terrifying manoeuvre for them. But at least the crossing would not be excessively long and hopefully the weather would behave. At last, to the sound of drums and trumpets and the loud hurrahs of the thousands of men aboard, at three in the afternoon on 11 August the ships upped anchor and started their slow progress south.

Despite the large number of ships that had been begged, seized or borrowed there were still not enough. Minutes of Henry's council meeting held later on Saturday 6 March 1417 show that one of the items discussed was whether or not men who were ready to embark on the Agincourt expedition but could not due to a shortage of vessels should nevertheless be paid. The minutes note that the cash-strapped king said that they should not.[3] It is clear that some men were left behind because there were not enough ships to go round.

As the king's vessel headed for the horizon, its path was crossed by several swans. This was a good sign; the swan was considered a regal bird and their presence was perceived as a positive omen. Less encouraging was the sight of three ships that caught fire even before the fleet was in the Channel. All three were totally lost, the ships running aground and burning themselves out with others nearby not wanting to approach too close in case they also caught alight. Their captains had perhaps heard that in the recent plot plans had been discussed to set the fleet ablaze and maybe feared that this part of the conspiracy was still going ahead.

Few men would have looked forward to the crossing, which in those days could be a dangerous enterprise. The loss of the three ships served to remind men of the fact. The vast majority of the men would have been archers, probably over 75 per cent of the total number of fighting men aboard. It is likely that a number of them would be crossing for the first time.

The composition of the army was important. The expeditions of the previous century had typically seen a one-to-one ratio between men-at-arms and archers. During recent times, especially in the campaigns in Wales, that ratio had changed to one-to-three (and possibly even higher in practice). This was a very different ratio than they would see among the French forces they were soon to face, which had a much greater preponderance of men-at-arms. It emphasised the greater reliance the English placed on their archers, a matter of great significance when it came to battle tactics.

Due to the existence of large numbers of English records concerning those on the expedition, something is known of where these men came from. There were about 500 archers each from Lancashire and south Wales. The north of that country was considered too volatile to recruit from given the recent uprising in that area; most of the recruits from the south of Wales came from the counties of Carmarthen, Brecon and Cardigan, though the twelfth-century writer Gerald of Wales had considered the men of Gwent to be the best archers.[4] Over 600 bowmen were theoretically called up from Cheshire although only 294 subsequently appeared on the pay records.[5] All three areas had special connections with the king given that Wales was a principality and that the earldom of Chester and the duchy of Lancaster were also crown properties.

The men of Cheshire were prized archers whose stock had risen in recent decades. Their reputation had been established during the previous century and some of the men from the county formed part of the personal bodyguard of the late Richard II. If this seemed ironic, what made it even more so was the fact that Henry V might well have been injured by one of their arrows at the Battle of Shrewsbury. But Henry subsequently became the Earl of Chester and had great respect for the skills of the county's archers. Nevertheless it was perhaps significant that numbers from Cheshire appear, judging from the pay records that have survived, to be short of those required; this may suggest a lukewarm attitude from the men of Cheshire towards the king.

There were many men from neighbouring Lancashire too. Among them were three archers who appear on the Muster Rolls of those troops who presented themselves on the south coast for embarkation to France: William, Thomas and John Lathom. Their shared surname does not necessarily imply kinship for they were probably named after the Lancashire village of the same name, where they came from.

Lathom is a village in Lancashire close to Ormskirk, where other archers on the campaign came from. It appeared in the Domesday Book survey in 1086. A lucrative marriage in 1385 brought it into the orbit of Sir John Stanley, a man who had made a name for himself in the French wars. This helped him when he was implicated in a murder in England in 1376. A one-time supporter of Richard II, like many others Stanley proved very talented at changing sides adroitly. He later served Henry IV and his son well, becoming a Knight of the Garter and latterly Henry V's Lord Lieutenant in Ireland. He had fought at the Battle of Shrewsbury where he was wounded in the throat with an arrow.

Stanley's death in 1414 prevented his taking part in Henry V's French venture but he may have been too old or too valuable where he was to go anyway even if he had lived. He was succeeded by a ten-year-old son who was clearly too young to be involved. Nevertheless the men of Lathom did their bit, as they did in other conflicts in this period; John of Lathom was a man-at-arms during the French campaign of 1375 and Thomas Lathom (perhaps the same man who served in 1415?) was in France in 1443.[6] The Stanley connection with the Lancastrian cause would be a long-lasting one: future generations would play a pivotal role at the Battle of Bosworth in 1485, which brought the Wars of the Roses to an end, dethroned the Yorkist Richard III and put Henry VII on the throne.

Although the archers that took part in the 1415 expedition are not nameless – the Muster Rolls of those who presented themselves for the departure give us thousands of names – they are largely faceless. We can know little of their individual histories. But there are clues in their names, especially as to their possible point of origin. Literally several hundred archers have names with the tell-tale inclusion of 'ap' (Welsh for 'son of'), giving a very clear indication of the general region from which they came. That story is a well-trodden furrow, talked up notably by Shakespeare. It reflected the fact that Wales was a poor country well stocked with tough and hardy fighting men who had a long tradition of fighting alongside the English, for example in previous campaigns to Scotland and France.

However, in many ways the English places suggested by some of the names are just as interesting. This truly seems to have been a national force even if there were sizeable elements from Lancashire and Cheshire. There were a number of archers with the surname Bolton, which probably often refers to the town in Lancashire though there are other places in Britain with the same name, such as another in Yorkshire. The names William Oldham and Peres Wigan also suggest a Lancastrian origin while Hugh Ollesmere probably emanated from Ellesmere in Cheshire. The origins of John Orkenay, on the other hand, suggest a potentially fascinating story and a point of origin far to the north. But William Tailor of Ormeskirk was presumably also a Lancashire man from a place just three miles from Lathom.

We have information of some other men from the region who were involved, such as Sir Peter de Legh of Lyme Hall, Sir John Savage of Runcorn, Sir Ralph Bostock from near Northwich, as well as Sir Richard Kyghley from Inskip in the Fylde in Lancashire. There was also the Sheriff of Lancashire, Robert Urswick, in command of the hundreds of archers from that county.[7] The north-west of England proved a fertile recruiting ground for Henry.

There were others from regions close to Lancashire if we judge from the surnames. Six archers bear the surname Kendale, which presumably refers to the town of Kendal in Cumbria. Other Cumbrian names that may be suggested include Richard Penreth and William Sedborough. This is in some ways surprising as it might be expected that men from this region would be required to participate in the defence of the borders against Scotland in the king's absence. There are also a number of Prestons, which probably refer to the town in Lancashire although again this is a place name that is found elsewhere in England.

However, there are definite indications of others from wider afield in England. Walter Somerby probably came from the village of that name in Leicestershire, suggesting strong Lancastrian connections. John of Leicester probably came from a nearby part of England in the Midlands as did Robert and William Lutterworth. A number of archers bear the surname Kent. Several archers have a surname which hints at an origin in Oswestry on the Welsh borders. John Spaldyng presumably came from Lincolnshire.

John, Richard and Thomas Notyngham's names clearly imply

their origins as do the even more unambiguous John of Coventry, Henry of Derbyshire and John of Grantham. John Norffolk presumably came from East Anglia and four archers bore the surname London. Three men, Henry, Robert and William, bore the surname Sheffield and there were several men with the surname Beverley. William Swaldale was presumably a Yorkshireman too, as were Thomas Halifax and several men with the surname York, while John Chesterfeld came from further south in Derbyshire. Kirkeby of Newcastle and Kirkeby of Gateshead, on the other hand, were from the north-east of England.

There are other names that suggest more of a West Country origin. Thomas Pokkeswell probably came from the small hamlet of Poxwell in West Dorset, while Laurence Poyntyngton may have emanated from Poyntington on the Somerset–Dorset border and several 'Shirbornes' possibly came from the abbey town of that name in the latter county, which was strongly connected to the Lancastrian cause through their landholdings there. There was also a Robert Pokeswelle, a man-at-arms in the retinue of the Lord Maltravers who probably came from the same area as Thomas. The names of about a dozen archers start with the syllable 'Tre', indicating a Cornish origin. On the other hand, Jacob Bewley may well be a Hampshire man from Beaulieu.

Some names are less helpful. John Englyssh tells us something of his national origins but little else and the surname Sutton that is carried by seventeen men could refer to a number of places in England. However, one interesting name is that of John Berthelot, which refers initially to a French surname which eventually became established in English as Bartlett.

While the metropolis of London was a bustling, busy port and there was a trend of movement away from rural to urban areas in England, the majority of people still lived in insignificant settlements scattered around the countryside or in small towns. Poxwell – 'Pokkeswell' – is an example of the many small settlements that still typified much of the country at the time. It was probably little more than a hamlet. Although predating Agincourt by over three centuries, the Domesday Book gives us some information about Poxwell in the eleventh century.

Back then (when it was part of the lands held by Cerne Abbey in Dorset) there were seven ploughs, fifteen acres of meadows as well as pasture enough to support one cob, six pigs and 200 sheep. Wool from the sheep may well have been sent for export from the nearby port of Melcombe (near Weymouth) to the Continent; much wool trading was done via the lands of the Duke of Burgundy in Flanders, which underscores one of the reasons for Henry's desire to be on good terms with him.

With a prominent hilltop position atop the chalky downs of south-central Dorset, Poxwell looked out over the English Channel across which the ships now sailed to France some fifty miles to the east. Little of the Poxwell of Thomas's time now remains in the small settlement that has survived. Even the church was destroyed by misguided Victorian do-gooders wishing to improve the landscape. Yet tantalising clues remain to that former era when perhaps a young man from the village left for the adventure of his life. Next to the churchyard that sits in a field without a church is a wall with a masonry door opening in it. This looks very much like a survival from a medieval church while a nearby barn incorporates a window built into it which suggests an initial origin in a Perpendicular ecclesiastical building using an architectural style that started to emerge in the mid-fourteenth century.

Of course there were practical reasons why Henry wanted to

spread his recruitment net as wide as possible across England and assemble as large an army as he could, leaving few stones unturned in the process. But there were very useful side-effects too. Recruiting across the country helped to bring the nation together, an important quality for a king who wished to rule a unified, single-minded realm. There were most definitely important benefits to this expedition in addition to the possible conquest of France.

From higher up the social ladder than the archers were men such as Sir Thomas Erpingham, a knight from Norfolk. In his late fifties, he had been a strong supporter of the House of Lancaster, and in particular Henry IV, for decades. His career had been extraordinary. He had been one of those who had called firstly for the deposition of Richard II and then for his complete elimination. He had become steward of Henry V's household and was undoubtedly in his inner circle of advisers. He had been present during many of the meetings at which the details of the current campaign had been hammered out. He had also, on 24 July just past, been a witness to the king's will and then, a week later, had sat in judgement on the Southampton plotters.

He had indentured with the king to bring eighty men to the expedition, twenty men-at-arms and sixty archers; the classic one-to-three ratio. This was in the mid-range in terms of size; the largest single contingent, 960 men, was provided by Thomas, Duke of Clarence, 800 by the Duke of Gloucester (both men were brothers of the king), and the Duke of York and Thomas Beaufort, Earl of Dorset, the king's uncle, had provided 400 each. Full details of Erpingham's company, fortunately for historians, have survived the ravages of time, enabling remarkable details to become known.[8]

There is even a surviving effigy of Erpingham that may give us an idea of what he looked like, though we cannot be sure that it was a true likeness. It probably comes from his tomb in Norwich Cathedral, which has now sadly been lost. It later reappeared on the so-called Erpingham Gate at the entrance to Norwich Cathedral Close. It shows a man, kneeling humbly in the position of prayer, with long, curly hair (although possibly balding) – the haircut was unfashionable, with close-cropped hair, as famously shown in Henry V's portrait, the preferred fashion, possibly to make wearing a helmet more comfortable[9] – and he had a flowing, full beard. He looks modest but determined. From eye-witness accounts we can colour in a few more details too, such as the fact that he was grey-headed, unsurprising given his stage in life.

From the very top notch of society were men like Edward of Langley, 2nd Duke of York. Here was a man with probably very mixed emotions, who had witnessed the traumatic events that led to the execution of his brother on the very eve of the armada's departure from England. He was closely connected to the royal family, being a grandson of Edward III, and he had served Richard II and Henry IV as well as the current king. Like many men in Henry's entourage he was a survivor who had managed to manoeuvre his way safely through some of the dangerous political mood-swings that had characterised recent decades. He was also an experienced soldier, having fought in England, Wales and Guienne. However, he was not by this stage in his physical prime and an exhausting campaign lay ahead.

His actions during the reign of Henry IV suggest a man who was hedging his bets. Although he never actively took up arms against the king, he was implicated indirectly – but quite closely – in several plots against him. Nevertheless he was far enough removed from their epicentre to survive (though he did spend several brief spells in prison). In all probability Henry IV did not want to make a martyr out of such an important man given the fact that he did not have to look very far for other enemies. By sending him off to the distant position of his commander in Guienne, he perhaps hoped to keep him away from English politics, though as it happened he did not spend very long in that posting.

York was in the good graces of Henry V when he came to the throne and had served in his embassies in the abortive attempts to negotiate for the hand of Catherine of Valois. He had married Philippa Mohun, a strange match to which she brought little, having not much in the way of possessions. She was also twenty years older than him. This perhaps helped to explain why they had no children and that their heir was York's nephew Richard, whose father, the Earl of Cambridge, had been executed in Southampton just a few days previously. York was known to be a keen hunter and had written a book on the subject, *The Master of Game* (in fact, a translation of a French book to which he had added a few chapters).

Few personal letters have survived from 1415 to relate the experiences of the men involved but one that has was penned by a royal esquire by the name of John Cheney on 12 July. It was written to Sir John Pelham and after the customary pleasantries it reveals that John Holland, the future Earl of Huntingdon, had set to sea with several ships in what was an advanced raiding party. Cheney went on to reveal the main purpose of his letter: he was short of money and requested Pelham 'to lend me some notable sum of gold'.[10] His king was clearly not the only man in Southampton at the time who was in need of more funding.

The exact purpose of Holland's expedition is not known for certain but it may well have been connected with violence at the town of Fécamp in Normandy which took place on 16 July 1415. It appears that a number of townspeople foresaw that this was just the start of yet greater trials and tribulations to come and packed up their belongings and left; refugees are not just a by-product of modern wars. But the presence in an important post of Holland, who was a young, inexperienced warrior at the time and whose family had not long before been in disgrace, suggests that something in this young man had attracted Henry's attention. Perhaps Henry recognised a kindred spirit, someone with something to prove.

As the rest of the ships prepared to make their way across the Channel many men, like soldiers of more recent times, took measures to ensure that, should they not come back, their affairs would be in order. One of those who did so was William Botreaux, the Lord of Cadbury in Somerset. He wished to be buried in the parish church of Cadbury. He left a good deal of his possessions to his wife. These included utensils and furniture, a basin and ewer of silver, five new goblets, a drinking cup of gold in the shape of a rose and vestments for her altar decorated in peacock feathers and velvet.

Botreaux was twenty-six years old and had two daughters but no son. He left £1,000 to them in his will but if they inherited his estate in the absence of a son then the money was to be distributed to the poor instead. This was a very generous act but Botreaux probably had a vested interest in making it, namely the well-being of his immortal soul. Such Christian charity would stand him in good stead with the Almighty. That he was a conventionally religious man for the time we can tell, as he asked that three priests should hold services at Cadbury for his soul and those of his ancestors. A number of friaries and monasteries were also remembered in the will.[11]

Although England did not have a standing army that did not mean that the arts of war were left to chance – far from it. English kings had long recognised the brutal stopping power of the archer; Edward I had employed it to devastating effect at the Battle of Falkirk as long ago as 1298 and the part played by them in the triumph of William the Conqueror at Hastings in 1066 is well known.[12] Yet it was Edward III who took fullest advantage of the opportunities given to him by the skill of his archers; his victories over the French, at Crécy in particular, relied significantly on the prowess and killing power of his archers and these had done much to inspire Henry V in his efforts to finish what that earlier King of England had started.

Henry was certainly not the first English king to understand the importance of the archer. Edward III had passed legislation in 1363 requiring that archers keep their skills well honed. This had been reinforced by further orders passed by Richard II in 1388 and Henry IV in 1410.[13] These orders stipulated that archers were required to practise their skills on Sundays and feast days so that when the time for war came they were properly prepared. Years of practice were about to be tested on the field of battle.

Of course, there were not just men and thousands of horses to ship, there were also large stocks of provisions to ferry across too. Although the army would have to live off the land to some extent, it would also need to have a large volume of supplies to start the campaign with before further stocks could be secured locally. These included bread, beans, cheese, ale, clothes, shoes and many live animals such as cattle, sheep and pigs.[14] The stench in the enclosed spaces of the small ships must have been overpowering.

News of the invasion was soon to spread further afield. The Venetian d'Antonio Morisini had been following developments from a distance. When he heard that the French delegation to England had achieved nothing, he noted, 'God help Christianity.' He had heard that a hugely inflated number of Englishmen (100,000) were to be involved. He had also learned that Venice's great rival, Genoa, had incurred the wrath of the English king so this was not all bad news, though like the good Venetian that he was he was concerned about any effect on commerce that the war might have.[15]

The size of the English army according to Morisini appears frankly ridiculous but there may be a good reason for this. Richard Courtenay, Bishop of Norwich, was a man who was seemingly involved in a most un-episcopal function, namely as one of the main men for Henry's spying activities. He had apparently tried to recruit a canon of Nôtre-Dame by the name of Jean de Fusoris and later sent him a message via a captured French cleric, Raoul le Gay, telling him that the English army was some 50,000 strong. This suggests that there was something of a campaign of disinformation going on, whereby the English were talking up the size of their army in some quarters, presumably to spread fear and despair among their enemies.[16]

The crossing took the English fleet two days. On 13 August, fishermen off the coast of France spotted the vast armada. When they returned to their home port of Boulogne the news was quickly despatched across France. Raiding by the English had already started from Calais at the beginning of August, possibly pre-planned to coincide with the original date scheduled for departure from Southampton but premature given the unfortunate events that forced the king to postpone his original plans.

At about 5 p.m. on the evening of 13 August, the *Trinity Royal* anchored off Chef de Caux, a hamlet (now named St Adresse) just three miles from Harfleur. There was now no doubt where the army was headed, no further need for any possible disinformation hinting that Guienne and the south were the target. A council of war was called by Henry. No one was to land on French soil before the king without his permission, on pain of death; he was worried that if men were to go ashore prematurely they would be distracted by the lure of plunder and discipline would be lost as a result.

He was quite probably also worried that an undisciplined landing could expose his force to counter-attack. He did not yet know if there were significant French forces nearby and even though his army was large by the standards of the time, if they were assaulted before a significant part of it was ashore and in a good defensive position then chaos could follow. In any era an amphibious attack was at its most vulnerable when it was in that no man's land, with some men on dry land, perched on the shoreline, and the others at sea; British, American and Canadian soldiers would find this out just over 500 years later nearby.

A small advance party was sent ashore that night. Its purpose was to reconnoitre and find out exactly what resistance could be expected. With them would be the hugely experienced John Cornwall and his young but talented stepson, John Holland. Holland was also the first cousin of the king, sharing a grandfather in John of Gaunt.

Cornwall was an important man too, being uncle by marriage to the king; he had been a warrior for a quarter of a century and would show himself to be one of the most effective of all soldiers present with the army. Other men-at-arms were also with them on this initial sortie to spy out the lie of the land. They returned the next day. Henry, a cautious commander by nature, would not move until he was confident that the landing was likely to succeed. It was crucial that the king's army should establish a bridgehead before they were counter-attacked.

Henry was taken ashore at about seven in the morning on Wednesday 14 August, in the religious calendar of the time the Vigil of the Assumption of the Blessed Virgin, commemorating the 'dormition' (or 'falling asleep') of Mary. As she was someone to whom the king was especially devoted, it was a particularly apposite moment to begin his great adventure.

It was a beautiful day and the sun shone down approvingly on his enterprise. Henry fell on his knees when he landed, praying that he might do justice to his enemies. A number of men were knighted on the beach in the hope that they might be inspired to fight more valiantly in honour of their new-found status; among them were two men in Erpingham's company, Thomas Geney and John Calthorpe.[17] Mass was then held for the religiously minded king and the camp was set up on Mont Leconte. The king lodged in the nearby priory at Graville.

The landing site was not ideal, though. The shoreline was lined with boulders which could potentially cause the ships much damage. Behind the shoreline were deep ditches, moats filled with water, and next to them were earthen ramparts. The causeways across the ditches were narrow. It could have been a perilous place to land but the landing site was devoid of any defenders. Even a small number could have created significant problems for Henry's force according to one who was there,[18] but there were no enemies in sight. A gilt-edged opportunity to intercept the landings had been missed.

But unlike the German defenders of Normandy in June 1944, the French in the region of Harfleur in 1415 were at that precise moment in no position to attempt to fight off the invasion. The nearest sizeable force, of some 1,500 men under Charles d'Albret, was at Honfleur on the southern side of the Seine Estuary. Even if he could have moved them up in time he had too few men with him to fight back the English as soon as they had started to come ashore in significant numbers. There were only a few hundred men in Harfleur itself, which meant that they would be vastly outnumbered. Without help their position already looked difficult.

The shoreline where the English came ashore was at the bottom of a valley overlooked by hills and just a few miles from Harfleur. The army made its way up the hill and established itself close to the port hoping for a successful, and short, siege. The clock was now ticking for those inside the town walls, which could as easily become their tomb as a means of defence. There was a small force under a knight, Raoul de Gaucourt, a few days off and if they could force their way into the town they could make a useful if hardly decisive contribution to the defence. But time was running short. It would take a little time for Henry to unload all those ships but with each passing day he grew stronger, as did his foothold in France. He would be able to lay a tight siege around Harfleur and slowly and deliberately squeeze the life out of it.

Except that Henry did not want to waste weeks in a siege of the port. Sieges were expensive and inglorious. They also introduced an unwelcome element of uncertainty into the equation. Sieges could drag on for months, the costs could escalate and men would start to drop, from malnutrition or disease, those invisible but lethal forces. Other men would become despondent and disillusioned and their morale would suffer; some would desert, although that would be a more difficult feat than it would have been if they had been in Britain.[19] Nevertheless, despite the distance and the fact that the English Channel cut men off from home, there would later be some evidence that desertion would indeed be a problem.

A siege also meant a loss of initiative. The besiegers were in danger of being attacked from the rear, finding themselves besieged as a result. Supply lines would be stretched too; although the English had a large fleet now, they could not keep it for long. Most of the vessels were 'arrested' or hired and would need to return to their normal business soon. Henry did not want to be held up at Harfleur for one second longer than he needed to be.

The choice of Harfleur for this initial assault was interesting. Although the main reasons were probably strategic ones, the target also conveyed a powerful message. The Treaty of Brétigny, the Great Peace, did not include Normandy as one of those territories to be handed over to the English king. Therefore under its terms Henry had no claim to it. But as the French had reneged on the terms of that treaty, Henry was effectively winding the clock further back than the time at which it was signed, to the moment when Edward III – in Henry's eyes, actions and words – became the King of France by right. Henry based his claim to Harfleur not on the treaty but on his divine right to be king of the whole of France.

The town had been a significant port from Roman times, when it was known as Caracotinum. As Heresfloth it had been a Viking seaport where it grew up opposite its sister, Onderfluth (now Honfleur), on the other side of the Seine. More recently it had formed part of the duchy of Normandy, in the hands of the kings of England until most of those territories had been lost in the time of King John (the Channel Islands alone stayed English). The French had come to realise its potential significance and usefulness to the English and a rebuilding programme had been undertaken between 1341 and 1361 to defend it more adequately. The walls were pierced by three gates, the Porte d'Eure, the Porte de Rouen and the Montivilliers Gate, each of them protected to the front by a barbican.

The newness of the walls was a help to the defence; on the other hand, the shortage of defenders was not. And Henry was well equipped with the latest available technology in cannon, which had at the time evolved to a stage where they were beginning to give a significant advantage over fixed fortifications, many of which had been constructed in a very different era when no such powerful artillery weaponry was available. However, the defenders had some artillery of their own which had been recently sent to them in anticipation that the English might land somewhere in the area.

Yet the effectiveness of cannon should not be overplayed; their efficacy was still in the process of improving. At the siege of the castle of Vexellon in 1409 the firing of 1,200 shots weighing up to 850 lbs did not manage to bring the defences down. They were also incredibly slow; at Tannenberg in 1399 some large cannon only managed to fire once a day. It was not until after the Agincourt campaign, and indeed beyond the reign of Henry V, that such weapons really began to change the balance of power in war.[20]

With a population of about 5,000 people, Harfleur was a large but not massive town by the norms of the day. Its encircling walls, liberally scattered with towers, stretched for some two and a half miles. These were given colourful names such as the Lion, the Dragon, the Stork, the Swan, the Snail, the Stag, the Tin Pot and the Pies' Nest.

Inside these all-embracing walls there was an inner port, making it one of the most significant seaports in north-west France opposite the coast of England. The harbour was protected, as many such sites were at the time (Constantinople being the most famous example), by thick chains that could be stretched across its mouth to prevent the entry and exit of enemy ships.

It was in peacetime a busy port with regular trade with England, Portugal, Venice, Genoa, Ireland, Flanders, Aragon and Castile. In wartime it would be an excellent harbour base for the English if they captured it, a place where more supplies could be shipped in as well as providing a good launch pad for a move deeper into Normandy. It was an attractive prize if it could be taken quickly at the start of the campaign.

The town was not unprepared for the attack that was now imminent. Additional bulwarks had been built up around the gates as an extra line of defence. These were circular in shape, constructed of tree trunks sunk into the ground vertically and lashed together. The interior was packed with earth as an early form of defence against the impact of artillery. A moat around each of them added further to the complexities of attacking them. There were gaps in the walls to allow cannon fire and crossbow bolts to be directed at any attacker who ventured too close.

Some of the roads leading out of the town had been dug up and the rubble created brought into Harfleur to be fired from catapults. The river approach into Harfleur had been booby-trapped with pointed stakes and sluice gates had been shut so that the valley to the north of the town was flooded. This prevented an approach from that particular direction, which added significantly to the complexities of an attack. There might be a shortage of defenders inside, and those that were there were hugely outnumbered, but it appeared that Harfleur would not fall without a fight.

A river, the Lézarde, ran down from the north. Before it reached the town, it split into two. One arm ran to the west of the walls, forming a natural moat to further strengthen the defences. The other was allowed egress to the town by sluices cut into the walls. This meant that a reliable supply of water was available to the defenders of Harfleur, boosting the chances of a successful defence. It also meant that French ships with reinforcements and supplies could still come into the town unless the English took command of the sea approaches. On the other side of the town, the south, marshland made an approach difficult too. This was a strong and very defensible position.

There was a need for the invasion force to top its provisions up right from the off. It was not feasible, nor was it expected, that such an invading force would rely solely on a shuttle service of supplies being brought over from England, though there would certainly be one in place. The army would to some extent have to live off the land, though the situation might ease should Harfleur fall and a new entry route into France be secured as a result.

Henry, realising that he would have to fight if he were to take Harfleur, meticulously made the preparations for the assault. The suburbs around the town were burned to the ground. This made it easier for his cannon and siege engines (which he had ferried with him across the Channel)[21] to move into position to begin the bombardment. Inside the walls, the citizens steeled themselves for what was to come. No doubt some of them made their way to the fine church of St Martin in the town to pray for salvation, either in this life or the next, and protection from the horrors of the assault that loomed.

The rules of medieval warfare were clear and extremely harsh. The citizens should be given a chance to surrender. However, if they rejected this and a fight began, then the prize would be for the captor to treat as he wished. Often in the aftermath of capture a period of rapine and pillage would follow in which no one would be safe.

Henry was a man with a strictly legalistic mind. He had developed such cogent and convincing arguments that France was rightfully his that he had convinced himself that no other interpretation of the position was possible. It followed, taken to its logical conclusion, that the citizens of Harfleur by refusing to let him in were not playing the parts of patriotic Frenchmen and women but were rebels, to whom the most awful punishment could be meted out.

Henry was an unknown quantity in France. However, the little that was known of him suggested a man of ruthless determination who would not shy away from harsh measures if required. His recent execution of the Southampton plotters and the burning alive of Lollard heretics in his own country suggested a man who would be fierce in his prosecution of this war. The siege was ready to begin and those inside Harfleur could only hope and pray that relief would be sent to them in time to protect their property and their lives from the enemy at the gates.

Henry was well aware of the importance of keeping discipline among his men though. Because armies were impromptu affairs, thrown together for a specific campaign, it was very difficult to keep control and this could have catastrophic results in battle. He therefore wanted to instil a strong sense of discipline and to facilitate this Henry issued some demanding ordinances for his men to abide by.

Much may be read into the ordinances that he issued regarding both his character as a man and his philosophy for the campaign.

Orders were to be obeyed without question. Crucially from a military standpoint, no one was to break ranks without being given leave to do so. Such actions were a real Achilles' heel in medieval warfare and defeat could be grasped from the jaws of victory when an over-enthusiastic force lost its discipline and the advantage with it. In a similar vein no one was to ride flying a banner unless he were a messenger, as if they did so it could be misconstrued as a signal to go on to the attack. An uncoordinated assault might follow with disastrous consequences for the cohesion of the army.

Non-combatants were especially referred to by Henry. Churches and religious buildings were to be protected and stealing from them was to be a serious offence; this offers an insight both into Henry's essential piety and also his need not to antagonise the Church, which was a major political power at the time. No clergymen or women were to be harmed or captured. Rape was forbidden and violators of this edict were to be put to death. No buildings were to be burned unless specific orders were given to do so.

The measures taken to protect civilians offer an important insight into Henry's thinking. A medieval army considered that rape and pillage were its right, especially if an injunction to surrender was ignored. The Hundred Years War was a terrible time for the citizens of France in the areas that were affected as they suffered dreadfully from depredations by both English and French troops. Indeed, the deliberate targeting of towns and cities was a core tactic of armies during the conflict in an attempt to destroy local economies and with it the will and ability to fight. Henry's rules for this particular campaign in 1415 contrast markedly with the ruthless *chevauchées* conducted during the time of Edward III.

Other rules were laid out by the king to deal with the vexed question of prisoners. The situation was problematic because prisoners had a value and whoever owned the rights to them could potentially earn large sums of money. Grooms and pages were not to argue over captured prisoners or equipment; if they did so, they were to have their left ear cut off. If a man were captured, his helmet and gauntlet should be taken to stake a claim to him. It was forbidden to kill a man if he were trying to submit. These injunctions to protect prisoners would assume a rather hollow ring on the field of Agincourt.

One final clause in the ordinances gives another dimension to all this. No women were to be allowed into the camp, in fact none were allowed within three miles of it. Some have interpreted this as an example of Henry's essential prudishness when it came to sex[22] and they may well be right. But there is another plausible reason too. Prostitutes could interfere with military discipline and could distract men from their main task: fighting. This had been so great a problem after the siege of Acre during the Third Crusade that Richard the Lionheart had ordered all females except washerwomen away from his camp. Henry, too, wanted no problems with prostitutes in the camp. A woman who was a first offender was to be thrown out of the camp. If she then tried again, she was to have her left arm broken.

The issuing of such ordinances was not innovative. Henry's instructions to protect church property, clerics and civilians echo closely others issued by Richard II in 1386.[23] And those issued by Richard I while on crusade were much harsher, perhaps unsurprisingly given his fierce reputation. These included stark warnings that any man who killed another at sea would be tied to the corpse and both would be thrown overboard. Any crusader who struck down his fellow on land would be buried alive with him. For merely drawing a knife against another, a man could have his hand cut off.[24]

Among those on board ship with the expedition was an unidentified cleric. This man without a name is one of the most important members of the expedition from a historian's perspective, for within a year or so of the Battle of Agincourt he would commit his thoughts to parchment. It is to him that we owe the work known as the *Gesta Henrici Quinti – The Deeds of Henry the Fifth –* on which much of our information on the campaign is based. Modern historians may claim that he was not an unbiased chronicler, and they would be right; no such writer produced his work without an agenda. But by the same token it would be unwise to reject everything he says out of hand for he can claim something that no modern historian can – he witnessed what he wrote about with his own eyes.

Much of what we know about the expedition and the battle that marked its climax comes from this unnamed man. He, along with his companions, must surely have wondered what now lay ahead. The Channel had been breached and the men were ashore. The army and its king were about to step into the unknown. For the great, like the Duke of York, and the humble, such as Thomas Pokkeswell from Dorset, a leap of faith had been taken and no one quite knew where it would yet lead them and how it would all end. They were now in the hands of Fate or, as most of them at the time would have seen it, of the Almighty Himself.

5

HARFLEUR: THE OBSTINATE DEFENCE (AUGUST – SEPTEMBER 1415)

Not only were the combatants laid flat but also the beautiful buildings of the town.

Thomas of Walsingham on the siege of Harfleur

On 17 August, the siege of Harfleur began. Henry divided his army into three contingents, or 'battles' (from which word the modern 'battalion' derives). He himself led the one in the centre, in keeping with his desire to reinforce his image as a warrior-king. In medieval times it was expected that a king would lead his army into battle. He would therefore run the risk of being captured or even killed, as for example King Harold had at Hastings or Richard I when he was mortally wounded while campaigning in France.

It is no coincidence that the two kings of England to be deposed and subsequently probably murdered, namely Edward II and Richard II, did not have positive reputations as warriors. A third unsuccessful general, King John, came within a hair's breadth of also losing his crown. It is also significant that Henry V's own son, the later Henry VI, would prove to be an unsuccessful warrior and he too would lose his throne and his life. Having a reputation as a soldier was not an option but a necessity for a successful medieval King of England.

One of the battles besieging Harfleur was under the command of Thomas, Duke of Clarence, already an experienced commander even though he was Henry's younger sibling. The other was probably under the Duke of York, the most prominent member of the nobility there (if one excludes the Duke of Gloucester, another brother of the king but a man with little experience) and a very seasoned campaigner.[1] In the later Middle Ages there were some paradoxical forces at play; even as society started to change and allow more opportunities for those lower down the social scale, military command was increasingly vested in the aristocracy or 'great men' of the country as the upper classes perhaps sought to protect their own position vis-à-vis the rest.[2]

Both men had some personal issues to face up to. Clarence had been the late king's favourite son and some had even suggested that Henry IV would rather have had him as his heir than his elder brother. It is significant that Clarence never received a major independent command from Henry V and neither was he left in England as regent in Henry's absence, which would have been an obvious move to make as he was next in line to the throne. It was as if Henry did not trust his brother to be in control of England while he was away campaigning in France.

This was also a big moment for York. He was in a key position in the campaign and would become more so as it went on. If he suffered any pangs of doubt following the death of his brother, he did not show it. His performance in the next few weeks suggested that he was fully behind his king and his cause. Like other men in times of war, he had his own mortality to think about and on the same day that the siege of Harfleur began he made out his will. In common with many other warriors over the years, he knew there was a real chance that he might not come back alive from this expedition.

He had experienced a long and eventful career so far, one not without its problems. Born in 1373 and later becoming the Earl of Rutland, in 1402 he inherited the dukedom of York on the death of his father, Edmund of Langley, who was the first man to hold that prestigious title. He had then become a valuable supporter of the then Prince of Wales, now King Henry V, during his campaigning in Wales. But despite these signs of preferment there were hints of suspicions about his loyalty over a number of years. As a grandson to Edward III he was rather close to the line of succession himself and he had also served in the administration of Richard II, who treated him well throughout his reign.

The favour shown to York by his cousin Richard II was seen when he was just a small boy, when he was knighted at the king's coronation in 1377. Ten years later he was admitted as a Knight of the Garter, the foremost chivalric order in England. Richard had then made him the Earl of Rutland in 1390, and he was soon after appointed admiral of England's northern fleet in 1391. This was followed by being granted the earldom of Cork in Ireland, where he campaigned with the king.

He also became a member of Richard II's council. Later in the 1390s he became Constable of England and further grants to him followed from the king as well as his installation as the Duke of Aumerle (as which he makes an appearance in Shakespeare's *Richard II*). He went with Richard to Ireland on his ill-fated campaign in 1399, during which Henry Bolingbroke, as he then was, had launched his invasion of England that eventually led to the deposition of Richard II and his own accession as King Henry IV.

The Duke of Aumerle quickly capitulated and changed sides, though the actions of his father, the first Duke of York, who did the same, maybe impacted on his decision to do so. Despite this, his loyalty was initially doubted – not surprising given his closeness to Richard – and he was put in prison at the Tower of London for a short time and deprived of his dukedom. He was soon released, and became a member of the new king's council. But at the end of 1399 he became aware of a plot to remove Henry IV, and although he told him of the conspiracy in time to stop it, it is not clear that he did so as quickly as he might have.

During the uprising against Henry IV when Owen Glendower and the Percys had sided against the king, York, as he had now become, was implicated in a plot to release Edmund Mortimer, the Earl of March – the same man who had so recently been involved in the conspiracy uncovered at Southampton. York was locked up once more, this time in Pevensey Castle. He was again released and his fortunes were restored to him after only a few months. He had then accompanied the man who was now King Henry V on campaign in Wales. But during the last years of Henry IV's reign he had sided with the king against his son and had favoured negotiations with the Armagnacs rather than the Burgundians.

This was something of a patchy record that must have raised a few doubts in some minds. It is perhaps surprising that York had managed to escape a closer implication in the plot that had just been foiled and brought to a bloody end at Southampton. But if it suggested some doubts as to his commitment to the Lancastrian cause, on the other hand his ability to manage to restore his fortunes in double-quick time suggested something else – this man was indeed a survivor *par excellence*. And his survival skills must surely have been tested again when he reflected on the fate of his late brother.

Whether the duke had brooded on these things as he stared over the gunwales and across the English Channel on his way to France is not known, but it was ironic that within a few weeks the current king would have to rely on York more than most. It was not a marriage made in heaven, but the end results would be rather more positive than some might have expected at the outset.

The king too had much to think about at this precise moment as the expedition to France represented something of a gamble. It was important for Henry to get the campaign off to a good start, for what happened here would set the tone for what came later. A quick triumph and he would maintain the momentum and dent the confidence of his adversary. On the other hand, a lengthy siege would allow the French to regroup. They had the advantage of shorter supply lines and of fighting in their own country, and the longer that Harfleur held out the more Henry's chances of a decisive campaign would decrease.

Reading between the lines, there had already been problems with discipline shortly after the troops had landed. It seems that Henry finally issued his ordinances, the code of conduct for the troops, after he landed – the chronicler who scribed the *Gesta* stated that Henry declared that 'under pain of death there should be no more setting fire to places (as there had been to begin with)'.[3] This implies that there had initially been looting and/or gratuitous violence, hardly what was needed when Henry claimed to come only to avail himself of his right to rule his French subjects in the name of justice.

This violence was perhaps understandable, if not justifiable. This was not a standing army but one brought together by indenture or contract. Effectively each new campaign saw a new army, with no doubt some men who had fought before but some who had not. We cannot be sure that men like Thomas Pokkeswell had not been on a previous campaign with the king (though there are no other records found that suggest that he did).[4] Pokkeswell was part of the Duke of York's retinue and as such was destined to see much of the action during the forthcoming campaign.

This was possibly his first time overseas. Here he was in a strange environment, with the tension building as an imminent confrontation loomed. It would be hard to keep control of raw soldiers such as he might have been and the king therefore needed to invoke stern discipline to keep any potential excesses in check. Henry's character was well-suited for such a task.

Quite how Thomas might have been recruited is a matter for speculation. It is not clear how the archers in retinues were recruited though it has been theorised that lords would first and foremost look to men from their own lands but also that there was a pool of skilled archers that could be dipped into, allowing the pick of the bunch to be selected from what was effectively a semi-professional group of bowmen.[5] Perhaps Thomas was one such man. Certainly the end result was a marked improvement in the potential quality of the troops selected as well as in the cohesion of leading them on campaign.

The king needed to set about Harfleur as quickly as possible, before the French could recover their balance and send forces to fight him off. Cannon and siege engines were put into position, ready to start an intense bombardment. But the reality was that if it were strongly defended by stout walls it could take some time to take a town by storm. Many medieval sieges lasted for months although the onset of much more powerful artillery weapons had started to tilt the balance and had already in some cases proved decisive. But the defences of Harfleur had been restored fairly recently and would prove a stubbornly hard nut to crack.

Time was also of the essence for other reasons. It was already mid-August and the campaigning season was well advanced. In a couple of months, autumn would be here with its rains and the risk of much harsher conditions in which to wage war. The impact of any delays could therefore be significant; Henry's strategy for the campaign could be completely blown off course.

The English troops set up camp to the west of the town. Foraging parties were sent out around the surrounding villages to gather all the food and other supplies they could. Tactics also needed to be formulated, and a council of war was held where the plans for the assault on Harfleur were finalised. Henry ordered his army to be circumspect; watches were posted to guard against any sorties that might be made from within the town.

Henry was quite capable of making mistakes as a military commander but one of his strengths was that he learned from them. If something did not work out as expected, it seemed to inspire him with a ruthless determination to right the error, almost as if he took it as a personal insult. One such mistake was about to happen. The siege of the town had not yet been tightly laid; it was difficult to do so as the river to the south and the flooded ground protecting some of Harfleur made a direct approach awkward.

The day after the siege began, the people of Harfleur were delighted to see 300 fresh troops arrive led by a redoubtable knight by the name of Raoul de Gaucourt. He was an experienced warrior who had already fought alongside and been captured with the famous French knight and marshal Boucicaut at the disastrous French defeat at the Battle of Nicopolis. De Gaucourt caught the English off guard and entered by the gates on the east of the town. Although the arrival of his men probably at least doubled the number of properly armed and trained defenders available in Harfleur, it hardly affected the balance compared to the large English army outside. Yet it was an invaluable fillip to morale for the citizens of Harfleur and a blow for Henry as well as being a dent to his pride.

Henry resolved to right the error at once. Thomas, Duke of Clarence, was deputed that same night to lead a party of men past the flooded valley and block all further approaches from the east. When the people of Harfleur awoke the next morning and looked out at Mont Cabert they could see that Clarence's force had been deployed there. Clarence had set up his headquarters near a chapel on the slope. He had with him a cannon with which to start blasting the walls of the town, hoping both to bring them down and also to crush the morale and the resistance of the defenders. He soon enjoyed a useful success when a convoy carrying guns and missiles making its way to Harfleur from Rouen, the historical capital of the duchy of Normandy, was captured by his men.

Henry had only brought a small number of guns with him, including cannon from the Tower of London and Bristol along with a stock of 10,000 gunshots;[6] the fact that there were not more artillery weapons suggested that his strategy was to fight a war of movement rather than one of sieges. However, those weapons that were with him were more than capable of causing serious damage. Stones weighing up to 500 lbs could be blasted at the walls and if they were directed at the right spot could bring large chunks of them down.

The impact that they could have on mere flesh and bone if they struck hardly bears consideration. These instruments of death were personalised by the giving of names to them, such as *London* and *Messenger*.[7] The message they sent to anyone on the receiving end was clear enough. The English were also equipped with more old-fashioned stone-throwing siege engines and not just devices that relied on gunpowder.

Henry ensured that his gunners were protected against any missiles the enemy could fire back at them. Ditches were dug around the cannons and earthen ramparts constructed. Wooden screens were placed in front of the cannon. These were hinged mechanisms that could be flipped upwards, allowing the cannons to fire their projectiles before the screens dropped down to hide them again. But these guns could only be fired very slowly, the larger ones only three times a day.

While Harfleur was now under siege, the news had also reached Paris and prompted an alarmed reaction. On 19 August, the dauphin and the council in the city sent out the bad tidings that the English army now had a beachhead in France and summoned their own forces to assemble and face up to the threat. The tactics of prevarication had not failed; they had succeeded in buying time. The failure rather lay in not taking advantage of that time wisely. Now the French had been caught on the back foot and needed to strike back quickly before the English were strongly established. Given the terrible internal divisions that the French had to contend with, the whole fabric of government might come tumbling down if the threat from the English king was not decisively and quickly dealt with.

Henry vigorously employed measures to ensure that the walls of Harfleur came tumbling down, too. The bombardment continued both day and night. Bright moonlight on the night of 20 August made it easy for the gunners, many of whom were continental mercenaries, reflecting one particular area where Henry had recruitment problems. The noose that had been placed around the town was progressively tightened, threatening to strangle the life out of it. By 23 August the encirclement of the town was virtually complete. A desperate message was sent out saying that the only way in now was by sea and that this means of egress would soon be closed as well. On the other hand, English command of the sea now gave them the possibility of bringing in fresh supplies from across the Channel.[8]

Henry was at the forefront of the efforts to bring the siege to a successful close. He was indefatigable in his attempts to encourage the men. He 'stayed awake night and day', encouraging and cajoling the men to yet greater efforts, leading from the front in the way that another great warrior king, Richard I, had. But the defenders fought staunchly in response. Any Englishman who got too close to the walls of Harfleur would find himself showered in hot oil or other similarly nasty substances. Even the anonymous chronicler who produced the *Gesta* commended those inside Harfleur for their stoicism. They used their guns skilfully in reply to the English army's efforts.

Now that the invasion had been launched and the gloves were off, the authorities in Paris realised that the time for talking was finally over. They had done well to buy time but they now stopped their efforts to negotiate further. A formal message was sent to Henry from Paris on 24 August. It stated unequivocally that in the eyes of the French government none of Henry's predecessors had any sustainable claim to France and neither did he.

The message came through loud and clear: the French would oppose 'force by force'.

It is our intention with the assistance of the Lord, in whom we have singular trust, and especially from the justice of our cause, and also with the aid of our good relations, friends, allies and subjects, to resist you in a way that shall be to the honour and glory of us and of our kingdom, and to the confusion, loss and dishonour of you and your party.[9]

Brave and defiant words; it remained to be seen whether the French party could support them with decisive action.

Small groups of French troops started to assemble in the north. They were not big enough at this stage to face up to the English force but they were able to interfere with foraging parties and began to constrain supply lines. The English soon started to feel the inconvenience as their movements were progressively hampered. Foraging continued but it was becoming more difficult to seize French settlements and supplies. There were French forces just a few miles away at Montivilliers, not big enough to inconvenience the whole English army but certainly capable of causing trouble for smaller raiding parties.

The defenders of Harfleur were also putting up a gallant fight. Crossbows, guns and catapults were firing back at the besiegers. The walls of the town were certainly badly damaged but the townsfolk fought on defiantly from behind the rubble. Where the walls threatened to fall completely they were propped up with any materials that came to hand. Holes were plugged and clay and mud were spread across the streets so that any stones that came crashing down would not shatter and spray like shrapnel but would be absorbed by the ground, lessening the impact.

Henry decided to launch his men into a direct assault with scaling ladders. Men ran towards the walls, determined to scramble up the ladders, over the battlements and into the town. Harfleur was ready for them. The defenders were armed with improvised bombs, jars filled with sulphur and quicklime. As the English moved on the walls and started to scramble up the ladders, the French flung down the bombs which exploded and burned the men, scorched their eyes and set fire to their bodies. Carnage ensued. The assault fizzled out and the English retreated.

A fightback against the English was now being organised from further afield. The French authorities in Paris planned to assemble their main force against the English at Rouen. A call to arms was sent out across Normandy. The dauphin would lead the army that would be raised and the soldiers were to wear a white cross to distinguish them from the red cross of the English (traditional crusading colours[10]). They were also given instructions that they were not to pillage the local population. King Charles would join the force later.

There was one conspicuous absentee from the call to arms. The Duke of Burgundy was not asked to attend. His dealings with Henry of England had been conducted largely out of the public eye but this was unlikely to have fooled anyone. Then as now walls had ears and the French spies would very likely have been fully informed as to what had been happening. John the Fearless was *persona non grata* for the simple reason that nobody trusted him, though it seems that he had not reached a formal agreement with the King of England. In essence the duke was playing off one king against the other, which meant that neither really knew where they stood with him.

In the meantime, other measures were being taken to help the defenders. The account of Jean Le Fèvre, a Burgundian with the English army who was about twenty years of age at the time, states that a force of five or six thousand men made its way to the region around Harfleur tasked with the objective of making life for the English as difficult as possible by launching ambushes against them. They were also to offer themselves as bait to the English and tempt them out into the open to fight. The sensible plan was not as successful as it might have been due to problems in its execution. The English were indeed lured out but the subsequent attack on them was launched too early and several important Frenchmen were captured as a result.[11]

With the initial direct assault on Harfleur beaten back, Henry now adopted different tactics. There were ditches around the walls of Harfleur, making it difficult for the English to approach. He planned to fill these in with faggots of wood that the men could then cross over but the resourceful French had a counter-strategy. They would set light to the wood and so foil Henry's plans. This was exactly what they succeeded in doing.

This plan was therefore unsuccessful too. Henry now tried another tactic. Walls were susceptible to mining and two tunnels were to be dug underneath them; a large party of miners, probably from the Forest of Dean (an area that had provided miners for many years, as it did during the siege of Bedford in 1224[12]), had been brought over to help with such operations. The plan was to prop the tunnel up and then, when the time was right, set the supports alight. As they were consumed by the flames there would be nothing to stop the roof crashing down, bringing the walls with it.

Such was the plan but it was hard to keep it a secret from the defenders. There had been instances of mining being used successfully in siege warfare in the past such as at the capture of the city of Edessa in Syria by Muslim forces from the Crusaders in 1144. But defenders of walled towns and castles were on their guard for the tell-tale signs of mining. As far back as Antiquity, the defenders of towns would place brass vessels filled with liquid on the ground and look for vibrations in them to see where mining was possibly taking place. They would then start to dig a counter-mine by which they could lay about the enemy sappers and drive them off.

Anyway, the defenders did not need much help in working out what the next step in the plan of attack at Harfleur was. The English used 'sows', effectively covered sheds on wheels, and rolled them towards the walls, advertising the fact that mining was taking place. Surprise was anyway difficult as the mines were to be dug on the side of the town where the Duke of Clarence was based and the close proximity of the hills there meant that the digging had to start quite close to the walls. The defenders, soon wise to what was happening, dug their own counter-mines and sent men down to fight off the English miners. Chaotic fighting broke out in the claustrophobic subterranean arena, fights which it seems the English did not particularly enjoy. Eventually the French undermined the English tunnel, bringing it down before it was in position to do any damage. Henry had been thwarted again.

By the end of August, the siege was two weeks old and the clock was now ticking. The town of Harfleur was increasingly a scene of jumbled rubble. Every day no doubt began with a feeling of abject fear in the pit of the stomach of many of the citizens, waking after nights of haunted dreams and snatched sleep (for the bombardment was carried on through the darkness). They wondered if the next projectile to come crashing down would smash through the roof of their home, despatching them to purgatory or shattering limbs and heads, creating fearful injuries and condemning them to days, weeks, months of unspeakable agony.

The impact of the bombardment of the town was vividly described by Thomas of Walsingham. The artillery may have been, in modern terms, incredibly crude but its impact was brutal: 'The stones that flew through the air from these guns with the huge force of their blows smashed everything that got in their way as they landed, not only killing the bodies which they flattened but also scattering around whole bleeding limbs, and the weapons of the besieged yielded one by one to their blows, and not only were the combatants laid flat but also the beautiful buildings of the town.'[13] In other words, Harfleur was slowly being transformed into a heap of rubble.

But although the walls of Harfleur were increasingly broken, the spirit of the defenders was not. They fought on bravely. Some of the chronicles speak of sorties, sallies out against careless English troops who got too close. The French crossbowmen could cause fearful damage too. One man-at-arms, Thomas Hostell, was struck in the eye with its full force. He lost the eye and a terrible wound in his cheek was also caused by the bolt. Amazingly, he lived. Only slightly less amazingly, less than two months later he would fight on the field of Agincourt.[14]

By now, an even more dangerous enemy than the French had appeared, silent and invisible yet deadly. A large body of men were living in a confined space in the English camp. Sanitary provision was poor and the terrain was flooded and as time went on the problem of hygiene would become increasingly serious. The smell of excrement was by now overpowering, the atmosphere was growing foetid and disease was in the air. It started to strike men down with one of the deadliest of all medieval sicknesses – dysentery.

It was the worst possible news. This was one enemy that, with the limited medical knowledge and range of remedies available, it was very hard to fight against. Even a master strategist had limited powers to launch a counter-attack against dysentery. There were probably a number of factors at play. The men were packed closely together in unsanitary conditions. Chroniclers came up with other reasons too: the number of rotting animal cadavers around, eating bad shellfish, the very hot weather.

A major factor in the outbreak of disease was that the army had simply been in one place for longer than it was planned to be. If Harfleur had fallen according to the timetable then the army would have left their unsanitary patches of ground long ago and would have marched off, lessening the risk of dysentery, though there would of course be other risks on the march. But war famously does not often run to pre-planned timetables, and Henry's plans were already veering off course.

Named individuals who had died of dysentery now started to appear in the records. One of them, Lord Fitzwalter, died on 1 September, barely more than a youth at just sixteen years old. There were other problems manifesting themselves too. Food supplies were already a concern, and on the same day as young Fitzwalter expired orders were sent to Richard Bokeland, a London merchant, to send two ships with food to France with all possible despatch. Two men in Henley were also required to send 100 quarters of wheat. Two days later, Henry was writing to his subjects in Guienne, assuring them that the assault on Harfleur was going well and also requesting them to send him wine and other supplies.[15]

The reality was that with the townsfolk as defiant as ever, with dysentery starting to appear in the camp and with food supplies already an issue, matters were already far from well. Every day that passed saw the length of the feasible campaigning season for the year decrease and the possibility of a relief force being sent by the French increase. Henry needed to do all he could to bring the siege to a quick close before all he had left to capture was a useless pile.

So on 1 September he attempted to persuade the citizens to negotiate a surrender. A safe conduct was given to a delegation from the town who duly made their way to the English camp to discuss one. But the defenders could see for themselves that the English had problems, and what they could not see their spies would tell them. There was no doubting that the threat from the English invaders was formidable, but as time went on disease might make it less so. There were also high hopes that help would come from a French army. They could still get messengers out of the town and one was sent to the dauphin to urge him to march to the rescue. But the people of Harfleur were not disposed to surrender and the negotiations got nowhere.

The dauphin had by now started to take some measures to aid them. He had left Paris and had sent orders to the dukes of Orléans and Burgundy that they were each to send 500 men-at-arms and 300 archers. The Duke of Burgundy was still not asked to attend in person, a request that both surprised and irritated him as it evidenced a lack of trust in him, though this was a stance that appeared quite justified given the violent disturbances that had fragmented France in recent times. But the English were still receiving reinforcements from across the Channel. The town walls were now a mess, with those on the landward side breached. Inside them, Harfleur was already turning into a ruin. The River Lézarde had been diverted by the

English so that the water supplies available to the townsfolk were seriously interrupted.

It was by now something of a stalemate. Outwardly Henry still breathed confidence. There were stories circulating that after Harfleur fell he would move on to take other important French cities like Dieppe, Rouen and even Paris. However, that was already looking like wishful thinking. On 3 September he sent orders to England requiring the fishing boats of the men of the Kent coast to make their way to France with their gear to help keep his men fed.

The situation was continuing to deteriorate for the English king. He had a large force with him, ironically probably too large for the task immediately at hand. There were French forces not too far off that according to some accounts interfered with the ability of the English to forage, making their position far from ideal. Problems were beginning to mount and the expedition had barely begun.

But the defenders too were in trouble, especially as the English had laid a blockade across the waterborne entrances to the town, stopping any reinforcements or new supplies from that direction. French attempts to break the blockade failed. The Duke of Clarence, as already noted, had intercepted an early attempt to resupply the town by road at night from the direction of Rouen, capturing carts carrying useful stocks of gunpowder, guns, missiles and catapults in the process. It was now a question of who had the greater stamina and whether or not the French authorities would make a determined effort to loosen the stranglehold.

The days passed and still Harfleur did not fall, but neither was there any sign of a relieving army on its way. Then, at last, on 10 September a drama of huge symbolism was played out in Paris. First of all, Charles VI, the titular if not practical head of the realm, attended Mass in the hallowed walls of Nôtre Dame. In those almost mystical surroundings, seeming to hold within their Gothic glory the very soul of France, as the light streamed in in heavenly brilliance through its great rose windows, the king prayed for his realm and for victory in the battle ahead.

He then moved to the great cathedral of St Denis; if Nôtre Dame represented France at prayer, Saint Denis represented the country at war. Here King Charles heard another Mass. More prayers were offered up for victory and then the ritual moved towards its climax. The great French war banner, the Oriflamme, was brought out and presented to Charles. He took it in his hands, the embodiment of the whole country of France. Cries of 'Montjoie! St Denis!' went up. It was a definitive symbolic statement that France was now at war. She too had taken her gloves off and was committed to defending the rights of the French against the English invaders. The blood-red banner spoke evocatively of a war to the death. But it had taken over three weeks from the start of the siege for the king to raise it.

The ceremony was powerful, poignant and moving but also too late. Even as it was acted out, the mood in Harfleur was already starting to shift. The pleas for help were still getting through to the dauphin but they were growing increasingly desperate. Even as the king handed the sacred war banner of France to the venerable Guillame Martel, a veteran of over sixty years of age, to carry into battle on his behalf, the sands of time were running rapidly through the hourglass for those defending Harfleur for their king.

Events at Harfleur were starting to edge towards a conclusion, although those two impostors, triumph and disaster, both paid court to Henry as September moved on. On the fifteenth of the month, personal catastrophe struck. One of his closest confidantes,

Richard Courtenay, Bishop of Norwich (a man who also held the responsible position of Keeper of the Royal Jewels), had shown signs of dysentery a few days earlier. Though only aged thirty-five, Courtenay had suffered from bouts of poor health for a time, being ill during two of the king's embassies to Paris in 1414 and 1415.[16] His situation now deteriorated. At last, he died with the king at his side in attendance. There were many indications that the king and the bishop were close; they had even shared a tent together during the campaign. As the last breath escaped from the Bishop's body, Henry touched the dead man's face and closed his eyes.

Henry was not a man prone to expressions of grief but that simple movement, that last uncomplicated but deeply symbolic action of sympathy, spoke volumes. Inwardly he was so distraught that he ordered that the bishop should be buried in that magnificent, sacred royal mausoleum, Westminster Abbey, a rare honour for a cleric.[17]

This was a black day for Henry, for a determined sally from Harfleur caught his men off guard; the *Gesta* chronicler criticises the English, accusing those on watch of 'inattention and indolence'.[18] The French were able to set some of the English defences alight and a pall of smoke wafted over their camp. The fire was eventually brought under control but the people of Harfleur were ecstatic, mocking the English for being half-asleep.

But it was in this moment of grief and potential despair that Henry began to show his greatness. His genius was not in devising magnificent stratagems; in that respect he was no Alexander, though he was not without his merits. Henry's greatness lay in far more human qualities, to display in the darkest moments a stubbornness and determination that we might now call Churchillian in its quality. When the obvious and perhaps only thing to do seemed to be to give up, Henry soared to heights that few other warrior kings in English history have ever done.

He had already pushed himself hard, patrolling the lines at night, making sure the guns were ready for action and urging his men to even greater efforts. Despite his great sense of personal loss due to the death of the Bishop, he was determined that the fiasco of the raid from the town would not be repeated again. He would go on to the attack. But he would do so in a very Henrician manner, in a calculated, thought-through move. There would be no all-out assault, which might win the town but would cost him many lives that he could ill afford to lose. Instead he identified a weak point in Harfleur's defensive perimeter and he chose a hand-picked group of men to assail it.

A small party was assembled, composed among others of the young John Holland – 'a knight brave and high-spirited'[19] – his father-in-law Sir John Cornwall, Sir Gilbert Umfraville and Sir William Bourchier. This was the same select band that had formed the party that had been sent ashore to scout the area before the main army had been offloaded near Harfleur at the start of the invasion. As such, they can be seen almost as Henry's storm troops, a commando-like outfit that were used for special operations.

The English storm troops were instructed to attack the barbican outside the Porte Leure gate to Harfleur on 16 September. The barbican, in the front line, had presumably already seen its walls badly damaged, allowing them to break in. When they did so, a party of men from the town sallied out to drive the English off. But the English were ready for them. They had come equipped with fire arrows and a fiery hailstorm was soon descending on the barbican and all those Frenchmen still in it. In the confined space, the scene quickly became one of terror. The battle turned the way of the

English and the French retreated back into the town through holes that they then hastily plugged after them with any materials that came to hand: earth, stones, timber, even dung. But the English had won the day, though the barbican itself was a wreck and would be smouldering for several weeks to come.

This appears to have been a tipping point, for on the following day serious negotiations for the town to be surrendered began. It is not completely clear whether the initiative for this came from Henry or from the defenders of Harfleur. There are some accounts that Henry, buoyed by the capture of the barbican, planned an all-out attack. These intentions were backed up by a mention of the Biblical law referred to in the Book of Deuteronomy, a scriptural reference point that the king and his advisers were clearly drawn to as it was mentioned on several occasions in correspondence with the French.

This might to modern eyes appear to be somewhat archaic but it was in fact a statement with terrifying undertones. For Deuteronomy said that if a king took a town through force of arms, once he had given it the chance to surrender but had been refused, then he should slay the men but spare the women and children though they were then effectively his property to do with as he wished.[20] The implication was clear and terrifying: the lives of all the men of Harfleur were in the balance and the rest of the population were faced with a complete loss of their freedom. And if the English were to suffer avoidable loss of life in storming the town, then their king was hardly likely to be in a merciful mood when he captured it.

That an all-out assault loomed was now apparent. The clarion calls of trumpets in the English camp summoning all available men, including sailors from the fleet, could be heard and told eloquently enough of the imminent attack, a terrifying sound that perhaps reminded the defenders of the build-up to the biblical Joshua's assault on Jericho. All this noise was quite possibly a calculated piece of psychological warfare on the part of the English. An artillery bombardment commenced once more at night, keeping the townsfolk awake and in a state of terrified anticipation. Bitter, intense warfare this was, preying on the mind as well as the body.

Other chroniclers suggest that the initiative to seek terms came from inside Harfleur. The defenders too were in an awful state by now, short of food, water and most of all hope, as well as also going down themselves with diseases like dysentery. And there was no sign of a relieving force. It appeared to them increasingly as if they had been abandoned to their fate and it was therefore time for them to negotiate the best outcome that they could.

It might be significant that the overtures to start negotiations from within the town were directed not at the king but first of all at his brother, Thomas, Duke of Clarence, as he was thought to be a more sympathetic figure. But news of course was quickly passed to the king so that he could strike while the iron was hot.

Negotiations began that very night, on 17 September. Lit up by the brilliance of the full moon, a delegation led by Thomas Beaufort, Lord Fitzhugh and Sir Thomas Erpingham later reported back to the king with news of the first round of discussions. The townsfolk had asked that they be given until 29 September, Michaelmas. If no relieving army came in that time, they would surrender.

This was not an unusual tactic. The Battle of Bannockburn just over a century before in 1314 had been fought when an English relieving force was on its way to Stirling Castle to fulfil such an arrangement as one example. Another was the defeat of the Scots at Halidon Hill in 1333 when they were trying to relieve Berwick in similar circumstances. But it was not enough for Henry. It gave the French too much time; it was theoretically possible that they could form an army and march it to the relief of Harfleur within that timescale. Henry therefore demanded that with the break of the next day the town must surrender or face the unpalatable consequences.

The negotiations were now approaching their endgame. Those inside Harfleur were considering the possibility of surrender and were merely negotiating about the timescale. They responded that it would not be possible to surrender in the morning but they would do so if no French force appeared by one o'clock on the afternoon of 22 September. It was practically impossible for a French army to be there in that time; Henry had won. So rather than pedantically stick to his demands he compromised, knowing that Harfleur would anyway be his.

As a mark of good faith, a delegation from the town would present themselves to Henry on the afternoon of 18 September. They would deposit twenty-four hostages with him. These terms proved acceptable and the deal was struck. It was a fantastic opportunity for Henry to present himself as a magnanimous, merciful ruler, in the spirit of Edward III half a century before when he had spared the lives of the burghers of Calais even though their town had resisted him for nearly a year. It was a chance for Henry to send a message to the French people; that he would be a just, benign ruler, driven by a desire to show mercy rather than exact stern justice. It rather went against the grain for Henry, who could be fierce in the execution of such justice, but it was nevertheless a propaganda coup that could not be ignored.

That same afternoon two delegations, one from the English side, the other from the town, approached each other. The former party was led by Benedict, the Bishop of Bangor, and the procession included Henry's thirty-two hooded chaplains from the Chapel Royal, who chanted as the two groups moved towards each other, giving the occasion an aura of great solemnity. The king had brought with him some of the finest singers in England. He had a fine ear for music and he loved to hear it well sung and even wrote some himself. These works have been described as 'musically competent, spiritually impeccable, another insight into his extreme piety'. In other words, this music is a window into the soul of Henry V himself.

This musical accomplishment was not for artistic merit but for spiritual benefit. But the musicians were by all accounts sublime in their execution; even French envoys who had heard them admitted that they had never witnessed musical perfection like it. It was no coincidence that one of the earliest famous names of English music, John Dunstable (or Dunstaple), a man who achieved a Continental reputation for his beautiful polyphonic works, had Henry as a patron. The king would also have a Chapel Royal of fifty singers, larger than any cathedral choir.[21] Not all of them went with him to France, of course, but there were also eighteen minstrels with the king according to one of the contemporary chroniclers. The names of fifteen of them survive; as well as one John Cliff there were three Pypers, three Trumpers and one Fyddler, many of these names presumably alluding to musical instruments that they were skilled with.[22]

The king in fact had a very large retinue with him. There were not just musicians, but also the German gunners and stuffers of bascinets (responsible for padding and adjusting the helmets). There were also kitchen staff, clerks of the spicery, poultry and scullery. Then there were carpenters, fletchers and bowyers, and members of the king's household brought with them their archers to add to the force. These included William Smith (the smith, of course) who brought along forty-one archers; even the chief minstrel, John Stiff, contributed some.[23]

The two negotiation parties met outside the Porte Leure, scene of the recent heroic action by John Holland, John Cornwall and their comrades. The townspeople swore a sacred oath to abide by the terms of the agreement. Formal documents were exchanged and the hostages handed over. They would be well fed and given comfortable billets in the English camp – another chance for Henry to demonstrate his magnanimity to those he wished to rule. This was not yet surrender; the formalities were not complete and had to be complied with before Harfleur finally changed owners. A messenger was to be allowed to ride to the dauphin. The man chosen to undertake this task was Guillame de Léon, with an escort of twelve men. His chances of returning with an army within four days were to all intents and purposes non-existent.

At least the imminent fall of Harfleur had shaken the French from their lethargy. In the words of the French chronicler and supporter of the French crown Enguerrand de Monstrelet, the king and his council 'instantly issued summonses for raising in every part of the kingdom the greatest possible force of men-at-arms'. This would not be an easy logistical feat to pull off and bailiffs and seneschals were sent out to oversee the process.[24]

These messengers were despatched to a number of places including to Picardy to the north-east. Not everywhere did they have the desired effect. Monstrelet writes that on 20 September the king (or his council in his name) was forced to send a sternly-worded second command to the bailiff of Amiens. The tardiness of forces from this region to assemble reflected its close affiliation with Charles VI's difficult subject the Duke of Burgundy. In fact, the bailiff of Amiens and others of his ilk were expressly singled out in the letter as being responsible for the subsequent fall of Harfleur. The French had already started playing a blame game among themselves, merely the beginning of a rather extended session of a counter-productive sport.

The dauphin was at Vernon, some seventy-five miles off from Harfleur. De Léon arrived there from Harfleur with the news of the proposed terms on the twentieth and was told that there was no chance of getting an army to the port in two days as the assembly of a force had barely begun (which was true enough). So after all the fighting, that was it. Harfleur was abandoned and left to the English. The townsfolk were left to make the most of the situation by themselves.

In its own way, the abandonment of Harfleur by the French rulers who had reacted far too late to make a difference provided a neat contrast between their own frailties and the determination of the English king. The possibility of Henry meekly letting the French take possession of a key port in England such as Portsmouth without fighting back did not exist. If the roles had been reversed, come hell or high water he would have done everything to march to its defence as quickly as possible. But France, divided, at war with herself and led by a man who from time to time thought he was made of glass, barely moved a finger to help Harfleur until it was too late to make a difference.

The situation inside the French government was chaotic. The men demanded of the dukes of Orléans and Burgundy had still not arrived and urgent orders were sent out reminding both of them of their obligations. Having failed miserably in their half-hearted, half-cocked measures to relieve Harfleur, those theoretically in command of France started to look everywhere for scapegoats to blame for the loss of the key port of Harfleur and the consequent threat to the rest of France.

At eight o'clock on the morning of 22 September, the feast day of St Maurice, the formalities concerning Harfleur moved towards an inevitable close. De Léon was back in the town with the bad news that no help was on its way from those who claimed to govern in France. He had ridden 150 miles in four days, a valiant and energetic effort in contrast to the pathetic attempts of men who were supposedly his betters. He, at least, was absolved of any blame in the loss of the town.

At one that same afternoon, a procession of the leading townsfolk of Harfleur made their way through the smoking ruins of the barbican – taken by the English a few days before – and trudged wearily up the hill on top of which Henry's tent had been pitched. The king's throne was placed before the royal pavilion, and grouped around Henry in a semi-circle were those of his nobles who were well enough to attend, dressed in their finest. To his right stood Sir Gilbert Umfraville, holding aloft the king's great war-helm on a staff. It was a triumphant, almost gloating, display.

In contrast, one chronicler wrote that the delegation from Harfleur, led by the commander of the town, Raoul de Gaucourt, and probably about sixty strong,[25] wore ropes around their necks, symbolising that they were at the king's mercy, an indication that their surrender was an unconditional one. This repeated neatly the scene at Calais over half a century earlier when the burghers had thrown themselves on the mercy of King Edward III. On that former occasion, the King of England had spared the lives of his captives (though only after the pleas of his wife, it was said by some of a romantic disposition). Henry knew full well that a similar performance was required from him and he duly obliged.

However, the moment was not without tension. Henry's Earl Marshal reminded the citizens of Harfleur that the king was well within his rights to treat them with extreme harshness. While he gave this stern speech, Henry started grimly ahead, not looking at the delegation nor showing the slightest sign that he was minded to be merciful. As has been pointed out by historians,[26] previous incidents in the Hundred Years War had led to massacre on a grand scale. The capture of Limoges in 1370 by the Black Prince saw that mighty warrior living up to his name when 3,000 men, women and children were slaughtered in cold blood, only the most extreme manifestation of violence in a series of *chevauchées* that became a byword for terror during these troubled times.

Of the sack of Limoges it was said at the time that 'it was a most melancholy business; for all ranks, ages and sexes cast themselves on their knees before the prince, begging for mercy; but he was so enflamed with passion and revenge that he listened to none, but all were put to the sword, wherever they could be found'.[27] This was total war from which no one, including civilians, was immune. These terrible precedents must have been foremost in the minds of those surrendering, for whom an awful fate beckoned.

Henry too could be cruel, harsh, haughty and vindictive, as later events during future conflicts in France would prove. We should not assume from his performance at Harfleur that being merciful came naturally to him. Indeed his first instincts may have been to exert the maximum penalties of the law as he saw it; he was just intelligent enough to realise that on this occasion it was expedient for him not to do that. Nevertheless, he kept the delegation from Harfleur guessing; he told them that he was minded to show some mercy but that he might change his mind on further reflection.[28] It was almost as if he was toying with their emotions and playing on their fears.

Having at last decided that he wished to play the part of magnanimous victor, Henry did so to the full. This threatening game of cat and mouse at last came to a halt. He informed the prisoners that their lives would be spared and invited them to dine in the English camp. Two banners, the Royal Standard and the cross of St George, were hoisted over the town and Thomas Beaufort, the Earl of Dorset, was appointed its lieutenant (he would be appointed the Duke of Exeter in 1416, although Shakespeare anomalously refers to him with this title throughout his drama *Henry V*).

The glad tidings of Harfleur's capture were sent to London post-haste; good news to justify the support previously granted to the king by the people of England. Parliament had been generous with its grants, as had the Church, and they needed to see results in return for their generosity. A picture was painted in these messages that the English were on the verge of a final decisive assault on the town when the people of Harfleur desperately sought an agreement to prevent the effusion of blood; part of the truth, perhaps, but not quite the whole truth as the English had had a far harder fight than the message made out.

The following day, 23 September, Henry processed into Harfleur to claim his prize. It was by now of doubtful worth. Its walls were shattered stumps, the smell of death and acrid smoke hung heavy in the air. Many of the houses had been reduced to rubble. Nevertheless, Henry determined to exact maximum benefit from the propaganda opportunities that he had achieved by its capture. The gates were opened and he walked barefoot through the streets to the historic church of St Martin in an act of pious humility. It too was a wreck: its steeple had crumpled to the ground along with its bells.

The banners flying the colours of the defenders around Harfleur were taken down. In their place went up the Royal Standard of England and crosses of St George. The women and children were rounded up while the men who swore allegiance to Henry could stay; the rest would be imprisoned until appropriate ransom had been paid for their release. The inhabitants were allowed to keep many of their possessions, though the English helped themselves to a useful stock of horses that they had captured.

The women and children were kept in the town overnight and the next day, the 24th, they were all marched through the gates of the town and told to leave. The women were given a small amount of money and then told they were free to go wherever they wished. Monstrelet also suggests in his account that two towers in the town stubbornly held out for an extra ten days but eventually the defenders of these too were forced to surrender.

Even though it has been argued by some that this was a merciful act,[29] this was a less generous side of Henry in evidence. Women and children were split up from their menfolk and left to their own devices; in the choice phrase of the *Gesta* chronicler, those who had thought themselves inhabitants now became travellers, homeless, their daily lives, the domestic round that had marked them just a few months before, gone. Insecurity and uncertainty marked their future as families without husbands, without fathers. Whatever else this was, it was not merciful.

A stream of perhaps 2,000 refugees wended a disconsolate course away from Harfleur. One source suggests that they were escorted by a convoy of English soldiers to Lillebonne where they were handed over to the famous French commander Marshall Boucicaut. Other French sources suggest that the women were systematically rounded up by French soldiers later, robbed and raped.[30] Their lot was certainly a harsh one, left to fend for themselves on the fringes of a warzone.

Henry also had a longer-term plan for Harfleur, namely to Anglicise it. With ruthless and dispassionate efficiency, within days of its capture he was sending letters to London asking that potential settlers be encouraged to come and set up home in the port. In the meantime the inhabitants of the captured town had watched as the French charters which established its position in the country were burned. This Anglicisation was a plan that had been adopted by other English would-be conquerors in the past, notably when Edward I had conquered north Wales at the end of the thirteenth century and populated many of the towns with English settlers. Henry also ensured that all the key officials in Harfleur were to be from England. This was his plan; to make Harfleur English, a policy he would develop in future campaigns post-Agincourt when he began the systematic conquest of all of Normandy.

So that was that. Harfleur had fallen, but was this battered town to be the sole reward for the massive expenditure and effort that had been committed to the king's great venture? In many ways the safe option now was to extract most of his forces from Harfleur back to England and leave a garrison to hold the port. Harfleur might not be much but it was something and it would prove a useful and potentially important base for future operations.

What was actually going through Henry's mind now in terms of his next steps we can never know for sure but we may surmise to some extent. Perhaps never again in his reign would Henry have the opportunity of launching a major invasion of France. It had taken him two years of hard work to arrive at this moment and some might argue that Harfleur on its own was insufficient to justify the material and human cost that had been incurred. There was even a danger that it might inspire a renewed period of opposition back in England.

Henry thought and he listened. Many men wished to call it a day and hundreds, if not thousands, were too ill to fight and must go home anyway due to the debilitating effects of dysentery. The king took guidance and then he thought the issue through for himself. His decision when it came was another huge gamble. He would not retreat from Harfleur but he would march his army defiantly across northern France and to Calais.

What was the point of this? It is true that many of the ships that had landed him at Harfleur were no longer there but they were not at Calais either, so if he stayed where he was or he marched to Calais, in either event logistics would be a huge problem if he were to order a mass evacuation. Henry's decision might make sense though if he wished to tease the French into a major battle, which he hoped would be a winner-takes-all confrontation. If he were to win, then perhaps France might be his after all; but if he were to lose, then his life might be forfeit. Even if it were not, he might lose not only France but England too.

Whatever his reasons, inspired by the glory of the feats of Edward III and the Black Prince, Henry resolved that a march to Calais would be his plan. The odds of success were deeply uncertain but, like a master gambler, Henry put all he had on the table and set himself up to play a game where the stakes involved were enormous. Having made up his mind that this would be his course, he commended himself to the hands of God and made ready for the most extraordinary month of his life.

6

NORTHERN FRANCE: THE LONG MARCH (SEPTEMBER – OCTOBER 1415)

After his opinion had been expressed, nobody dared to contradict the king's decision.

The Pseudo-Elmham chronicler on the character of Henry V

Although the fall of Harfleur led to an end to the fighting in France for a short while, it did not mean that the dying had stopped. The ravages of disease continued to hit home. One of England's most prominent noblemen, Michael de la Pole, the Earl of Suffolk, an experienced warrior in his own right (he had been involved in Clarence's expedition to France in 1412), had expired on 18 September, shortly before Harfleur surrendered.

A few days after the town's capitulation, on 25 September, Sir John Chidiock, Lord Fitzpayn, a Dorset knight, also joined the list of the dead.[1] He knew all about problems with the French; his castle dated back to 1380, when the family were given permission to crenellate (fortify with battlements) their manor house in response to raids on the nearby Dorset coast. Dysentery was no glorious death on the field of battle. It was known as 'the bloody flux', and involved severe stomach pains and diarrhoea; when the victims of dysentery defecated they passed blood and mucus. At Harfleur, it had taken a high toll on the English. Shakespeare glosses over these deaths. This is not surprising; there is nothing very glorious in them.

Dysentery is a bacterial disease that eats away at the *mucosa* of the intestines, hence the blood (and indeed mucus) passed from the body. It also has the effect of creating exhaustion to the point of prostration to many of those unlucky enough to suffer from it. Despite the chroniclers' assertion that exotic food such as oysters was a likely cause of the outbreak, it was probably instead just bad hygiene that led to the problem. Here there were men in cramped conditions sharing water sources and food which could easily act as a carrier for bacteria and with little idea of the importance of hygiene. Factors such as the hot summer temperatures and the damp marshy ground would also help to breed bacteria, so the cause was probably multifactorial.[2]

While the support of prominent men like the Duke of York and the Earl of Suffolk was of course vital to the king, men of the 'middling' class like Sir John Chidiock were also very useful indeed. Dorset was an area where the duchy of Lancaster had extensive landholdings and the Lancastrians' natural strength there was further increased by men such as Sir John. He had been one of the MPs for Dorset in the November 1414 parliament (another prominent supporter of Henry, William Stourton, at one time his steward in Wales, was also chosen for one of the county's MPs several times during this period). An immediate ancestor had fought at Crécy. A writ dated 13 October 1415 listed his landholdings as being at Pulham and worth 100 shillings (£5) a year, in East Chalborough worth £10 a year and Chidiock worth £40 a year; all these lands were in Dorset. Now he left behind him a wife, Alianora (Eleanor), and a young teenage son, also John, who would inherit.

The loss of de la Pole, an experienced warrior, was a particularly hard blow for the king. His body was taken back home to be buried in the church at Wingfield in Suffolk, accompanied by an escort of two esquires and four archers from his retinue.[3] Other knights known to have died at Harfleur included William Beaumont from Devon, Roger Trumpington from Cambridgeshire, Edward Burnell from Norfolk, John Marland from Somerset, three Lancashire knights (namely John Southworth, Hugh Standish and William Butler) and John Phelip of Kidderminster.[4] The last named was thirty-one years of age and he was married to Alice Chaucer, the granddaughter of the great poet and daughter of Speaker Thomas; Alice was a sprightly eleven years old at the time of her husband's death. She later married two earls, the first of Salisbury, the second of Suffolk (another de la Pole).

There was a loss of men from humbler stock too. On 29 September several archers like William Thornton died (he had been involved in the deadly scrimmage on the way to join the fleet when four men were killed but had clearly not suffered the ultimate penalty for his actions), as did several others like Roger Piper and Roger Pemberton. This was a very serious outbreak of the disease.

In modern times, dysentery is eminently treatable. However, in the medieval period it was often a killer. It is thought that King John of England had died from it and that Henry V may also have been a victim in 1422. The Black Prince's army had suffered very badly after the Battle of Nájera from a serious outbreak of dysentery. Even into the modern era it could decimate armies. Napoleon Bonaparte's invasion force in Russia in 1812 was badly hit by it and one estimate suggests that up to 18,000 soldiers may have died of it in the American Civil War (1861–65).[5] There were also outbreaks amongst Allied captives in Japanese POW camps during the Second World War.

We will never truly know what the effect of these losses on Henry's army were, though the words of Thomas Elmham that 'this dysentery weakened many unto death' suggests that they were regarded as high.[6] But medieval chroniclers are notoriously unreliable in working with statistics; record books are a better and more trustworthy source of data. It has been estimated that Henry started the campaign with about 12,000 fighting men.[7] The number subsequently sent home after the siege of Harfleur was between 1,693 and 2,550, of whom between 1,300 and 1,900 were fighting men (the rest were camp followers and non-combatants of various types).[8] Among those returning home were fifty archers from Wales and eleven from Cheshire. However, there is evidence that replacements took over from them, at least in some cases, so not all these losses were permanent in the sense that they were partially replaced.

It has been contended that deaths at Harfleur, as opposed to more general incapacity due to illness in particular, were much lower than some chroniclers suggest, perhaps as few as fifty men.[9] But among them were the two new knights in Erpingham's company, Thomas Geney and John Calthorpe, who would die soon after going back to England, a salutary reminder of the transience of earthly glory if there ever was one. Two of Erpingham's archers had also died during the siege and a third was sent back home.[10]

One of the more ghoulish elements of the campaign was what happened to the bodies of the more important dead during the campaign. If they could not be embalmed then alternative arrangements were made which were definitely not for the squeamish. A large cauldron was carried with the army. In it, the body of the dead man was boiled in water. When it had stewed in there for the requisite amount of time, it was taken out and stripped of its flesh, the heart already being removed before the process began. The bones and the heart would then be sent back to England for burial.[11]

This was by no means a new innovation. No less a man than King Edward I had allegedly instructed that his body should be boiled in a cauldron when he was dead, his flesh buried and his bones then carried at the head of his army in the subsequent attack on Scotland that he had planned (his heart should be despatched to the Holy Land). But his instructions were ignored by his son Edward II, and he was buried more conventionally in Westminster Abbey.[12]

Amid all the death, there was still the inglorious game of politics to be played. Shakespeare makes much of the antagonism between Henry and the dauphin. Although he naturally exaggerates a good deal in the interests of poetic licence, there was an element of underlying truth in their rivalry, as evidenced by the issuing by Henry on 26 September of a challenge to the dauphin to meet him in single combat. This echoed the actions of Edward III seventy-five years earlier when he did the same with his French opponent; but then, as on the current occasion, no duel followed.

This was in theory a way of avoiding a massive effusion of blood by letting the foremost warriors fight it out among themselves.

There was never any chance that such a duel could happen, even though the dauphin himself was an experienced warrior (though he was ill and would die of his ailments not long after Agincourt); the formality of issuing a challenge along these lines was simply chivalric convention. In some campaigns impromptu duels would indeed break out, most notably when the English lord Henry de Bohun charged headlong at the Scottish king Robert the Bruce as the two armies lined up on the eve of Bannockburn. It made no difference to whether or not a battle was fought; de Bohun fell dead with an axe in his head for his troubles and the battle went ahead as planned.[13]

Henry's challenge to the dauphin was penned in such a way that it recognised that the infirmity of Charles VI meant there could be no battle between Henry and him; the remedy therefore lay between the English king and the dauphin. There was much that tugged at the heartstrings in it, in words which also summed up the horrors of war:

> And well considering that the effects of our wars are the deaths of men, destruction of countries, lamentations of women and children, and so many general evils that every good Christian must lament it and have pity, and us especially, whom this matter particularly concerns, we are minded to seek diligently all possible means to avoid the above-mentioned evils, and to acquire the approbation of God and the praise of the world.[14]

There was an important item of pragmatism displayed by the challenge. Should the single combat go England's way, then the throne would not pass to Henry until Charles died – an interesting precursor of the deal between Charles and Henry that would finally be made a number of years in the future at the Treaty of Troyes.

The message was sent and the dauphin was given eight days to reply. No one seriously thought that he would take up the gauntlet. In the meantime, there were many other things to be done. The damaged walls of Harfleur needed to be repaired and the port strengthened as a core part of England's territories in France. It was unlikely that the French would delay for long before trying to take such a key town back. In practice, they would attempt unsuccessfully to do so within a year of its capture by Henry.

The leading captives that Henry held were released, on condition that they would re-present themselves at Calais on 11 November (which was Martinmas, the festival of St Martin of Tours, a day when the slaughter of fattened cattle in preparation for the winter took place). A total of about sixty French knights and 200 other gentlemen were released. If a battle had been fought by 11 November, they simply had to pay their ransoms. If not, or if the ransoms could not be paid, then they were to be imprisoned again.

By 28 September, ships were returning to England with the invalided troops on board. A number of leading men were on them, warriors that Henry could ill afford to be without, most of all the formidable Thomas, Duke of Clarence. There is an interesting reference in a slightly later account that suggests that Clarence wanted the army to return home rather than carry on with the campaign.[15] It comes from the pen of an Italian called Tito Livio Frulovisi, who wrote his account in 1438. As it may well have been commissioned by Humphrey, Duke of Gloucester, who was one of Henry's main commanders on the Agincourt campaign as well as being brother to both the king and Clarence, it cannot be lightly dismissed as inaccurate.

In any event, something had to be done with the English invalids at Harfleur. They could not join the march, both for their own sakes and also because they would slow the rest of the army down. Neither could they stay in Harfleur, which was now a shattered wreck and in danger of further attack, both from disease and from the French. They would also be a drain on provisions without offering very much in return, so the only viable course of action was to ship them back home.

Several accounts of the time also refer to problems that the king was experiencing with regard to desertion[16] and it is noticeable how careful the king was to meticulously record all those men who were invalided home once Harfleur fell, presumably in an attempt to make sure that all who did so were entitled to – every man counted.

Many chronicles at least hint at the fact that there was a desire on the whole for the army to return home. A slightly later chronicle, known as the 'Pseudo-Elmham',[17] states that the king wanted to pass through lands he believed were rightfully his to make a point that his adversary was powerless to stop him. He also did not want to give the French reason to crow over his withdrawal without bringing them to battle. The writer noted that 'since, after his opinion had been expressed, nobody dared to contradict the king's decision', they marched on.[18]

On the ships sailing north were Edmund Mortimer, the Earl of March, and the Earl Marshal, John Mowbray, Duke of Norfolk. Their departure meant that half of the leading magnates who were meant to leave England with Henry (including the Earl of Cambridge and Henry, Lord Scrope) were now either dead or had returned home. Another, the Earl of Dorset, was to stay behind at Harfleur as its commander and the Earl of Warwick was in

Calais to ensure that the defences there were in good repair and that the garrison was prepared to help the king's army as much as possible. Warwick had been one of Henry's closest confidantes and had been posted to Calais in 1414, a sign of both how important it was to the king and also how, even a year before the expedition to France set forth, a conflict with the French seemed probable.

There were a number of ships available to ferry these men back to England, helped by the fact that the evacuees mostly left their horses behind and only required enough provisions to make the crossing. However, some extra vessels still needed to be found. Ships from across England were hired for the task as well as making use of the king's own vessels; the hired craft came from a number of ports including Seaton, Plymouth, Hartlepool, Dartmouth, Sandwich, Boston and Colchester.[19]

The traffic was two-way, as supplies had to be brought over from England while there was just a small foothold in Normandy and limited provisions available locally. Records state that two of the king's ships, the *Catherine* and the *Holy Ghost*, crossed from Winchelsea and Rye, bringing with them English beer, corn, hay and oats, along with ropes, winches, bowstrings, glue and coal, while other supplies were shipped in from the ports of Chichester, Dartmouth, Melcombe, Plymouth and Southampton.[20]

At this time a serious problem was emerging: only a handful of potential commanders were left to accompany Henry as he moved across northern France, namely Humphrey, the Duke of Gloucester (Henry's younger and largely inexperienced brother), Edward, the Duke of York, Lord Fitzhugh and Sir Thomas Erpingham (we must also add Thomas, Lord Camoys, to this short list). This created significant challenges in terms of the army's leadership and placed an enormous burden on Henry himself. Now that Clarence had gone and the Earl of Suffolk was dead, much rested on the shoulders of the small group remaining.

The army was also much depleted. Although modern historians have suggested that the small size of the English army has been overplayed as a factor in this campaign, research has shown that slightly less than 12,000 men were in the army when it left England and of these some 2,000 had been shipped back, though some had been replaced. Another 1,200 men had been left in the garrison installed at Harfleur, including probably some who were sick but not sick enough to be shipped home. Other men had probably deserted, as some of the chroniclers suggest, though their numbers are not recorded.

Given this, the estimate of Thomas of Walsingham that the army was now about 8,000 archers and armed men might not be too far off the mark. But it may also be the case that a number of those who were not shipped home had nevertheless been badly affected by the onset of dysentery and this will have impacted upon their potential vitality in a battle situation, not to mention the energy that would be drained from them on the long march that lay ahead.[21]

By this stage a French force was at last gathering to face up to the English. They were assembling at Rouen, down the Seine from Harfleur. If Henry had wanted to meet the French in battle and force a decisive result, he would certainly have wanted to do so on ground that would give him the greatest advantage. But the French were cautious. Rouen would be a major prize for Henry, not least because both the king and the dauphin were close by. Noticeably neither man moved personally into the city until it was obvious that Henry was not headed in their direction. They had no wish to make a present of themselves to the English; the ransom of King Jean II after the Battle of Poitiers in 1356 had created enormous problems for France and was a disturbing precedent.

The French also had major internal tensions to distract them. There was still widespread distrust of the Duke of Burgundy by many of the French and the Armagnac supporters in particular. The Parisians offered 6,000 men to help their king but they were refused. Some, seeking to make a social point, suggested that this was because the men were not of high birth and would dilute the quality of the French army. A much more likely hypothesis though was that any man loyal to the king should stay in Paris to guard against any attempted coup by the Duke of Burgundy when the Armagnacs' backs were turned.

The French were at any rate slow to move out and preferred to stay on the defensive in Rouen while Guillaume Martel took command of the key fortress of the nearby Château Gaillard, the 'Saucy Castle', once the pride and joy of Richard the Lionheart when Normandy was still firmly held by the English. But Henry decided not to attack such a strong position, perhaps nervous after the tough fight at Harfleur as Rouen was an infinitely tougher nut to crack.

The plan to march to Calais was a bold one. Why did Henry choose this course? History was again perhaps something of an inspiration. Moving his army towards Calais would take him over ground that his great ancestor Edward III had also crossed. He would be moving towards northern France, through which flowed the River Somme and close by where the fabled field of Crécy was located. By giving the French eight days to respond to his demands sent from Harfleur, he was effectively telling them that he would be leaving the town after that. Perhaps he was using his army as a bait, enticing the French into a battle on ground of his own choosing.

If this was indeed the case, it was a great gamble. It is certainly very feasible to suggest, as some have done, that the very pious king believed that God was indeed on his side and that this was some sort of divine mission.[22] Be that as it may, this was effectively an all-or-nothing strategy, and if it backfired then the consequences for Henry would probably be disastrous. It is also possible that Henry believed that the French would not choose to fight, which had been their strategy in recent times.

The time limit for a French response to Henry's demands expired on 4 October. There was, predictably, no response at all and Henry therefore had to take the initiative in making the next move. He would certainly have assumed that there would be no immediate response to the ultimatum he had sent and therefore would have mulled over the options for some time. A decision about what to do next would presumably have crystallised in his mind before 4 October.

He had to give some thought as to what should be done with Harfleur for the French would no doubt take steps to recapture it as soon as possible. He decided to leave a garrison of 1,200 men with the Earl of Dorset in the town in the customary three-to-one ratio of archers to men-at-arms. Also remaining in Harfleur were various lords and knights, including Lord Botreaux of Cadbury. Botreaux would later be attacked by dysentery and shipped back to Dover, though he would recover and live on for nearly half a century.

But more black clouds were brewing for Henry, in this case literally. A heavy storm on 5 October resulted in several ships off Harfleur being lost. Other vessels were picked off by pirates shortly after. This further raised Henry's stress levels and added to the tension. It was a salutary reminder that the seasons were changing and that the conventional time for campaigning was drawing to a close.

Some aspects of Henry's strategy may be worked out from other sources. There was a letter exchange between the Duke of Bedford, Henry's regent in England in his absence, and the commander of Calais, Sir William Bardolf (the Earl of Warwick had not yet arrived there to take up his post as the man in charge of the crucial seaport). On 7 October, Bardolf wrote to Bedford and stated that 'it is well understood that it is your will that we make the hardest war that we can against the French, enemies of our most feared noble lord, in order to prevent those on the frontier crossing or advancing near to where he is now in person'.[23] In other words, the garrison in Calais were to attack the French in the region and distract them though he also pointed out that he was aware that the French were guarding the borders of Calais to prevent such a move.

Bardolf also said that men who had come into Calais (that is to say spies) from both France and Flanders told him that a decisive battle was expected in the next fifteen days (in actuality it would be seventeen). This clearly demonstrates that it was common knowledge that both the English king and his French adversaries were already believed to be committed to meeting each other on the field of battle. The bait, if such it was, was proving to be successful. If on the other hand Henry did not wish to fight but merely to promenade across France to make a point, then his plan was already seriously awry.

That same day Charles VI met his son the dauphin at Vernon, on the banks of the Seine in Normandy, complete with the

Oriflamme, the flag of war. More disconcerting news was coming Henry's way. The Duke of Lorraine was en route with a force to join the French army. He was a close ally of John the Fearless, the Duke of Burgundy, and the decision of a supporter of a man who it was hoped would throw in his lot with the English to join the other side was hardly encouraging for Henry.

But the French too did not have far to seek for their problems. For one thing, theirs too was a paid army and it was not easy to pay for it. Unlike Henry's army, there was no time limit for how long they would be needed as that would depend on just how sustained the English assault was. There was also a problem with obtaining and paying for provisions. A Benedictine monk from an abbey near Rouen lamented how the French damaged his foundation and the surrounding area. The dauphin was forced to issue orders that French soldiers should stop annoying monks and stealing provisions from their lands.[24] This might reflect hooliganism on the part of the soldiers but it might equally have resulted from a shortage of provisions and the money to pay for them.

The English got ready to leave Harfleur. There would be three 'battles' or main divisions as the army marched, the vanguard, the centre and the rear. The repercussions of the departure of the Duke of Clarence now showed themselves. He would have almost certainly have led one of the battles, with Henry in command of another and the Duke of York the third. With Clarence's departure there were limited replacements available.

Henry decided to lead the centre and York was given one of the divisions – in fact, it is not clear who led the third and some accounts suggest that York may have been responsible for both the vanguard and the rear. This seems unlikely for pragmatic reasons as much as any other, but it certainly added to the risk that the king was forced to rely so much on a man, namely York, whose brother had been executed on Henry's orders just two months before.

It certainly appears that in the latter part of the campaign the vanguard was led by York, who had with him some of the top warriors in the army such as Cornwall and Sir Gilbert Umfraville (though at the beginning of the march it seems that York was in command of the rearguard along with the Earl of Oxford). They eventually spearheaded the advance of the army with the men carrying eight days' supply with them to see them through the journey to Calais of approximately 150 miles. According to the 'Pseudo-Elmham' chronicler they were not to take wagons with them but were to ferry their supplies on horseback.[25]

This suggests that the English were planning to march across the territory as quickly as possible without the added risk of a battle being fought. The assumption therefore seems to have been that the French would not fight or try to impede their progress and that this would be little more than a demonstration or even a procession – a highly flawed analysis as it would turn out. This suggests that Henry's intention was not to fight, but to demonstrate both to the King of France and to the domestic audience back in England that he was not afraid of the French and that he could march across their territory with impunity. It was not much to show for the large investment that his country had made in the expedition, but it was something.

However, if the French did decide to fight, then a whole different scenario came into play. If the king's order regarding the restrictions on the amount of supplies to be taken was followed, it would create a massive problem for the English if their progress was blocked. Any battle could cause a significant delay and a corresponding food shortage of nightmare proportions. Agincourt was still over fifteen days away, leaving a gap of a week or so between the supplies that the men had with them running out and the likely date of any battle. Unless this shortfall was somehow made up by very effective foraging en route, then it was probable that it would be a very hungry army that eventually met the French in battle. According to some accounts the French were also engaging in a scorched earth policy to further discomfort the English.[26]

Henry's army was now facing one of the perennial challenges of a large group of soldiers in the field in any era, namely how to obtain sufficient provisions to meet their needs. Based on records from other campaigns, an army of around 10,000 men (the probable approximate size of the English force if camp followers and servants were included) would have needed about 250 tons of grain per week. 5,000 horses would need 400 tons of oats or fodder.[27] It was likely that many more horses than this were with the army at this stage as it appeared that there were plenty to go around when the army set out from Harfleur.[28]

In previous times, kings like Edward I of England had put a huge strain on domestic resources by demanding large volumes of supplies from their lands during times of war via the highly unpopular mechanism of prises or purveyance, basically a form of compulsory purchase that was very open to abuse. That had changed in the fourteenth century and anyway France, unlike Wales or Scotland where Edward I was often campaigning, offered a much greater opportunity to live off the land. But that was in itself a risky strategy as a regular supply could not be guaranteed and would sometimes have to be fought for.

There is plenty of evidence that, during this campaign, Henry

V had simply not brought sufficient supplies with him.[29] This problem was further exacerbated by the delay resulting from the siege of Harfleur. Despite these challenges, the long march to Calais began. Little time passed before further fighting began. There was a sharp skirmish at Montivilliers, just a couple of miles from Harfleur. The French had installed a garrison here and there were some English casualties in the scrap, though they did not hinder Henry's further progress.

The army would initially travel via Fauville. Outlying units attacked the partially abandoned town at Fécamp which had been the target of an English raid in July (though details of this action are vague and we cannot be certain what specifically happened here). By 11 October, the English were at Arques, just four miles from Dieppe, which the French feared could be a target for an assault.

At Arques there was an engagement with the castle garrison who fired gun-stones at the English with their cannon though they did not succeed in hurting anyone. The castle was in a formidable position on a precipitous hillside that dominated Arques but the town itself was not walled. Nevertheless it was in a crucial position as it controlled bridges over a river that the English army needed to cross. The castle was a particularly tough nut to crack given its situation; no such structure is truly ever impregnable but there could have been a long and frustrating delay here if a siege were necessary.

The locals were determined to put up a defence and had laid their hands on any materials they could – trees and other barricade materials – in order to impede the English. Henry could not afford a long delay here given the tight supply scenario, so he tried to disarm the situation. He proposed to the people of Arques that, if they provided him with bread and wine for his army, he would not harm the town and instead move on, leaving the people unmolested.

Henry's army was a large one and could have done much damage. It made sense to the townsfolk to accept the deal and they duly did so. The agreement held and the people of Arques breathed a sigh of relief. Henry continued north towards Calais and it would have been clear by now where he was headed and broadly what road he would follow. Ahead of the English lay a crucial crossing over the Somme at Blanchetaque and Henry headed towards it. He was now in a race, for the French were headed there too.

By the next day, the English were outside the much stronger town of Eu, which marked the outer limits of Normandy before the English entered the county of Ponthieu, to which Henry had specifically laid claim before invading France. Probably the whole army was not with him there; it would have been tight to reach Eu from Arques in the time available so perhaps a detachment was sent ahead to neutralise it.

Eu was an important spot, not least because it contained a shrine to St Lawrence O'Toole, Archbishop of Dublin, who had died there in 1180 and was later buried in the crypt of the magnificent collegiate church in the town. Here he was in good company for this also housed the tombs of the counts of Eu – today the church contains a magnificent family vault with superbly decorated tombs that form a striking memorial to this important French noble dynasty.

At Eu there was far less chance of a deal being brokered and serious fighting between the inhabitants and the English followed. There was a sally out of the town and in the scrap that followed both sides lost men. One of them, noted by Monstrelet, was a renowned knight by the name of Lancelot Pierres who was impaled through the belly with a lance and died what was presumably an agonising death, much to the grief of many of the French. The men of Eu had been forced back inside the town, though some of the English were 'cruelly wounded by missiles hurled across the walls of the town'.[30] Negotiations followed in which Henry offered the same terms that he had agreed at Arques. In return for provisions from the town, Henry agreed to desist from burning the outlying settlements that his men had occupied.

In the meantime, John the Fearless had been sending positive messages to the French king and the dauphin which suggested that he was fully behind their cause, though whether anyone truly believed him or not must remain a matter of some doubt. By this time another French force was being assembled to the north to be led by the vastly experienced and much-respected Marshall Boucicaut and Charles d'Albret, the Constable of France.[31] Henry faced the unwelcome prospect of being caught between two French forces, one emerging from Rouen and chasing his rear, the other coming down from the north. The odds against him had worsened again.

Both Boucicaut and d'Albret were experienced if not necessarily always successful commanders. John le Maingre, Boucicaut, was a veteran fighter who had a practical knowledge of warfare that stretched back over three decades, his first campaign taking place when he was aged twelve. Surviving portraits of him suggest a man of experience and a pugnacious, determined commander; almost, as one writer has described it, a 'prize-fighter's face'.[32] He was a hugely travelled warrior, who had fought in Prussia, Spain, the Near East, the Balkans and Cyprus.

He had been captured by the Turks under Sultan Bayezid,

'The Lightning', at the disastrous Crusader defeat at Nicopolis in Bulgaria in 1396. Nicopolis was an interesting precursor of Agincourt, involving a disorganised French charge against a well-prepared Turkish position, with the latter protected by a manufactured hedge of wooden stakes. Turkish archers protected by them caused considerable damage. Also fighting in the French ranks that day was none other than John the Fearless, the Duke of Burgundy, who had earned his nickname as a result of his heroic if somewhat rash actions during the battle. He was also captured, though the vast resources available to his father meant that he was quickly ransomed.

Boucicaut only narrowly escaped death in a slaughter of captives by the Turks after the battle, which was done in retaliation for a similar incident earlier in the campaign when Crusaders had slaughtered Turkish captives, a stark demonstration of the danger of revenge killings when such outrages occurred. He was not a prisoner for long before he was ransomed and released after Nicopolis. However, he did not return to France and found himself involved in the defence of Constantinople against Turkish forces in 1399. He then became governor of the French-held Italian maritime city of Genoa. He had been immortalised in chivalric literature and was one of the best-known knights of his day.

Charles d'Albret, the Constable of France, had held his important post since 1402. He had a reputation as a cautious commander. Born in Guienne, for long the location of England's strongest foothold in France (and therefore nominally a vassal of the English king, as some chroniclers eagerly point out), he had served under the renowned Bertrand de Guesclin, one of the foremost knights of the medieval period. D'Albret had briefly lost his position as constable when the Burgundians gained control of the French government but recovered it again when Armagnac fortunes were restored. It was to these two men that the initial task of blocking Henry's progress was given.

Henry's advance from Harfleur had initially kept the French guessing. Charles VI and the dauphin did not enter Rouen until 12 October, the same day as the Duke of Berry. The Duke of Bourbon would not arrive until 17 October and the Duke of Anjou not until the twentieth. Two months had passed since the invasion force had landed, and the French had known long before this that such a move was likely. But the response was still patchy, uncoordinated and fragmentary, an appropriate symbolic summary of the state of France itself at this particular time.

It was not immediately clear to them what the English were up to. Although with each step away from Rouen and Paris and the heartland of France the French command might breathe more easily, there were other possible targets nearer the coast which would be attractive to the English. One of the most significant was the port of Boulogne near Calais. French hearts must have skipped more than a beat if, as some chroniclers claim, the Duke of Clarence suddenly arrived at nearby Calais, possibly not quite as infirm as reports had suggested.

At the break of day on Sunday 13 October, the English packed their tents and left Eu. With the benefit of hindsight it would become clear that a critical point had been reached, a crossroads moment when the countdown to Agincourt truly began. In anticipation of crossing the Somme, the vanguard pushed ahead towards that vital ford at Blanchetaque. This was a passage near the mouth of the river used for cattle when the tide was out.

The crossing at Blanchetaque played a pivotal role in the story of Edward III's Crécy campaign, as it would now do during the events that led up to the Battle of Agincourt. Despite being defended by French forces, two of Edward's knights, William de Bohun and Sir Reginald Cobham, had heroically forced a crossing. The action had become legendary and Henry would have been delighted to repeat this earlier triumph. The crossing also presented a superb opportunity for Henry to get his men over and complete the march to Calais quickly, proving a point in the process that the King of England could pass with impunity over land that rightfully belonged to him, and that there was nothing that the forces of France could do to stop him.

A thunderbolt was about to strike home and threatened to blow Henry's plans asunder. A man from the retinue of Charles d'Albret was brought in whom some accounts say was a Gascon. Brought before the English for questioning, he delivered a hammer blow. He had not long before been with the Constable of France at Abbeville (where d'Albret and Boucicaut, previously operating independently, had joined forces on 13 October). When asked about the situation at the ford, he responded that it was heavily guarded and also staked against any attempt to cross. The prospect of forcing a crossing against a well-prepared position was not a welcome one.

A council of war discussed the situation for several hours after this worrying news was received. At the end of what may have been a difficult meeting it was decided that the risks of forcing a way across at Blanchetaque were too great. Henry therefore decided that he would seek another way across the Somme. Intriguingly it was later suggested by at least one chronicler, a Burgundian supporter called Jean Le Fèvre who was actually with the English army at the time, that the whole story was a fabrication made up by the captive and that there were no Frenchmen guarding the crossing until over a week later. Some Frenchmen reportedly later cursed this man, for if Henry had crossed without opposition at Blanchetaque then there would have been no Agincourt.

It was nevertheless a crushing blow to Henry's army. One English chronicler, betraying his national bias, called the French tactics of using stakes 'refined tricks' as if they somehow had breached the rules of fair play, although the use of them at Agincourt was apparently acceptable.[33] But the whole plan of action for the English army had now been thrown well off course.

The French were now in a position of decided advantage. The Somme, although crossed in a number of places by bridges, was easily defensible as the crossings could be defended and the bridges destroyed. Further along the front just on the far side of the Somme from the English were several key towns like Abbeville and Amiens. Local militia would be called upon to guard the river along with those from places slightly further back such as Montreuil, which would form a vital communications point between the French-held territory to the north and that to the south of the English army. Near the coast the land was marshy and the river wide. And even if the Somme were crossed there were other smaller rivers such as the Canche, the Ternoise and the Authie which, although less formidable, would still form useful lines of defence.

It seems that there had been a debate within the English camp for several days as to whether or not the French would fight. Some were confident that the internal dissension fuelled by the ongoing shenanigans of the Duke of Burgundy meant that they would be able to complete their journey to Calais unmolested. Others felt that the loss of Harfleur was too great a stain on French honour to go unavenged, that the world would judge their enemy to be 'irresolute and cowardly'[34] if they did not try to right the wrong.

Now it appeared that the French were finally determined to fight and were taking active steps to bar the English army's progress.

This represented a serious deterioration in the English position. With French forces believed to be approaching from several sides, a net was closing around Henry. Increasingly, the only way out was to cut that snare apart by winning a decisive battle or alternatively agreeing to humiliating terms that would seriously compromise Henry's position not just in France but also in England. The latter was unthinkable to a man of Henry's character, so a battle was probable. But if the battle were lost, there was nowhere to run and nowhere to hide. There was no way out for the English and their king save to crush the French on the battlefield. From this point on, Henry's plan to march defiantly from Harfleur to Calais without a fight was in serious trouble.

Nor was that the only hammer blow to hit the king, for on that same day, back in England, the Earl of Arundel, who had been invalided home shortly before, died. He was one of the foremost men in England and a close friend of Henry; he was as much a victim of the king's war in France as if he had been struck down in battle.

Arundel had led the English force that had gone to aid the Duke of Burgundy in 1411 and had helped him win his triumph at St Cloud. The loss of an experienced commander and a close aide to the king was a bitter blow to Henry both on a personal a military level (though of course Henry would not get the news of Arundel's death for some time). He could have done with him at his side now. Further, allied to the loss of Richard Courtenay, the Bishop of Norwich, a heavy double blow had been struck. The campaign had turned into a sobering experience for Henry and with the immediate future uncertain these were worrying times for the king.

All in all, this was a terrible day for Henry. His inability to force the crossing at Blanchetaque, or at least his unwillingness to attempt to do so, would mean a massive diversion though quite how much of one would not become clear until he had seen for himself if a crossing further down the Somme could be accessed. In the event he would move fifty miles inland before he found an alternative way across the River Somme and, in so doing, he ceded the momentum to his opponent. The situation in which the English army found itself would deteriorate by the day from this point on.

The failure to get across at Blanchetaque, close to Abbeville, created major logistical difficulties. It also contrasted adversely with what had happened previously during the reign of Edward III, who was able to force the Somme there. It was even thought by the English that they might have to march all the way up to the source of the river, over sixty miles off. It was believed that the French would be waiting in force here, and that a major battle should be expected as a result. By the time that they arrived there, they would be in a poor position to fight.

The region through which Henry would be passing was on full alert for the English army. As far back as 15 September, the inhabitants of Boulogne had been told to place extra sentries at night and to post watchdogs to guard against a sudden English attack. A good deal of work was undertaken to prepare the defences including the destruction of suburbs that would have hampered the defence and a widening of arrow-slits to allow more effective crossbow fire. Guards were posted in the hills around the port too but as Henry and his army were increasingly pushed further inland the threat to Boulogne receded.[35]

The French forces in the region had been active in preparing their defence. Local militias had been prevailed upon to assist in this. The inhabitants of Amiens were informed of the arrangements that had been made at a meeting held on 13 October. The local forces appear to have been under the coordination of Charles d'Albret and he probably ordered them to help stake the crossing at Blanchetaque. They also sent a number of crossbowmen as well as cannons to Abbeville.

The day after this shattering blow, Henry and his army reached Pont Rémy where a strong French force could be seen on the opposite bank of the Somme.[36] They teased and mocked the English. For a time it seemed that a battle was imminent and in preparation for it a number of men were dubbed knights, including Lord Ferrers of Groby, Ralph Greystoke, Peter Tempest, Christopher Moresby, Thomas Pickering, William Hodelston, John Hosbalton, John Mortimer, James Ormonde and Philip and William Hale.

The tension ratcheted up further as the two sides faced each other from a distance. But the 'pont' that spanned the river was broken and marshland on either bank prevented the two sides from closing without great difficulty. Nevertheless, in the account of at least one chronicler, the Frenchman Pierre de Fenin, the English army made an attempt to get across but 'could not effect a crossing and lost many of their number'.[37] We can perhaps read into this that some of Henry's troops tried to force a crossing against a well-entrenched force and suffered heavily as a result. The situation of the English had deteriorated still further.

There would be no decisive battle that day and the English were starting to experience serious food shortages by now. They were living off horsemeat and filbert nuts (hazelnuts) instead of bread. 'It was on such luxuries and dainties that the champions of the King of England were nourished and fed, as they prepared to join battle with all those thousands of giants.'[38] Hunger gnawed at the empty stomachs and fear at the hearts of the invading army.

Morale was, unsurprisingly, dropping like a stone. The English army were like pieces on a chessboard and their opponent was putting up a blocking defence that was forcing them further and further off course. They were being pushed deeper inland, into an ever-tightening noose. Despite Henry's injunctions against any loss of discipline, looting had started to break out, precipitated by the increasingly dire position that the English were in and the impact of such harsh deprivations.

On 15 October, the important city of Amiens was approached by the English. Nearby at Abbeville a large French force stood ready to move against Henry. A number of the potential defenders of Amiens had been ordered across to Abbeville, weakening the capacity of the city to fight off the English. But Henry was in no position to lay siege to Amiens, even if the strength of the defenders had been denuded. The English marched on by, probably nervous of being attacked from that place as they did so but unaware that the militia of the town had largely been redeployed elsewhere.

The pace of the English advance was now noticeably slowing down. Hunger had started to do its job and increasing instances of looting also reduced the speed of the army's progress. To make matters worse, the autumn rains had broken and the nights were turning cold. The roads along which the increasingly demoralised English trudged were turning into quagmires. The damp and cold gnawed at the bones of the army, slowing the advance even more.

For men who had recently endured the ravages of dysentery, the march was turning into a nightmare. Many a prayer was offered up for help, including some from our unnamed *Gesta* chronicler. But it was not just the hunger, the cold and the damp that sucked the life out of the men; it was the thought that in all probability a large French host was assembling with the aim of forcing a decisive confrontation when the English would be poorly equipped to fight an effective battle.

Boves was reached on 16 October and here a truce was negotiated with the garrison of the castle. This was at least a positive development. Boves was connected to the Duke of Burgundy and the lack of aggressive action by the garrison suggested that he had still not thrown himself fully behind the French king and his government in reality. The local lord, the Count of Vaudémont, was absent with part of Boucicaut's force and in his stead command had passed to Jean de Matringueham, who had presumably led the negotiations with Henry. Bread was sent across to the English in eight large baskets to help alleviate the hunger pangs for a short while at least. There was some better news when it was arranged that two sick men were to be left behind with Matringueham to recuperate.

Nearby vineyards were pillaged, much to the anger of Henry who knew too well how poorly a drunken army would fight. The region was well supplied with wine to which the grateful English helped themselves ; it should be remembered that this was often drunk instead of water at the time as it was much safer in terms of sanitation to do so, though the dangers of overindulgence were of course obvious and had often occurred in the past. Hostages were supplied by the townsfolk of Boves and in return Henry agreed not to burn the villages or the vineyards in the area.

The following day the army moved towards Nesle. There was a foray from the French at Corbie, which the English were passing on their left, when a group of cavalry charged out to attack passing English archers. The fighting was short but sharp and several of the attacking French were taken prisoner. At one stage, the standard of Guienne, which was being carried by Hugh Stafford, was lost but it was retrieved by a Cheshire squire named John Bromley who killed two of his foes and captured two others in the process. It was a heroic action but the far side of the Somme remained as unreachable as ever.[39]

There was an unsavoury incident on the way to Nesle when a pyx, a sacred vessel containing the Eucharist, was pilfered from a church that was passed by the army. It was made of copper-gilt, which may have been confused by the thief with gold.[40] This was an outrage to the king's religious sensibilities. It was one thing for his men to ignore his orders and steal food to live, quite another to indulge in such a sacrilegious act.

Reports of looting and the fact that some of the men had resorted to alcohol suggested that order was starting to break down. Henry resolved to take decisive action now that a church had been robbed; this was not the kind of message that a king claiming the support of the Almighty desired to send. The march was stopped and his captains ordered to search the men until the stolen object was found. Eventually an archer was identified who was hiding the sacred vessel up his sleeve.

The pyx was returned to the church while the archer was hanged in full sight of the army (according to some chroniclers close to the church he had robbed) to serve as an object lesson that the king's patience must not be pushed too far. It was an important signal to send in terms of reinforcing discipline but would hardly have helped to increase the men's morale. The story certainly resonated down to the time of Shakespeare, who gives the hanged man the identity of Bardolph, the roistering companion of the king's misspent youth.

All the bridges they reached were down and any fords were guarded. With nowhere to cross, and the Somme bending, they were forced further away from the river. As there was no chance of forcing a crossing, the pace of the march picked up. Nesle was reached in the evening of the eighteenth. An unwelcome sight met the eyes of the English when they arrived. The northern French army was at Péronne just sixteen miles off and bolstered by this the townsfolk in Nesle refused point-blank to surrender. They hung red cloths over the walls, a mark of disrespect and defiance against the English.

An insight into Henry's own state of mind can be found in his reaction to these signs of resistance. He ordered that the villages around Nesle should be razed. But before these draconian measures were carried out, the mood changed. News came in, possibly with the help of inside information from a Frenchman in the area, that there was a nearby ford that was not defended. Important though this was, it did not stop Henry from going through with his plans to burn some villages near Nesle as an example, 'out of anger' as one chronicler, Thomas Elmham, a monk of St Augustine's, Canterbury, put it.[41] It is an enlightening insight into the sternness of the king who, even though his fortunes had suddenly improved, still resolved to teach the rebellious locals (as he saw them) a lesson.

The burning of the villages was something of a return to type for the Hundred Years War. Violence against non-combatants was a feature of earlier campaigns in France. Society was at something of a crossroads with regard to such issues. On the one hand, the campaign in France in particular represented a form of 'total war' where there appeared to be no such thing as a non-combatant. Most people paid taxes and provided food and other supplies for

French armies on campaign, so they were regarded as legitimate economic targets.

On the other hand, some commentators were starting to query both the moral and legal aspects of this harsh situation when non-combatants were subject to rape and pillage at the hands of campaigning armies. One such was the French monk Honoré Bonet in his *L'Arbre des Batailles* (*The Tree of Battles*, which appeared in 1387), where he said plainly that 'valiant men and wise, however, who follow arms should take pains, so far as they can, not to bear hard on simple and innocent folk, but only on those who make and continue war, and fear peace'.[42]

Bonet also remarked caustically how 'in these days [namely the closing years of the fourteenth century] all wars are directed against the poor labouring people and against their goods and chattels, I do not call that war but it seems to me to be pillage and robbery. Further that way of warfare does not follow the ordinances of worthy chivalry.'[43] Clearly such men were not blindly taken in when comparing the harsh realities of a real-life war as against the romantic musings of authors and troubadours in their quest to conjure up visions of a world ruled by chivalric conventions. The period in question was, like most epochs in human history, an age of paradox but men have rarely found it difficult to live in such times with apparently clear consciences.

In the campaign of 1415, the English were well equipped with spies or, alternatively, cooperative prisoners. Rumours were by now circulating of the tactics that the French planned to use in any forthcoming battle. They were well aware of the threat posed by the English archers and planned to designate a strong cavalry force to break them up. In response, Henry had developed his own tactics. He issued orders that each archer was to cut himself a stake about six feet long and pointed at both ends. When they were faced by a French cavalry charge they were to hammer the stake into the ground, with one pointed end facing at above waist-height towards the enemy. Any mounted warrior charging towards the English lines then faced the unpleasant prospect of having his horse impaled on the hedge of stakes.[44]

Early on the following morning, 19 October, a scouting party was sent out by Henry to test out the situation with regard to the possible crossing of the Somme that had been discovered. They made their way stealthily towards the river, taking great care not to alert the enemy to their presence. They returned with uplifting news. There was indeed an unguarded ford; there were two of them, in fact. Causeways that led to them had been deliberately damaged by the French but not thoroughly enough. They could still be crossed, even if only in single file. The Somme could indeed be traversed; even after the rains the water did not pass beyond the belly of a horse.

Furthermore, the crossings were not guarded. The task of doing so had been deputed to the men of St Quentin but they had failed to do it properly, nor had they destroyed the causeways leading up to the crossing. They had partially done so, meaning that men could only cross in single file and then with difficulty, but they had not been rigorous enough to stop the English altogether.[45]

Speed was of the essence; the French could realise the error of their ways and rush forces to the crossing at any moment. So Henry ordered the advance at once, though the nearby villages were still burned as threatened. Those two staunch warriors, Cornwall and Umfraville, assisted by other knights such as William Porter and William Bourchier, once more led the charge. They moved across the Somme and established defences on the far side to hamper any French attack that might be launched and to guard the army behind them. They held the bridgehead from midday until one hour before nightfall, by which time it was firmly secured.

Archers were also sent out as an advance party to discourage any French forces who might try to intervene, showing that the military tactics were very much reliant on a combination of forces and that both men-at-arms and bowmen supported each other in the process. Bridges were thrown up to help speed up the crossing. They were put together with any materials that could be obtained, including stairs, doors and window frames from houses.[46]

Henry ensured that full advantage was taken of his unexpected opportunity. The partially damaged causeways were hastily repaired, with the gaps that had been gouged out by the French filled in. Men could now cross over three abreast, enabling the bridgehead to be more firmly secured with each passing minute. In the race against time, the English were winning. The army's baggage was sent across one ford, the men the other, lessening the chances of confusion or delay. The king personally oversaw the crossing of the men, directing the traffic with an efficient eye. There was every possibility of confusion and congestion and Henry was keen to ensure that this was avoided at all costs.

The tension began to mount. Before even one hundred men had crossed over, French cavalry were seen not far off. There was a danger of an attack being launched before the English were across in sufficient proportion. There were unhappy precedents of which some may have been aware. The English army had suffered a catastrophic defeat against the Scottish warrior William Wallace at Stirling Bridge in 1297; in that battle they had been crossing a river when the Scots attacked while they had only managed to get half their force across and had been decimated as a result.

The bridgehead grew stronger and the English army waded across the two fords, one at Béthencourt, the other close by at Voyennes. Nowadays the Somme at Béthencourt is a sleepy and tranquil backwater that would not look out of place in a Monet landscape – very different than what might be expected of such a crucial spot in history. Then it was a place of destiny. The French in the area awoke to the threat, but too late. Because the English had been forced away from the river during the past two days, the French had lost sight of where the invader was headed. Now they called up reinforcements, but not enough men were available to mount a successful counter-attack. What few attacks did take place were easily beaten off.[47]

Fortunately for the English, there would be no repeat of Stirling Bridge today. The French were either not present in sufficient force to repulse the crossing or were not coordinated well enough to do so. Henry sent out mounted patrols to break up any opposition, and they succeeded in forcing the French away from the fords. It was dusk on the nineteenth by the time all the English were across. They continued the march for a while under the light of the full moon, eventually coming across several hamlets where they established their base for the night.

Henry put up for the night in a house at Athies (though some chroniclers place the army at nearby Monchy-Lagache; perhaps in close enough proximity for both places to have been used). Morale, much battered during preceding days and weeks, climbed again, partly because the English had shortened their march by as much as eight days and partly because a number of the men believed that the French would now be disinclined to fight. Few of the English had much stomach for a battle now, and many merely wanted to get back home without further hindrance or suffering.

Just ten miles off, the French held their own council of war at Péronne, a sturdy town with a strong castle that the English would want to avoid. Boucicaut and d'Albret had by now been joined by the Duke of Bourbon, who had made his way to them from Rouen, showing that the two French forces were coordinating their actions to some extent. The duke came with news that Charles VI planned to bring the English to battle within a week. Bourbon was up for a fight; earlier in the year he had established the Order of the Prisoner's Shackle for such a purpose. Letters were also sent to the Duke of Brabant ordering him to bring his men-at-arms and join them as quickly as possible. It is interesting that the message, which was received on 19 October, intimated that the plan at this stage was that Charles VI and the dauphin still planned to be present with the army.[48]

Also present at this meeting in Péronne was the Duke of Alençon and the counts of Richemont, Eu and Vendôme. In their message to the Duke of Brabant to the north at Louvain, they told him that his presence was urgently required as a battle was likely during the next week. The two armies were now effectively on a collision course and, although they had known for some time where Henry was approximately headed, the French were still assembling their forces. The presence of Arthur, Count of Richemont (the brother of the Duke of Brittany), at this meeting would have been of particular interest to Henry V, as they had something in common: the king's stepmother was Richemont's natural mother from her first marriage.

However, there was a worrying development emerging from the French side. The arrival of a number of prominent noblemen meant that the command structure of their army was already starting to get complicated. There was a real risk that the more cooks who had an input in preparing the broth, the greater the chance that it would spoil. This was a situation that would become increasingly problematic as the days passed.

When the Duke of Brabant received the news from Péronne, he assembled his secretaries and told them to send summonses to his lords and nobles to assemble their retinues for battle. They sent word around his territories including to Antwerp. The troops were to assemble at Cambrai, to which place the duke made his way. He also spoke to the assemblies of Brussels, Louvain and Anvers as he moved around, asking them to get together as many soldiers as they could. He may have been a member of the Burgundian dynasty but clearly he had no intention of missing out on a fight.

The march from Harfleur to Béthencourt where the Somme had finally been crossed was a period of shadow-boxing when the English and French forces in the region jostled for position, throwing feints here and there to catch their opponent off balance. The use of Péronne by the French appears to have been, according to Monstrelet, mainly as a headquarters from where forces could be despatched to block all the crossings of the Somme that would otherwise be available to the English. The French had had the better of it so far. They had succeeded in forcing the English away from the coast and deeper into France. They had bought time in which to bring their armies together. In the process there had been some English losses, though how many is not clear. But among those who died during this phase of the fighting was one Richard Charman, a member of Erpingham's company.[49]

If the French had only succeeded in delaying Henry for a little longer, for perhaps even a day, the entire course of the campaign might have changed, as by the time that the Battle of Agincourt was fought some of the French troops were still on their way to their rendezvous point. As things transpired, the chain of events at Agincourt could have worked out differently if timings had changed even by just a few hours. If God really was on the side of Henry, He showed it by allowing the king to discover the fords at Béthencourt when he did. With the Somme crossed at last, the English and the French were finally on a collision course. By the time another week had passed, the whole of France would be turned on its head and the world would seem a very different place indeed.

7

AGINCOURT: THE EVE OF BATTLE (20–24 OCTOBER 1415)

Such a huge host that it cannot be numbered.
An English observer on seeing the French army for the first time

So Henry and his increasingly bedraggled army had at last succeeded in breaching the watery walls of the Somme. They were wet, hungry and exhausted after the long march. They had been under enormous mental stress over the past few days too, pushed deeper and deeper into France, knowing that all the might of their foe was converging on them, intent on bringing them to battle, forcing them always further away from the coast and the promise of safety. In reality, one serious problem had now been replaced by another, for the path to Calais and home now lay before them but it was far from being an open one. Battle in the next few days was almost inevitable given the presence of sizeable French forces in front of them in the region. There were few signs that the French would meekly let them pass without a fight. Wishful thinking about avoiding a battle was turning to pessimism at a rate of knots.

On 20 October, the day after crossing the Somme, the English decided to do something very sensible: nothing. They needed to recover their strength as far as they were able to prepare themselves for the looming battle. In case they were in any doubt that they were now bound to fight, during the day a delegation came over from the French to lay down the challenge. They came in the first instance to the Duke of York (once more suggesting that he was in the van of the army), who sent them on to the king. Among the French delegation was Jacques de Heilly, who had broken out from a prison in England a few years previously and run off to France accompanied by a beautiful paramour.[1]

Chivalric pleasantries were duly observed. The challenge to meet on the field of battle was formally presented to Henry and he obligingly accepted, also giving the envoys gifts for their pains. This was all in all a very polite precursor to a fight to the death. It was also extremely bad news for those in the English army who wished to avoid a battle. Henry himself realised that a fight was now highly likely and steeled himself for the challenge ahead, encouraging his men to do the same and putting on his coat of arms as a signal that he was ready for action. According to the Berry Herald, a site for the battle was agreed, at Aubigny in Artois.[2] If this is true, then it appears from subsequent events that Henry had little intention of complying with this agreement for his route would not take him past this place, an interesting snippet of information that hints that Henry was not at all keen for a fight.

While the French army in the north was ready for battle, those who were still in Rouen were taking their time deciding what to do next. A council of war was held there on the same day that the meeting of the representatives of the northern army with Henry took place, with a majority of those present wishing to fight.

However, it was not a unanimous decision. The Duke of Brittany was one of the French king's more independently minded vassals. He had in fact been negotiating surreptitiously with Henry for months. Indeed, one of Henry's envoys had arrived at his court on 19 August, even as instructions were delivered by the King of France telling the duke to lead a force to his side.

In something of a difficult position now that he had obeyed Charles VI's summons to bring up his men, the duke said that he had no wish to take the field against the English unless his cousin the Duke of Burgundy was there too. It was a canny move for there was little likelihood of the Duke of Burgundy arriving in person and previous exchanges had already suggested that the French did not really want him to. But the tactics of avoiding a fight against invading English forces had been the norm in more recent times and had worked rather well, so there were sound military reasons for opposing a pitched battle too.

But the Duke of Brittany was heavily outvoted and the will of the council was to fight. Word of their decision was sent post-haste to Charles d'Albret. But there was a surprise. Neither the king nor the dauphin would be present with the army that was now making its way towards the northern French force. This was perhaps understandable in the case of the king given his mental state. It was much less so in the case of the dauphin, who was far from happy with the situation. It had been argued that it was too much of a security risk; the capture and imprisonment of the French king Jean II after the Battle of Poitiers set a most unhappy precedent, one for which the French were still in some ways paying over half a century later; part of Henry's package of claims against France was the unpaid ransom for him that had not yet been cleared.

In fact, this move reflected contemporary French policy thinking.

In 1404, a work called *The Book of the Deeds and Good Habits of King Charles the Wise* was produced by a quite remarkable female figure of the time called Christine de Pizan. She was a Venetian by birth but had spent most of her life in France, married at fourteen and widowed a decade later with two young children. As well as producing poetry she also wrote military treatises – a most unladylike pursuit for the time, one might think, but one in which she showed a well-informed mind.

In her work Christine de Pizan praised Charles, saying that 'he judged wisely that it was not healthy for the prince to put himself into battle save in dire necessity. For the whole body and its limbs will be weakened if the head is damaged. The capture or death of the king leads to the effective death of all his subjects.'[3] This was exactly the policy that Charles was now adopting a decade or so later.

The leading member of the French royal family who would therefore be present at any battle in the near future would be the Duke of Orléans, the king's nephew. He would, because of his standing, be in command of the army. Other important men alongside him would be Charles d'Albret, the constable, along with the dukes of Alençon and Brittany, the latter compelled to participate despite his lack of enthusiasm. Other positions of command were allocated. The vanguard would be led by Marshal Boucicaut, with the Duke of Bourbon and Guichard Dauphin; the last two were connected by family ties.

The rear would be under the command of the Duke of Bar, supported by the counts of Nevers, Charolais and Vaudémont while Tanneguy du Chastel and the Count of Richemont would each lead a wing. The heavy cavalry, who would be given the task of cutting up the English archers, would be led by the seneschal of Hainault. For the Count of Nevers it would be a baptism of fire, a very appropriate phrase as just three days previously he had been present at the christening of his son near Vézelay.[4]

There were stories current that the French forces had been undisciplined as they made their way towards the English. Some French accounts accused them of being more interested in plunder and helping themselves freely to the possessions of the villages through which they passed than in fighting the English. They stole the animals of the peasants they came into contact with, leaving a desperate scene behind them.[5] These accounts even suggested that the behaviour of the French contrasted poorly with that of the English.[6]

On the other hand, although most English accounts dodge round the issue of pillaging, some of the French chroniclers specifically accuse the English of ravaging the country through which they passed. In reality, probably both sides were short of food, and helping themselves to what they could might have been unfair but it was necessary. The rights and needs of the civilian populace were, as ever during this terrible extended period of conflict between England and France, swept to one side.

Indeed, there are enough of these accounts to paint a consistent picture. It is unlikely that Henry's army marched across France without helping itself to much-needed provisions. It is almost inconceivable that hungry soldiers would not grab all that they could while they were marching through what, to them, seemed like enemy territory regardless of what their king and his propagandists might say. The chronicler Monstrelet tells how at one stage the English marched on, 'burning and destroying the whole country, taking prisoners and acquiring great booty'. Neither was it unlikely that the French army, equally in need of provisions, would rob its own people to meet requirements.

Henry had issued his orders at the start of the invasion and he clearly intended his men to be kept under strict discipline. He would not hesitate to use it either, as the archer who had unwisely stolen the pyx had found out to his cost. But it was one thing for a king who wished to appear as pious as possible to hang a man for robbing from a church, quite another for him to punish hungry, dispirited men for stealing food. Overall, the most likely situation is that Henry managed to avoid excesses in the actions of his men – if there had been any specific examples, then his opponents would have made more of them – but it is probable that there were some breaches of discipline, as would be the norm for any army of that time.

Henry took the issue of discipline very seriously. He was a very visible commander and his stern visage would be enough to discourage most of his men from going too far. His instructions were that only selected men, his 'herbergers', should go out in advance of the army and look for food. In addition, each retinue was to keep its men together on the march, which would help cohesion and control significantly.[7] Given the levels of authority that Henry enjoyed, it is probable that the army was largely kept under control and that most seizures of provisions were done in a coordinated fashion, though the hardship that would cause for the lands through which they passed would still be substantial.

Neither were there just moral or propagandist reasons for Henry's tight control of his army. The king by this stage was giving the impression of a man in a hurry. Avoidable distractions such as unwarranted pillaging should not, therefore, be undertaken. They also introduced unnecessary risks – of his men being dispersed and more vulnerable to attack, of discipline starting to deteriorate. Once lost, discipline was hard to regain; such loss of discipline would lead to a serious English defeat at Baugé six years later.

Some French chronicles also tell a story about which the English versions of the time are largely silent. This concerns the English garrison of Calais, which was a strong one. They sallied out to meet their king and got rather the worst of it in the fighting that followed. Some were killed and others captured and held for ransom. It is an intriguing story and one that comes from a source written by the so-called Religieux, believed to be in all probability a monk at St Denis who is by no means uncritical of the French ruling regime, so his account cannot be dismissed out of hand as propaganda. There have been some suggestions – and these are more part of the 'legend' of Agincourt than being based on documentary information – that the raid out from Calais was repulsed by the French close to the pivotal crossing at Blanchetaque.[8]

That night there was a rather strange incident at Chauny, near St Quentin, some miles off the English army's line of march. The mayor of that place had heard rumours that the invaders were heading his way and went out to investigate. Finding the rumours to be unfounded, he returned to his home only to find his wife naked in bed and a man named Jean Mairel nearby with the minimum of clothing on. Putting two and two together and probably making four, he lashed out at the unwelcome guest, who later died of his injuries, an odd if indirect casualty of war.[9]

After resting up on the 20th, the following day the English set out once more, marching north from Athies and Monchy-Lagache. Henry was ready for anything. He was dressed in his armour and told all his men-at-arms to do the same. They made for the important town of Péronne, where the French command had been not long before though they had by now left. The English army was nervous; 'their hearts were quaking with fear', as Thomas Elmham put it.[10]

The English and the French forces were now so proximate that there were frequent skirmishes between them, though these were not at this stage major. As Henry's army passed Péronne on its left, the French sent out sorties from the town to harass the English, possibly in an attempt to lure them closer to the walls where they could be shot at by artillery. However, the English succeeded in driving back the skirmishers without allowing themselves to be brought into range.

In the wider context, large bodies of French reinforcements were even now coming up. The Duke of Brittany, for example, had left Rouen with 6,000 men. To the north, Duke Anthony of Brabant, the brother of the Duke of Burgundy, had received news that a fight was imminent. There was no apparent prevarication on his part, as we have seen. Summonses were issued to all the lords in his retinue to make their way with their men to Cambrai as quickly as possible.

But the fact that men like the Duke of Brabant were receiving this news at late notice suggests again that the French response was not well coordinated. It was no surprise that the English were making for Calais, in fact it had been common knowledge that this was a likely destination for weeks. The response to this by the French had up to now been inefficient in a number of respects. Instead of having time to get together his men in an organised and coherent fashion, the Duke of Brabant and others like him were rushing around at the last moment grabbing all the resources they could in a short space of time.

It was now becoming increasingly obvious to the English that, despite these problems of coordination, a large French force was in the area. As the English resumed their advance along the mud-caked roads just out from Péronne, they could see that they were badly churned up as if thousands of the enemy had been marching and riding along them not long before. This depressed morale once more. The English turned their thoughts heavenward, praying that God would have pity on them and help them to avoid the violence of the French.[11]

After crossing the Somme at long last, Henry billeted at Forceville and at Acheux while the French moved towards Saint-Pôl. The pace of the march increased, exerting an already tired English army even more although the rest day on the 20th would have helped. On 23 October they marched twenty miles along roads that were really mud tracks, badly churned up after the heavy autumn rains. They crossed the River Authie and camped at Bonnières and in the surrounding area on the night of the 23rd. The Duke of York was proving himself invaluable, leading the vanguard and pushing himself to the limit. He moved on to Frévent, where the French were already present in some force. There was a fight and the duke and his men succeeded in pushing the French out of the town and repairing the broken bridge that he found there. This secured the crossing of the River Canche, another significant barrier to cross though one that was on a smaller scale than the Somme.

The French had moved their army away from Péronne on the twentieth and would have been well aware of where the English were approximately headed. The route their opponent was taking, north-west towards Calais, could have suggested that the English were now keen to avoid a fight. The French moved therefore to block their progress and force one, believing that they now had the upper hand. Messages were once more sent north to the Duke of Brabant, who was now heading for Mons, telling him to expect a fight on the 25 October. The English and the French were now so close to each other that they could almost touch.

The tension was palpable and was to ratchet up still further on the 24th. By the end of that day it would be clear that a major battle was now almost certain. The day began with the English crossing the River Canche and heading towards Blagny. Their progress was not uncontested. The Duke of York and his forces were in the thick of the action, which soon grew intense. The skirmishing was frequent and heavy and there were some English casualties. The two forces were in a race for the River Ternoise. If the English could be prevented from crossing it or at least moving far beyond it, then a battle would be inevitable.

Henry's main priority was now to avoid a fight but this seemed increasingly unlikely. His army was weak, tired and hungry. Although the French too had had to march some way to reach the region, they had the advantage of freshness relative to the English. They also knew the area better, something that is often overlooked by historians but a potential advantage nevertheless. All the best cards appeared to be in French hands. Reports came in that many thousands of Frenchmen had been seen on the far bank of the river. The English army was now in serious trouble; to one chronicler 'it was a wonder that they were able to stand at all, when you add in that they were exhausted by their marches, hollow-eyed from keeping watch and weakened by the cold at night'.[12]

The king was distracted. He mistakenly rode past a village where some food had been found and set aside for him and refused to go back when told about it. Though he explained that he was dressed for war and he did not think it appropriate to frighten the villagers, it was more likely that he was just too busy with too many crucial matters on his mind to waste time, which was of the essence now that a battle loomed so close. Stopping to eat was an avoidable luxury at moments such as this.

The redoubtable Duke of York and his men came across some French troops at Blagny in the process of destroying a bridge which was crucial if the English army was to cross safely. He immediately led his men in a charge against the enemy, putting them to flight, killing some and capturing others in the process. The river that ran through Blagny, the Ternoise, had also carved a valley that hid the way ahead behind a fairly steep ridge. What lay beyond could not be seen from down in the town.

One of York's men rode forward again, riding up the hill to see what was ahead. He was not prepared for the sight that was about to unfold before him. As he reached the summit and looked beyond, a terrifying vista met his eyes. He returned to the duke almost at once with a 'trembling heart' and frightening news. He told the duke that he was 'astonished at the size of the French army' that he had seen, talking of 'such a huge host that it cannot be numbered'.[13]

This disturbing news of the great French army that had been spotted was hurried back to Henry, who continued to move forward, riding hard up the slope to see for himself what lay ahead. The main English force succeeded in crossing the Ternoise but the French army hove into view shortly afterwards. There was indeed some fighting during the day, and records note the capture of some English archers so clearly it did not all go Henry's way. Among those captured were seven of the men from Lancashire, and another man from that county had been taken the day previously.[14]

To the anonymous chronicler of the *Gesta*, who was actually present and witnessed these things with his own eyes, the massed ranks of the French were 'grim-looking'. They seemed 'like a countless swarm of locusts', taking up position just half a mile off. There was just a shallow valley between the English and the French forces now, all that kept them apart from a decisive confrontation. Not far beyond in the middle distance there was a small village, marked by a castle that at this moment meant little to the English. The name of the village was Agincourt. Henry, whatever his innermost feelings, outwardly stayed the picture of calm and got his own men into position in case a battle were to start soon after.[15] The reality was that, just three days' march from Calais, the English army's progress was blocked by a substantially larger force.

What should not be overlooked was the remarkable speed at which Henry and his army had travelled from Harfleur to this point. With diversions and other factors taken into consideration, the English had covered perhaps 260 miles in seventeen days, an average of over fifteen miles a day. In contrast Edward III's army in France in 1359 had barely travelled six miles a day. Even the American Civil War leader General Sherman only managed twelve miles a day in his march from Atlanta to the sea.[16] It would therefore be no surprise if as well as being hungry and attacked by disease, Henry's army was also on the point of exhaustion.

Despite the reservations of some modern historians on the subject, there are many contemporary accounts suggesting that the English believed they were facing up to a much larger army than their own. Chroniclers are notorious for playing fast and loose with numbers in the interests of exaggerating the prowess and achievements of their main character, in this case Henry V. But it would be wrong to completely ignore them on these grounds unless there is compelling evidence available to disprove their thesis. For a demoralised English army there may well have seemed to be more French troops than there actually were, fearing perhaps what they could not see as much as what they could. But most accounts are consistent in stating that the French enjoyed a substantial numerical advantage over the English and this collective picture should not be dismissed out of hand.

What made things worse for Henry's army was the fact that many of the French forces despatched to bring the English to book had not yet arrived on the scene. Probably the Count of Nevers was not yet there. He was an inexperienced warrior who had not yet been dubbed a knight before the Agincourt campaign and was only made so by Marshal Boucicaut on the eve of the battle. Neither had the dukes of Brittany or Brabant arrived. Other French nobles were still on their way.[17] In other words, if the English were already heavily outnumbered, the situation would become far worse when the missing French forces turned up. It was a frightening scenario.

When the disturbing news of the large forces ahead reached him via the Duke of York's frantic messenger, Henry reacted as any good commander would; he went to see for himself. His reaction in doing so is compelling evidence that the news was disturbing. He rode forward and consulted with the Duke of York as to their next steps. Then he returned to the main force and drew up his men in battle formation. Perhaps this intimated that he feared an attack would be launched at once and he wished to make sure that his men were not caught off balance.

In some French accounts,[18] Henry sent messengers to his opponents asking for a short truce. It would buy him time to ensure that he and his army were ready but it would also allow more French troops to arrive so it would help them too. Therefore it was agreed that there would be no fighting that day (with the shortening of the days as the year moved towards winter a fight now was probably an unlikely scenario anyway). Not trusting that the truce would hold, the English were kept in battle formation just in case. They made their way to the village of Maisoncelle a few miles off to the north-west, where they prepared to set up camp for the night.

Other French accounts were more explicit in claiming that the English sought to bargain themselves out of the situation in which they found themselves. These claimed that the English offered reparations for the damage that they had caused during the campaign and to return any loot that they had taken. The French, confident as they enjoyed superior numbers, rejected these approaches which therefore came to nothing.[19]

It would be a very disturbed night for Henry and his army for more than one reason. Alarmed and frightened by the scale of the task before them, the English were further discomfited by a turn in the weather. It began to rain heavily, soaking the English, mostly without shelter, to the skin. A few of the leading men in the army billeted in the few houses in Maisoncelle; the king certainly did. It was dark, but the white road to the village was possible to follow in the blackness.

For the rest, there were only orchards and gardens to try and shelter in. The downpour made their night miserable and in all probability mostly sleepless as large puddles started to form across the ground. It was ironic that the bad weather, which made their night so uncomfortable, was in fact a gift from God which would help deliver them the victory on the following day.

Above left: 1. A statue of King Henry V (central figure) in York Minster.
Above right: 2. Housed in Winchester Cathedral is the tomb effigy of Cardinal Henry Beaufort, Henry's uncle and a crucial political figure behind the Agincourt campaign.
Below: 3. The Battle of Shrewsbury, 21 July 1403. Henry V, then Prince of Wales, fought bravely at the battle although only sixteen years old.

4. Wolvesey Castle in Winchester, where a French delegation made a futile last-ditch effort to stop Henry V's invasion of France.

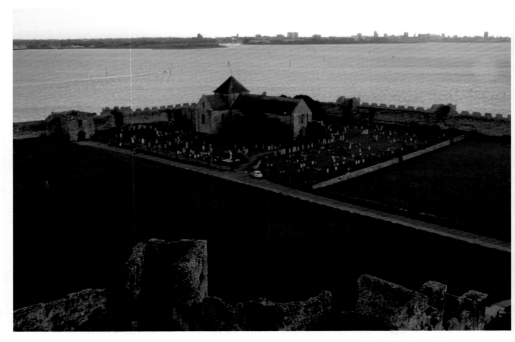

5. Looking over Portsmouth Harbour from Portchester Castle and the Solent beyond, where the English armada assembled.

Right: 6. Fifteenth-century archers. Detail from the *Pageant* of Richard Beauchamp, Earl of Warwick, Captain of Calais, 1414.

Top left: 7. The keep of Portchester Castle, where Henry V first learned of the Southampton plot to replace him.

Bottom left: 8. The Micklegate, York. The quartered royal arms of England and France can be clearly seen. The head of the executed Henry Scrope, Lord Masham, one of the Southampton plotters, was placed over the gate.

Bottom: 9. Before the launch of the Agincourt campaign there was a flurry of diplomacy between Henry V and the King of France, Charles VI. Here, Henry V receives a letter from Charles.

Above: 10. The West Gate, Southampton. Many of the troops departing for France marched through the city walls on to the waiting ships.

Left: 11. Thomas, Duke of Bedford, Henry V's eldest brother. Thomas was invalided back to England after the siege of Harfleur.

12. Chateau Gaillard, Richard the Lionheart's famous castle, which by Henry V's time formed part of the French defences of the Seine guarding Paris.

13. The formidable castle at Arques, which fired on Henry's army as it passed by.

14. Looking down on the town of Arques from the castle, showing the rolling country through which Henry would soon pass.

15. The battlefield of Crécy. The achievements of Edward III were a source of significant inspiration for Henry V.

16. The castle at Péronne, a major part of the French defences of the Somme.

Opposite: 17. A fifteenth-century siege, manuscript illumination.

Left: 18. The Somme at Bethencourt, one of the crossing points that Henry's army discovered which allowed them to ford the river.

19. The church at Athies. The English army rested for a day here to recuperate after their long march.

20. Dartmoor Cemetery near Albert. Henry V's army passed close to this spot, now the resting place of 760 First World War British and Commonwealth soldiers, including Private J. T. Bartlett.

21. Frévent, where the Duke of York and the English vanguard stopped shortly before Agincourt was reached.

22. The Ternoise near Blagny, where the English managed to fight their way across.

23. The top of the ridge near Blagny; from somewhere around here the massive French army was spotted for the first time.

Top to bottom: 24. The village of Maisoncelle, where Henry V spent the night before the Battle of Agincourt.

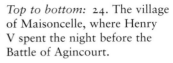

25. Looking back from the approximate spot of the first English position at Agincourt to the village of Maisoncelle.

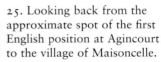

26. The woods by the village of Tramecourt that protected the right wing of the English army at Agincourt.

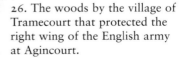

27. Looking across the battlefield towards the village of Agincourt.

28. Humphrey, Duke of Gloucester, Henry V's youngest brother. He fought at the Battle of Agincourt.

29. Brass of John Peryent and his wife. This was made in 1415 so is a very good representation of the armour that would have been used at the time. Peryent fought at Agincourt.

30. Men-at-arms from the Hundred Years War, from the Black Prince's monument in Leeds.

31. Archers from the Hundred Years War, from the Leeds monument.

Above: 32. The road from Agincourt to Maisoncelle, hard to see from the battlefield and a possible route for the French attack on the English baggage.

Right: 33. This brass shows Lord Camoys, probable commander of the English left wing at Agincourt, and his wife; from Trotton Church in West Sussex.

34. The Calvarie at Agincourt, reputedly the site of mass graves from the battle, though archaeology has failed to find firm evidence of this.

Here shewes howe Erle Richard when he w[i]t[h] his [shyp] toke the salt wat[er]
short space rose a grevous tempest and drofe the shippes into d[i]u[er]se [places]
so moch that they al [sup]posed to be p[er]isshed / And the noble Erle for [out]
leke bound hym self   and his lady and [how] his [sone] [Clyn]
after Due of warr   w[i]t[h] to the mast of the [vessel] to the[y]
that where did they   were founde / they myght have [be]
buried to gedder .   worshipfully by [the] k[n]owleg[e] of [hym]
[ar]riue[r] the shippes vpon   hym / but yet [the] p[er]isshed them
[&] so returned to England   and after to Normandy .

Opposite: 35. The French captives, strapped to the masts for their own safety, groaned and prayed. They were shipped back to England on 16 November.

Top: 36. The tomb of the Count of Eu in the family vault in the collegiate church in the town. The count spent many years after Agincourt as an English captive.

Right: 37. The date '1838', scratched in the walls of Agincourt church, allegedly marks the spot where human remains unearthed by Lieutenant-Colonel John Woodford on the battlefield were reinterred.

Bottom right: 38. The battlefield memorial at Agincourt at the bottom of the road from Maisoncelle to Tramecourt.

39. Tretower Castle in the Welsh Marches, ancestral home of the Vaughans, whose family members fought and died alongside Henry V at Agincourt.

40. A statue of Joan of Arc from Winchester Cathedral. Her efforts helped to undo much of what had been achieved in France by Henry V.

Despite the rain, there is some evidence that, in material terms at least, the English spent a slightly better night than they had for a while. Tito Livio said in his later account that 'they came into a village [Maisoncelle] where they were [more] nourished with food and drink than they had been on other days'.[20] The French were close in front of them, blocking their path. Watchmen were posted to keep an eye on things as the armies were 'scarcely 250 paces' away from each other, though many of the French lords were lodged slightly further off at Ruisseauville as well as in the village of Agincourt and others close by.[21] Their men were not so lucky, and would have mainly spent their night camping out in the open, probably in the fields between Agincourt and Tramecourt to the north of the English line.[22]

For those in the French army other than the nobility, it is doubtful that their position was preferable to those of their English opponents. They too were tired and hungry, having been on the move for several weeks. They would find it difficult to get shelter too. Sleep was difficult. There was much to worry them: few of them had the benefits of the heavy armour available to their social superiors and a battle with the English was something of a lottery; even if the battle were won it was probable that a number of lives would be lost and each soldier pondered on whether or not they might be the losers in this game of life and death. They were all too aware of the reputation of the English archers, earned on the bloody fields of Crécy and Poitiers.

The ordinary soldier probably thought more of his own humble life and possible fate than on matters of military strategy. Yet it was with respect to the overall strategy that the French were in a weaker position than might have been thought. The overall commander, the Duke of Orléans, arrived late and consequently he knew little of the ground or his men. He also lacked Henry's experience and was not yet twenty-one years old. Other French forces were still on their way and likely to arrive late in dribs and drabs. This made coordination of the disjointed forces potentially very difficult.

Given the inexperience of the Duke of Orléans it was probable, and certainly advisable, that he would listen to the advice of other, more battle-hardened warriors. All well and good as long as they all offered the same advice. But from what we can ascertain judging from the confused tactics and poor organisation on the following day, this was not the case. The situation, which encouraged management of the battle by committee, did not lend itself to a clear and logical choice of tactics or indeed of battleground.

Contrast the position of the English. They may have been suffering from a number of disadvantages but they had a few good cards in their hands nevertheless. Most of all they had significant advantages in leadership. At their head was an experienced tactician, possessed also of great personal courage and fortitude. In addition, Henry seems to have had a strong belief in the justice of his cause. Whether it was really just mattered not; he believed that it was and this conviction shone through in his leadership: always measured, usually avoiding the impression of panic whatever demons might have been gnawing away inside, always focused on the task ahead and how best to fulfil his ambitions.

He was not alone either; he had capable leaders around him. The performance of the Duke of York, who may have had good reason to be lukewarm given the fact that the king had metaphorically signed his brother's death warrant just a few months back, had in the event been very convincing. In the absence of the Duke of Clarence, a man with widely respected military credentials, he had stepped forward and enjoyed his finest hour. His contribution to the campaign was not yet over.

Then there were his elite fighting troops: Cornwall, Umfraville and Holland for example. York was not in the prime of life and therefore his fighting skills at a personal level may have been limited so he relied on those around him. They had fought valiantly, with superb results. Above all, they knew how to fight and win a battle.

It was on the eve of battle that a knight, Sir Walter Hungerford, spoke some words that would later be given full dramatic impact through the incomparable words of Shakespeare. Seeing that the English were heavily outnumbered he expressed a wish that the ten thousand archers back home in England doing nothing could have been with them now. In response Henry told him that his words were foolish; he asked him, 'Do you not believe that the Almighty, with these His humble few, is able to overcome the opposing arrogance of the French who boast of their great number and their own strength?'[23]

And so were conceived the roots of one of the most moving, eloquent moments in all of English literature, of the idea of 'we few, we happy few, we band of brothers',[24] the inspiration to Churchill and the 'Few' who saved the country during the Battle of Britain in 1940, another perceived triumph against the odds. The 'Band of Brothers' was also the name given by Nelson to his fellow captains before his epic triumph at the Battle of the Nile in 1798. It is significant that the great seaman's favourite Shakespearian work was *Henry V*.[25] This small scene and Hungerford's words, almost an off-stage moment, was to become a seminal part of the legend of Henry V.

Hungerford was a close adviser to the king. He had been a Member of Parliament for Wiltshire, and sheriff at different times of Wiltshire, Dorset and Somerset. He was also an experienced warrior and had famously beaten the King of France during a duel near Calais over a decade before. He had brought twenty men-at-arms and sixty archers with him during the current expedition. He had also been an ambassador to the crucial church Council of Constance which in the same year as Agincourt had decided on the future fate of the papacy with its three competing popes. He would later be an executor of Henry V's will. In short, Hungerford was most definitely in the king's inner circle.

It is maybe tempting to speculate that the exchange never happened as it fits so easily into the legend of the king who was able to lead his men to victory when even they believed it was impossible. The allusion to the power of the Almighty too could be seen as a classic idealised representation of a king who is Holier than Holy, too good to be true, nothing more than a *topos*, a literary device.

There were strong Biblical precedents to follow after all, such as when the Israelite warrior Gideon was instructed by God to send men away from his army because there were too many of them and God would receive little glory from giving him a victory unless it was one gained against overwhelming odds.[26] And another strong precedent, often referred to in medieval times, was the heroic Jewish leader Judas Maccabeus, who in the second century BC achieved a remarkable victory against much larger forces, said to be through the intervention and support of the Almighty.

Yet this may also be too cynical an interpretation. As a member of the king's inner circle it is entirely probable that Hungerford would feel that he was able to speak his mind. He would have been perhaps careful how he did so and would only have spoken in the king's presence when few others were around to hear, which incidentally suggests that the *Gesta* chronicler was a close confidante of the king, perhaps a royal chaplain, if he were within earshot to write such things down. It is quite plausible that the odds did appear to be overwhelming, even to an experienced campaigner like Hungerford.

The king's response is very much in character too. His deep piety has been much remarked on and his knowledge of Biblical precedent had featured in the campaign before, such as when he suggested to the townsfolk of Harfleur that he would use the powers allocated by God to a king chastising his subjects as outlined in the Book of Deuteronomy. The whole expedition had been given the impression of something approaching a Crusade by the king, an act sanctioned and approved by God. Given all this, his response to Hungerford's defeatist – or more likely realistic – comments appears entirely believable.

There was now some jostling for position between the two armies. The region was quite heavily wooded at the time and the movements of the French, when observed by the English, suggested that they were trying to use the cover of the trees to creep up behind them. There was a danger of encirclement to guard against, which would leave the English surrounded and completely at the mercy of their adversary. So Henry redeployed his men to guard against such a threat.

There was to be no battle that day, though few in the vicinity were in any doubt now that one was imminent. To some in the English camp, it appeared that they were trapped. To some of the French perhaps the major challenge was to keep them so. There were even stories that said that the French cast lots for who would have possession of which captive.[27]

Henry spent the night in a house in Maisoncelle. His innermost thoughts were not written up later in any campaign diary but some informed speculation can be made even so. He knew that it was now highly likely that a battle loomed and that it may well define his kingship, not just of France but also of England. Although his claim to the throne of England was now to all practical purposes mostly accepted, a humiliating defeat involving his capture and ransom could change all that. The recent Southampton plot, still fresh in the memory, showed that he could not take his position for granted.

A major battle was a great and rare event in the life of a king. Medieval warfare was epitomised much more by minor skirmishes, raids and sieges. A king could spend a whole reign without being involved in a major confrontation and often great efforts were made to avoid one. There was just too much riding on the result to engage in one, as the French had found out at Poitiers half a century before when King Jean had been captured with disastrous consequences. But it seemed that Henry now had little choice but to fight.

To any man possessed of any degree of self-doubt, the possibility of defeat would have been present, festering away and undermining his confidence. But Henry's actions around this time do not suggest that any such self-doubt existed. Perhaps he was a consummate actor, but more likely based on what we know of him was that he really did believe in the justice of his cause. With his deep piety, it is quite possible that he was sure that God was on his side; it is easy to be cynical of this in our modern, secular society but a vastly different proposition in a world where the presence of God and the existence of Everlasting Life or Eternal Damnation were as much a reality as the existence of the Sun and the Moon.

Henry maintained strict discipline during that night. Orders were given that silence was to be maintained during the hours of darkness. Men-at-arms who made too much noise were to have arms and armour confiscated. Archers who did so were to have an ear sliced off, a powerful reminder that, however much we might think of the yeomen of England as a fledgling middle class, they still came from a different social planet than the nobility.

It was a dark night; the moon was in its dying phase and was anyway concealed by the rainclouds. Bonfires were therefore lit. There was no point in trying to hide where the English camp was; the *Gesta* chronicler says that the English were so close they could even hear the conversation of the French from where they were.[28] The bonfires would help the English see if the French should launch a sortie in the night; the silence in the camp would assist them in guarding against this too as they could hear any imminent assault coming.

It is suggested by some that the field was scouted that night 'by some valiant knights by moonlight'.[29] This seems inherently unlikely. Not only were clouds reducing visibility, the full moon had appeared a week before and was now in its last quarter.[30] While of course the English would have taken great care to scout out the site of battle, this would have been much more easily done in the daylight.

On the French side it was later noted by Monstrelet that, although they were on the surface confident of victory, 'they had but little music to cheer their spirits'. He also suggested that their horses were abnormally quiet during the night; in an age when omens and portents were fastidiously analysed this was of no little significance, suggesting that they were nervous about what lay ahead. In contrast, he says that the English were noisy – there were sounds of the trumpets' blare in the night sky and the English appeared to be putting on an unusually positive show – though deep down, he suggested, many of them expected the following day to be their last. Perhaps we should take this description of the noisy English with a generous pinch of salt. If their king had told them to be quiet, it would have been a brave, or more probably a foolish, man who did the opposite.

Not all accounts say that the French were quiet. The *Gesta* says that they could be heard calling out to each other to establish their relative positions, so spread out were they. Other Burgundian-supporting writers said that the French made so much noise that the English could easily hear it.

So through the long, dark watches of the night the English steeled themselves for the trial by fire that was now inevitable. Around the camp, thousands of men, a number of Hughs, Thomases, Johns, Williams, Nicholases, Geoffreys, Richards, Ralphs and Roberts (all of these first names feature prominently in the Agincourt Muster Roll) prepared for whatever critical events the morrow might bring. Among them perhaps was Thomas Pokkeswell thinking of his humble homestead on the chalky downs overlooking the English Channel in Dorset and wondering if he would ever see it again. The French in the meantime established patrols to keep an eye on the English probably more to try and ensure that they did not try and sneak away in the night rather than to forestall any attacks during the hours of darkness.

Nevertheless it seems that there was a brief clash during the night when the Count of Richemont came close to the English camp and was driven off after what Monstrelet called a 'smart skirmish'. Richemont's presence at Agincourt reveals something of how divided France was; when the English had landed in France he was busy at a siege of the castle of Parthenay – Deux-Sèvres

– in the west of France, trying to capture it from a supporter of the Duke of Burgundy. The veneer of peace in the country was not very deep.

It was unlikely that the French considered a major attack during the night, though some probing raids may well have been planned. Once it was decided that a major battle would be fought, it was perhaps unlikely that anything other than an all-out assault was ever considered by the French command as this would not have given the glorious victory that they craved. Creeping up like a thief in the night was not in the standard French manual of battle tactics.

Nevertheless the French appeared confident, certain of their imminent victory and the prizes that would be theirs, though the relatively small size of the English army and its current demeanour did not suggest that there would be much honour or reward from overcoming them on the morrow. In the words of one chronicler, 'the two armies presented a different appearance and a dissimilar look'.[31]

The French army was still not complete. The Duke of Brittany, that reluctant warrior, was on his way with 6,000 soldiers but most probably would be very happy indeed to arrive too late to fight. Also on his way, probably more enthusiastically, was the marshal of Longny with another 600 men to bring to the battlefield.

But troops under the command of the constable, Charles d'Albret, and the dukes of Bourbon and Bar, were already moving into position from the area of Amiens, Corbie, Péronne and St-Quentin, responding to the instructions of the Duke of Alençon. Several of the men en route were prominent Burgundians, showing that a degree of unity had been achieved among the French if only on a short-term basis, although the Duke of Burgundy himself was not present.

The English remained short of food and even, despite the heavy rain, clean water to drink though quite possibly the French were little better off too. Across this small patch of ground of a few square miles at most, men prepared themselves spiritually for battle. They confessed, or in the language of the time were shriven, easing their passage into the Hereafter should the next day be their last.

However brutal and harsh the medieval world may have been, however full of contradiction and hypocrisy, it would be wrong to think that the majority of men and women did not hold sincere religious feelings. Following the religious rulebook may have been mechanistic – thinking for oneself was not encouraged and was at the heart of Henry and other's resistance to movements such as Lollardy – but it was a reality in the lives of the majority. Dying was a real fear as in all eras, but Death, what came next, was far more terrifying than in a secular world. This life was nothing save a dry run for the one that really mattered: Eternity.

So most of those there, in the words of the *Gesta* chronicler, 'put on the armour of penitence', no doubt an allusion to Holy Scripture and its injunctions for true believers to put on the whole armour of God.[32] There was, according to his description, no shortage of penitential intent, only of priests to hear confessions.[33]

Many a vow was no doubt made that night that, if the horrors of the following day were survived, those who benefited from the grace of God would repay Him with their penitence and homage. This is more than a speculative assumption, as it is known that two of the Welshmen to survive the battle, Thomas Bassegle from Cardiff and John William ap Howell, were later arrested at

Sawston in Cambridgeshire while journeying to Walsingham to fulfil a solemn promise to do so made at Agincourt.[34]

Yet there are some accounts that suggest that that night was almost as much a trial for the French as it was for the English. These note that they did not sleep well and 'they had to bivouac in a terrain of considerable extent, newly worked over, and that torrents of rain had converted into a quagmire'. The mud was so thick that in places they sank down in it up to their knees. They would be fatigued even before they reached the front line in the morning to begin the fight.[35]

The English army realised that tomorrow would see a fight for their lives. There was no real hope of escape should the battle be lost. The rich and the noble might be spared in return for ransom but no such prospect was there to comfort the masses, the humble archers, the Thomas Pokkeswells of this world. In such circumstances, when faced by desperate odds, one of two outcomes was possible; either that men would be inspired to fight tenaciously to live or, devoid of hope, that their morale would evaporate altogether. All too often, the difference is to be found in the quality of the man who leads them.

The words of Thomas of Walsingham stirringly suggest the true standard of leadership to be found in the English army at that precise moment. Henry's soldiers believed that 'the French had boasted of their intention to spare no one except the famous English lords and the king himself and to slay everyone else without pity, or at least mutilate their limbs beyond repair. And so our men were the more keyed up. They worked themselves up to a pitch of anger and comforted one another to face all the chances of war.'[36]

So all men, from kings and great nobles down to the humblest archer and servant, put themselves in the hands of God. Tomorrow there would be a great battle, a massive melee, a scrum of heaving bodies. Or so it would seem from a distance. But it was not so. There would instead be countless individual battles in which the thousands of French and English soldiers involved would fight man to man for their own lives in an area of a few square feet, blind to the fighting and dying that was going on to their left or their right. At the end of it all, the lucky, those who won in this lottery of death, would celebrate their valour in battle, the wealth and honour they would gain through victory but most of all their survival. For the losers a terrifying face-to-face interview with their Lord and Maker loomed.

8

AGINCOURT: THE FALSE START (DAWN TO 10 A.M., 25 OCTOBER 1415)

... when thou goest out to battle against thine enemies, and seest horses, and chariots, and a people more than thou be not afraid of them.

Deuteronomy 20:1

It was Friday 25 October 1415, the feast day of St Crispin, St Crispinian and also of St John of Beverley. At the time, the latter saint meant more to the King of England than the former two. Friday was always a special day in the Christian calendar as it was the day of Christ's death. It was specially venerated because of this by Marshal Boucicaut, a deeply devout man who always ate frugally and dressed in black on Friday in weekly remembrance of the Passion. But today was something different again. The scene was set for one of the most memorable events of medieval English history and an action that would resonate down the ages.

Inspired by the glorious gift of hindsight and his knowledge of how magnificent a victory now loomed, Thomas of Walsingham,

writing of Agincourt some seven years later, was moved to quote
the classics in his description of the opening of that fateful day:
'And so in the king's camp the rising day the mountains scarce
had spread with heaven's light, when sounded from afar the
trumpets brazen blare, and our men hurried from all sides to fall
in before their leader, doubly prepared with bold spirits and pure
consciences to face the challenge of Mars.'[1]

Henry was up before the sun was; sunrise would have been
at around 6.45 a.m. at this time of the year, though on cloudy
mornings such as this daylight might not be obvious until later.
There were religious duties to be attended to first. Before dawn
the king heard Mass, commending himself into God's hands in
the battle that was now only a few hours away. It was the time of
Prime, the first religious service of the day.[2] This was always an
especially sacred moment for religious men, for the terrors of the
darkness of the night had been survived and the light had come,
the mark of goodness and holiness. This particular day must have
assumed a special significance for the king. He was about to face
by far the greatest challenge of his life. It was something of a
role-reversal; today the terrors of the day might well surpass those
of the darkness.

The deeply religious Henry noted the significance of the time
and remarked on it. England would be waking up to the new day
at the same time and religious men and women across the land
would be saying their own prayers. The king commented on it:
'Now is good time for all of England prayeth for us. Therefore be
of good cheer and let us go to our day's work.'[3]

Perhaps Henry referred once more in his devotions to the Book
of Deuteronomy. In it he would find these words: 'When thou
goest out to battle against thine enemies, and seest horses, and

chariots, and a people more than thou be not afraid of them.'4 For if the chroniclers were right, then the English would be hugely outnumbered in the battle that loomed. Henry's trial by combat had at last arrived.

Some miles away, Anthony, Duke of Brabant, was also hearing Mass. At the supreme moment of that sacred ceremony, even as the Host was being elevated by the priest, a messenger by the name of Robin Daule entered. He came with urgent news: a battle would be fought that very day before noon. Time was indeed of the essence; Agincourt was some considerable distance away. Yet important formalities could not be neglected and the duke instructed that he and his company should have crosses attached to their clothing before mounting their horses and galloping frantically westwards.

In the quietness of Henry's billet at the very place where the Duke of Brabant was headed, the king prepared his soul for whatever fate beckoned during the coming hours. This most necessary action over, he changed his mindset to one of action instead of contemplation. He got together a small detachment of men, some thirty strong, and ordered them to keep guard over the baggage which would be left behind in front of Maisoncelle. Thomas Elmham says that he deputed this task to the Duke of York, who resisted it, saying that he would rather be at the front of any fighting rather than the rear.5

There would be only a few men left to guard the baggage, which could have had some unfortunate repercussions, but presumably there were just not enough men to go around. The small rearguard and the lack of any reserve suggests that there was certainly a sizeable numerical disparity between the English and French forces, meaning that there were not enough men spare to deploy.

Military discipline and order would be critical in the battle ahead. Keeping the English army tight and coordinated was key if Henry was to counteract any numerical advantage enjoyed by the French. An insight into the importance of such matters can be found in the works of Christine de Pizan, who wrote that 'two great evils ... can follow from a disordered formation: one is that the enemies can more easily break into it; the other is that the formations may be so compressed that they cannot fight. Thus it is necessary to keep a formation in ranks, and tight and joined together like a wall.'[6]

'Tight and joined together like a wall'; this was the mantra for the English army on the day. With the sun now up, the king sent a few of his senior knights to examine the field of battle, though given his own eye for detail it is not an unreasonable speculation that he would have had a good look himself too. The potential field of battle was roughly in the shape of a triangle with Maisoncelle at its inverted apex (i.e. to the south), the village of Agincourt (now called Azincourt) to the north-west and that of Tramecourt to the north-east. The road to Calais ran northward across this triangle and right at the top of it the French army was blocking any further English progress.

The English army was probably drawn up a few hundred metres in front of Maisoncelle, although we cannot be sure exactly where either army was. It was a good position and although there were a few bumps and depressions in the ground the view over the road that ran across from Tramecourt to Agincourt at the top of the inverted triangle was a good one.

Only on the left of the English line was there a problem. Here there was a marked depression in the ground that partially hid the road from Agincourt down to Maisoncelle from view. This would have unfortunate consequences for the English later in the battle but otherwise this was a decent position for them.

But there is one thing that must be emphasised about the battlefield of Agincourt and that is that remarkably little evidence has survived to tell us exactly where it is. There is very little battlefield archaeology that has been found. The excellent museum that is now placed in the village of Agincourt has very little that has been dug up in the area and the few examples that are there, for example a spur recovered from the area, are not on their own conclusive as they may not even be from the battle at all. Neither have any massed graves been found that would help build confidence in the specific locations of the battle. When we talk of the field of Agincourt, then, we cannot be sure which precise field we are talking about.

But some general comments may be made. If the whole army had been placed in Maisoncelle (in itself not possible as the settlement is hardly more than a hamlet) then it would have hampered the English army's view of their French opponents. Therefore it seems probable that the bulk of the army was a few hundred metres north of the hamlet where they would have had better sight of the enemy.

In the main the battlefield was remarkable for its unremarkableness. An early twentieth-century historian described it well in the following terms: 'The field between the English and French was open, devoid of hedges, thickets, valleys, ravines, or other obstacles, and had been chosen by the French themselves. For our purpose the country was like a table; rarely is a battlefield so simple and easy to describe.'[7] The only caveat to this otherwise laudable description is that the rutted furrows in the newly ploughed field gave it a most unsuitable surface for any tabletop. If anything it was a slightly uneven tabletop that tilted slightly from right to the left as the English looked at it. But this farmer's field was hardly a dramatic setting for the great epic that was about to unfold.

Henry then gave a speech to his men. In fact, even though the numbers of the English were relatively small, he cannot have been heard by them all at once (the line probably stretched for about half a mile) so he must either have delivered a number of orations or only spoken to a select few. It was apparently not with the eloquent oratory scribed by Shakespeare that he spoke but with humbler words which reminded his listeners of the righteousness of their cause and the obstinacy of the French:

My fellow men, prepare arms! English rights are referred to God. Memories noted many battles given for the right of King Edward and Prince Edward [Edward III's son, the Black Prince]. Many a victory occurred with only a few English troops. This could never have been by their strength alone. England must never lament me as a prisoner or as to be ransomed. I am ready to die for my right in the conflict. St George, George, saint and knight be with us! Holy Mary, bestow your favour on the English in their right. At this very hour many righteous English people pray for us with their hearts. France, hasten to give up your fraud![8]

There is a tendency to assume in modern times that all such battlefield speeches are to a significant extent the result of the interventions of monkish chroniclers rather than being based on any words that might have actually been used. In this respect it is interesting that the *Gesta* author, who was present at the battle, does not mention such an oration on the morning of the battle at all. Indeed attributing such speeches to great commanders on the eve of battle was not just a medieval phenomenon. Classical writers of Ancient Greece and Rome repeatedly put highly unlikely words in the mouths of their heroes and the medieval world, often emulating the Classical, may have been inspired to follow suit.

Yet there is much that rings true in this speech with its evocations to the saints and the Virgin as well as St George, very much in keeping with the king's temper and his oft-repeated motivations for the war. There was realism too, in that Henry's words suggested that he knew that there was a very real possibility that the battle might be lost but that he had resolved to die rather than surrender.

If there was any speaking to the troops by the king it was probably done by riding along the line and giving a number of short exhortations to those in earshot. In so doing he would also have been emulating ancient heroes such as Alexander the Great, who rode up and down the line before his decisive battle against the Persians at Issus encouraging individuals and specific units to fight bravely in the fight that was imminent.[9]

Having done what he could to exhort his troops to superhuman efforts, Henry put on his crown so that he might be recognised. This was a contrast to some contemporary monarchs who would send in lookalikes to the battle to confuse the enemy. He wore a surcoat emblazoned with the arms of England and France 'from which a celestial splendour gleamed on the one side with three golden flowers, planted on an azure field; on the other, from three golden leopards, sporting in a ruby field'.[10] Then, seated on a small grey horse, he crossed himself and prepared for battle.[11]

The use of such surcoats with coats of arms displayed on them was crucially important and in some cases literally a matter of life and death. They showed an enemy that the wearer was worth something. They demonstrated that a sizeable ransom could be expected if the captive owner of such an important heraldic device was traded in. This increased a man's chances of living considerably. At least one man at Agincourt would have cause to regret arriving too late to put his coat of arms on in time for the battle.

Sometime during the morning, three French heralds were sent to speak with Henry by the dukes of Orléans and Bourbon to ask the king what his plans were. The fact that the message emanated from these two men rather than the constable or Marshal of France was significant and for the French potentially serious. It shows that command had switched and, instead of being led by two experienced and cautious campaigners, younger, more hot-headed voices had emerged. The equilibrium of command had been disturbed and for the French it could not have happened at a worse time – at the last minute.

The king responded that he intended to march on to Calais and he hoped that no one would seek to impede him. It was a bold statement but one which he must have had some inner reservations about given the disparity in numbers and the condition of his army. Several French accounts mention that Jacques de Heilly also came across to Henry to ask him to concede that the imminent fight would be a hopeless one and that he would be best served by surrendering.[12] De Heilly was well known to the English, and for some recollections of him were no doubt far from positive; for example, he had led a French expedition that was sent to support the Scots against the English in 1402.

Others perhaps had more positive and recent memories of him. At the confrontation at St Cloud in October 1411 the Burgundians, supported by over 2,000 English archers led by the recently deceased Earl of Arundel, had managed to drive off an Armagnac force that was besieging Paris. Among those in the Burgundian force fighting alongside the English that day was Jacques de Heilly.

After St Cloud the wheel had turned again and when there had been a brief flare-up of trouble in Guienne in 1413 between the English and their French neighbours, Jacques de Heilly was prominent among those fighting off the former. In the course of this confrontation, he had been captured and imprisoned but had subsequently escaped and so was still, in chivalric terms, un-ransomed. He therefore had no right to be on a battlefield about to fight those from whom he had escaped. De Heilly's relationship with the English was complicated to say the least.

Boucicaut, the Marshal of France and the man who had recently advised without success that the French should let the English travel to Calais untroubled, had also fought alongside the English at St Cloud. With him had been the Count of Nevers. Now men such as these three prominent French lords, and no doubt many humbler soldiers who were in the ranks at Agincourt, were facing up to an English army that included men like Gilbert Umfraville, who had also been at St Cloud.

It is not clear when exactly the Duke of Orléans arrived, with some chroniclers suggesting that he did not reach the French army until the morning of the day of battle, though apparently he brought few men with him.[13] Reinforcements for the French were still arriving piecemeal even now but were nevertheless having a positive effect on morale. Some French accounts state that Henry tried to bargain with the French and offered to surrender Harfleur and pay 100,000 crowns if they were allowed to march freely on to Calais but that the marshal was not prepared to agree.[14] Interpreting such differences between English and French chronicles almost becomes a matter of faith (or national pride) rather than history.

It was now clear that neither side would come to terms without a fight, so Henry led the bulk of his army towards a recently ploughed field that had been sown with wheat where the ground was as a result uneven and soft. The condition of the ground made it extremely heavy going. The mud sucked at the feet of the soldiers as they trudged forward, clinging with tentacle-like tenacity to them as they moved cumbrously across the ground. For any mounted men it was just as bad, as the ground was 'so soft that the horses could scarcely lift their hooves out of it'.[15]

Given the fact that he was outnumbered, it was especially critical that the English king chose the most advantageous position he could. In this respect Henry's dispositions were masterful. His army was positioned between the villages of Agincourt and Tramecourt with the baggage close behind him at Maisoncelle. On either side of the English position were woods, difficult for the French forces to pass through.

The trees on either side of the battlefield would have the effect of funnelling the French forces with their large numbers into an enclosed position between them. This space, demarcated on either side by the woods, would effectively become a killing zone for the English archers to take advantage of. One of the most striking features that can still be generally perceived even in modern times is how small an area is covered by the main battlefield, though due to our lack of precise knowledge we cannot know exactly how small. But the compact area covered by the battle meant that the concentration of English arrow-fire would have a particularly devastating effect.

How many men were actually in the English army by now remains a matter of much uncertainty. The muster rolls that have survived and may now be examined in the English National Archives are a very good guide to how many went to France but that force had now been denuded by disease, by the retention of a garrison at Harfleur and by further losses in the campaign since. Few men might have been lost in battle since Harfleur but it is very probable that more had dropped out due to illness or exhaustion, and desertion even in France would always be a danger.

English accounts vary, suggesting that there were about 1,000 men-at-arms and 3,000–5,000 archers in Henry's army.[16] French accounts go higher; Le Fèvre notes 10,000, Monstrelet 13,000.[17] The large majority of the English army, some 75 per cent and probably more, were made up of the archers though the partial records that were to find their way into what became known as 'the Agincourt Roll' show a heavy diminution of the numbers that had set out, with 209 Lancashire and 180 Cheshire archers left out of the possible 500 and 650 that had originally set out, though as noted earlier there are signs that a number of the latter never arrived at the muster in the first place.[18]

The archers had with them their stakes of wood some six feet long with which they could quickly put up a palisade. These would be slanted forwards at an angle of forty-five degrees, straight at the chest of an approaching horse or a dismounted man-at-arms. Many of the archers' carried a mallet, often tipped with lead, with which to hammer the stake into the ground, which would not have been too difficult a task on this day given the sodden state of it. These mallets would also be useful auxiliary weapons for the archers later on in the battle.

Just who were these archers such as Thomas of Pokkeswell or

the men from Kendal? There is a good deal of uncertainty as to who exactly was present at Agincourt. The Muster Rolls give us information about who set out on the mission from Southampton but it is not easy to work out who remained by the time that Agincourt was fought. Some general inferences may be made, though.

The stock of the archers had risen during the course of the Hundred Years War on the back of their performances during it. They were not seen as the lowest level of society but were regarded as 'yeoman'. A yeoman was normally a reasonably well-off freeholder or tenant, though he might still have an area of land that he worked. To give this some context, a writ of arms issued in 1342 stated that a £2 tenant was deemed to be a foot-archer, a man with holdings worth £5 a mounted archer and one with land worth £25 as a man-at-arms.[19]

Archers were well paid when on campaign. Their daily rate of sixpence contrasted rather well with that paid to a skilled artisan back home in England who could hope to earn ten to fifteen shillings a year.[20] That theoretically meant that they could earn in a month what an artisan could earn annually. Their relatively comfortable economic status is borne out by the large number who were by now mounted; a horse was an expensive acquisition. However, that was not quite the whole story. For one thing wars did not provide full-time employment, though subsequent campaigning in France in the years following Agincourt did allow something close to that to happen. And then there was also the knotty issue of just when a man might actually get paid for his service.

Their weapon, the bow (it was not called the longbow until the sixteenth century), was simple in concept but deadly in the hands of a well-trained man as most of the English archers were. There is a perception that the bows would be made of yew but this was not true of all of them; ash and elm were also used and a law of 1416 forbade the use of ash for the making of clogs and shoes so that the wood could be used for military purposes. Ash was also used for making arrows along with other types of wood including oak, birch, elder and beech.[21]

English yew was not the best from which to make the bows, for the wet climate weakened the wood and Continental yew was much sought after instead. There are records of Spanish merchants being required to pay import taxes in the form of yew wood when they brought goods into England.[22] An act of 1566 allowed bowyers to charge 6s 8d for a bow made of foreign yew but only 2s for one of English yew, which gives a strong suggestion of the difference in quality.[23]

The inner side of the bow, the 'belly', was made of strong older hardwood from which it derived its strength. The outer side, the 'back', was made of younger softwood from which came the bow's flexibility. An archer would be compelled to start training with the weapon when he was just a boy, moving up to bigger bows as his strength developed as he grew. By the time he reached manhood, he would be capable of exerting extraordinary strength when he pulled back the bowstring of his weapon.

The bow, which could have been six feet or more in length – longer, in other words, than the man firing it – was of course of little use without arrows. Many archers of the time may have carried their missiles in an arrow bag which perhaps carried two sheaves of them (a sheaf being twenty-four arrows). An archer might have another sheaf hung in his belt that he could quickly access if he needed to. Given the fact that an archer was expected to be able to shoot ten arrows a minute as a minimum standard of efficiency, then he could theoretically run out of ammunition in about seven minutes. It follows then that there must have been provision of large reserve stocks just behind the lines with runners, probably little more than boys, to bring fresh provisions up when needed.

The English and the Welsh had become experts in the use of the bow but such a weapon was far from a new one. After all, although it was a skill to make one well, the design concept itself was a simple enough one. Bows have been found in Scandinavia and Ireland that attest to the use of the weapon in Roman and Viking times. The Normans too used the bow effectively, though it was shorter than those used by archers later in the Middle Ages.[24] But it was the English armies of the fourteenth and fifteenth century who managed to marry the weapon to tactics that maximised its benefits.

There were large supplies of arrows available at the start of Henry's 1415 expedition, vital given the fact that the archers would be the English army's main weapon. Before Henry left England, orders had been sent around the counties ordering sheriffs to ensure that six tail feathers were to be plucked from each goose (any birds who were breeding were exempted) though it was said that those that dropped from the bird naturally worked better in flight. Geese were not good enough for some; there were even records of peacock feathers being used for arrows for a few select archers and other medieval records suggested that those of swans were also used on occasion.[25] Stocks of arrows taken with the expedition were numbered in the millions.

But the archers were not just bowmen when they fought. They also played an important and, in the coming battle, crucial role as auxiliary light infantry. Most of them carried swords, the most popular type being a falchion, which was something like a cleaver. It was ideal for butchering an enemy in close-quarter combat when the man wielding it was not an especially skilled swordsman.

Most would have carried knives, too, such as the so-called 'bollock knife' (named because of the two small roundels that were positioned at the foot of the hilt; sometimes described as a 'ballock knife' in a doffing of the cap to political correctness) or the 'misericordia', sharp, pointed knives whose name ('mercy') came from the fact that they were ideally designed to finish off a prone enemy by sliding it through his visor into his face.[26]

The archers also had some form of body-protecting clothing. Many wore padded jackets, 'jacks', which would have been of some use in protecting them against the thrust of an enemy sword. A number also carried a small shield, a 'buckler', about a foot across, which offered some protection and could also be used as an additional weapon to smash into an enemy's face. Judging from evidence from the wreck of the *Mary Rose* and contemporary illustrations as well as plain commonsense, the archers would also have worn wrist guards (bracers) to protect them from the whiplash of the bowstring.

There was no standard uniform for the archers, though some may have worn surcoats to distinguish connected bodies of men and many would have worn some form of head protection. There was also of course the distinguishing sign of the red St George's Cross to mark them out as English. In terms of helmets there was again no uniformity and every man did the best that he could from his own resources. There were two popular types. The more old-fashioned of these was called a 'kettle hat' (in French called a *chapel de fer*); it had a round skull and a rim around it, something like a standard-issue First World War British army helmet. It could be turned upside down when not being worn and used as a cooking pot, hence its name.

The second type, more recently developed, was a bascinet. This had no rim and broadly followed the contour of the head. It was sometimes attached to a mail coif that also covered the neck and shoulders, thereby widening the area protected. The absence of a rim would also make it slightly easier for an archer – who pulled the bowstring back as far as his ear – to loose his arrow without any interference. For these reasons the bascinet may have been more popular but not all archers would be able to afford one and would have to make do with whatever they could get; indeed, according to the chronicler Monstrelet it would appear that a number had none at all.[27] They would, however, have a wide choice of replacements by the time the day was out.

Although the archers did not form part of a standing army, they were in their own way professional in their approach. The law of the land required all men between sixteen and sixty to practice archery on Sundays and Holy Days after Mass (and incidentally prohibited men from engaging in sports of 'null value' such as football). The requirement to practice archery and for all men to own certain weapons in accordance with their wealth was codified in the Statute of Westminster of 1285. It is interesting to note that one related command, issued by Edward III in 1363, also encouraged as an alternative to archery practice with pellets or bolts, suggesting that slingshot and crossbows still played a part in thinking even after Crécy and Poitiers.[28] But this practice did not conform to any quaint general picture of archers shooting at a painted target with a bull's-eye in the middle.

Instead a range of training was used. There was shooting at the 'poppingjay', the medieval name for a parrot, a target positioned in a tree or something similar, or at a mark placed in the ground. Then there was 'clout shooting', when an arrow was fired high in the air and at a great distance to drop on to a target. Although its primary purpose was to train the archer for siege warfare, this kind of practice was to become extremely useful in the battle today.[29]

This undoubtedly made many of the archers good shots, though perhaps it was not quite as a historian once said in the splendidly quaint language of the early twentieth century that they could hit the bull's-eye 'with the nicety of a Thames fisherman garfangling an eel'.[30] But the reality was that in the battle which was now not far off accuracy other than in a general sense would not be much called for. All that was needed was to aim the arrow in the general area of the mass that would be before them and that alone was almost enough to guarantee a hit of some sort.

Physically the archer put his body under enormous strain with his repetitive practice week after week and year after year. Evidence from the skeletons of archers recovered from the wreck of the sixteenth-century English warship Mary Rose shows that many of them had curvature of the spine. This suggests that the back action of the archer was as important as the musculature of the arms, and the use of these special techniques, while being wearing on the body, might also help to explain the effectiveness of English archers. There was also significant strain apparent on the shoulder bones of skeletons recovered from the Mary Rose in the form of a condition called os acromiale, which is effectively a form of repetitive strain injury.[31]

Skeletal evidence from the ship even shows that some known archers had grooves etched in their finger bones, due again to the repetitive action of shooting a bow. In the longer term it was always probable that the physical demands on archers, as well as the years of training required, would lead to the disappearance as the bow as a weapon of war as it was replaced by new, more technically advanced arms which were also easier to use. Certainly it is a much-discussed fact among recent historians that medieval bows required huge drawing power, about twice as much as their modern equivalents, and this would have required great strength on the part of the archers.[32]

According to some chroniclers the English archers were an unkempt bunch by this stage of the expedition. A number of them had rolled their hose (single-legged without a crotch to join them together) down to their knees for the very practical reason that this would allow them to defecate more easily if they were suffering from dysentery. It has also been suggested more prosaically that wearing their hose in this way was simply because it allowed the archer to move around more freely. A number of them may by this stage also have been barefoot.

Many archers would have been mounted by this time in history and indeed some of the indentures issued prescribed the assembly of mounted archers specifically.[33] This reflected developments in the fourteenth century particularly when the widespread use of mounted bowmen was a core element in allowing the English to launch their devastating *chevauchées* in France. But there is also compelling evidence of the widespread use of them several centuries earlier in the invasion of Ireland when a large contingent of them was present.

However a number of horses would have been lost during the current campaign – there are references to some of the men eating horseflesh. Today their mounts were anyway left behind the lines. The battle ahead was to be almost exclusively fought between foot soldiers with the exception of an initial French flank attack by cavalry.

One writer, Jean Le Fèvre, was a close-up observer to events at Agincourt. Despite his French surname (which means 'smith') he was in the English lines. His Burgundian sympathies made him no friend of the Armagnacs. He presumably had no reason to make it up when he said that many archers were 'without armour in their doublets, their hosen loosened, having hatchets and axes or long swords hanging from their girdles, and some with their feet naked',[34] painting a picture of an unkempt and squalid English army.

The French army continued to block the road to Calais, a seemingly impenetrable barrier to Henry's progress, perhaps some three bow-shots (about 600–750 feet) away.[35] They were eager for the fight, the vanguard 'full of brave men and bright with gleaming armour, while on the flanks of both armies the cavalry rode in front on noble horses of good stock',[36] though the reference to cavalry, particularly on the English side, contradicts other accounts.

The discovery just a few decades ago of the French battle plan gives an amazing insight into what their tactics were supposed to be on the day.[37] From this we learn that there was planned to be a large vanguard, in which would be Constable d'Albret and Marshal Boucicaut and their troops. Next to them would be the Duke of Alençon and the Count of Eu with their men. There were also to be two large wings of infantry, one led by the Lord of Richemont and the other on the left commanded by the Count of Vêndome. In front of them were to be deployed the French archers.

Behind was to be a cavalry force led by the Master of the Crossbowmen, David of Rambures, with the specific task of moving in on the English archers and dispersing them. This was a tactic that had been used before against English bowmen; Robert the Bruce had adopted similar measures against them at Bannockburn in 1314. One thousand mounted men-at-arms were to be allocated to Rambures to deliver this plan. As they launched their charge the main French force was also to step out towards the foe. Another smaller group of mounted men under Lord Bosredon was to sweep around the English lines and attack them from the rear.

The French chroniclers Waurin and Le Fèvre said that at some stage negotiations were entered into (both men were present at the battle, though on opposing sides; the fifteen-year-old Waurin with the French and the nineteen-year-old Le Fèvre with the English). Representatives from both sides rode out into no man's land though Henry did not take part directly in the discussions. These chroniclers state that they had been told that the French offered to let Henry keep his lands in Guienne and around Calais if he would renounce his claims to the throne of France and give up Harfleur.[38] It was, not to be frank, much of an offer as it was only allowing Henry to keep what he had started off with; this was not much of a return considering what he and his country had invested in the expedition.

The English envoys responded that they should be allowed to keep certain named cities as well as Guienne. They should also be given Ponthieu and Henry should be married to Catherine of Valois, who was to be accompanied by a sizeable dowry. In return they would give up Harfleur. The negotiations started such a long time before, when delegations had made their way to and fro between England and France without success, still continued right up until the very last moment. By now they were less likely to achieve a result than ever. The French believed they had the upper hand and the English could not possibly leave with nothing unless King Henry was to suffer a huge loss of face. The required formalities to try and avoid a fight had been duly observed and came to nothing. Both sides withdrew to prepare for the battle. Many a Christian life was about to be ended.

Some chroniclers suggest that all was not well with the French army as the time for battle approached. The writer known as the Religieux noted that the French argued among themselves about who was to have the honour of leading the vanguard. They were unable to arrive at a solution so a number of the more prominent French lords decided to position themselves in the front line, which did nothing for the tactical cohesion of the French forces. This did not bode well for the fight that was to come.[39]

This version of events is echoed in another French account, the *Geste des nobles François*, written probably in the late 1420s, which stated unequivocally that 'all the lords wanted to be in the vanguard, against the opinion of the constable and the experienced knights'.[40] This suggests that what could almost be termed youthful enthusiasm was present among many of the knights who were on the verge of battle, some for the first time, and was clouding their judgement. More sagacious, wiser voices were being drowned out.

There was no other way now for the English but to fight their way through and beyond the massed French forces. The *Gesta* chronicler looked out at numbers which to him seemed 'really terrifying'. He could see squadrons of cavalry on either side of the French vanguard, presumably tasked with the job of breaking up the English archers. The vanguard included large numbers of foot soldiers, with 'forests of spears'. Many of the other French soldiers were still mounted at this stage, though by the time that they actually fought they would be on foot.[41]

Henry took up position in command of the centre of the English line, which according to a number of chroniclers was four ranks deep.[42] His vanguard, under the Duke of York, was placed on the right and Thomas, Lord Camoys, led the 'battle' on the left with the king in the centre. It is unfortunate that more is not known of Camoys, who died in 1421; his splendid memorial brass can still be seen at Trotton near Chichester. But he was certainly an experienced warrior who had seen battle in Wales and France and against the Scots.[43]

There is no conclusive evidence that he had fought for several decades but his advanced age – he was about sixty-five years old – and his peerage perhaps gave him a perceived natural leadership quality. The army was closely deployed with few spaces between the four ranks. That said, only the *Gesta* chronicler names Camoys as the commander of the rearguard, while others give a range of candidates for the role.[44]

In fact, the disposition of the troops at Agincourt makes the terms 'rearguard' and 'vanguard' actively misleading. The names imply that the English ranks were drawn up behind each other whereas the *Gesta* chronicler suggests that they were drawn up in something approximating to a straight line across the field. This made sense given the relatively limited number of men at-arms that Henry had available to deploy. It was logical to stretch them out along the line between the two woods that protected either flank.

Just where the archers were positioned in these lines vis-à-vis the men-at-arms is much more debatable. Some chroniclers put them on the flanks. This accorded with the disposition of archers during previous campaigns fought by the English in France; it also matched the tactics used by the English in previous battles.[45] But other accounts suggested that the archers were placed in chevron-shaped formations interspersed right along the line as well as on the flanks.[46]

Understanding the deployment of the archers is of course fundamental to understanding the wider battle. Opinions are divided as far as historians are concerned. However, reference has been made to the writings of chroniclers such as the Religieux, who notes that there were archers in between each 'battle' as well as on the flanks. So too did the *Gesta* chronicler, who was of course there.

These arguments are made the more convincing by practicalities. Is it really plausible to believe that 1,000 men-at-arms were spread out in a thin line in the centre with about 3,500 archers on either flank in what would have been large masses? It seems unlikely, though this does not mean that there was not a greater proportion on the wings than in the centre. A greater concentration of arrows shot from either side would have had the effect of funnelling the French army even more into the centre.[47] The interspersing of groups of archers along the line seems to be the most likely deployment of the English archers at the battle, though it is not possible to prove this one way or the other. But even in this formation it would still make sense to have a stronger concentration of archers on each flank.

The men-at-arms would be fighting on foot. This was a tactic that had been developed, or more accurately re-developed, in the fourteenth century. It was used by Henry I of England at the Battle of Tinchebrai as far back as 1106 but had subsequently fallen out of favour with the evolution of tactics that revolved around heavy cavalry.

However, the use of dismounted men-at-arms had been employed anew in the time of Edward III, not just in the Hundred Years War but even before that in Scotland at the Battle of Dupplin Moor (9

August 1332, though the king was not personally present there). Here, in a pre-echo of Agincourt, many of the attacking Scots were massed so closely together that the bodies of the fallen piled up and many men suffocated. Soon after at Halidon Hill, fought on 19 July 1333, where King Edward was very much in command, a similar use of English foot soldiers led to a rather similar outcome. It is also worthy of note that the Battle of Boroughbridge, fought between supporters of Edward II and rebels under Thomas, Duke of Lancaster, in March 1322 saw tactics that involved the alliance of archers with men-at-arms, so even the great Edward III was not completely innovative.

Fighting dismounted would be very much the norm from the mid-thirteenth century on, though there were occasions, such as at Poitiers, where mounted warriors would charge an enemy before dismounting and it was still important that horses were close at hand to help pursue a defeated enemy or, alternatively, to flee from the scene of a defeat. Horses were still crucial for other reasons; they gave an army mobility, helped it to move more quickly and allowed men to potentially arrive fresher than if they had been marching.

There are more examples of mixing dismounted men-at-arms with archers such as at the small-scale confrontation at Bourgthéroulde involving English troops in Normandy in 1124 and then more emphatically at the decisive English victory at the so-called Battle of the Standard in 1138. At the latter the English archers caused huge casualties among many of their unarmoured enemy while the dismounted men-at-arms had robustly resisted the attacks of Scottish cavalry.

Edward III had typically deployed archers on the flank, a tactic first seemingly deployed at Dupplin Moor. But there are suggestions that in a number of other battles the archers were interspersed with the men-at-arms as well as being on their flanks, a tactical set-up that closely mirrored that which some of the chroniclers said was in use at Agincourt. Whatever the precise formations used in these earlier battles, the tactic of enfilade fire from the archers had proved itself stunningly effective.[48]

More recent battles elsewhere in Europe had proved that well-armed infantry were more than a match for cavalry. In Britain Bannockburn had helped to demonstrate this and more recently both Flemish and Swiss troops had fought successfully as infantry. In response even in chivalric circles in France it was now the custom for most knights to fight dismounted and this was the preferred tactic as discussed by contemporary military writers such as Christine de Pizan.[49]

The legend of the battle of Agincourt extols the virtues of the archers and in many ways rightly so. Yet this perception oversimplifies matters, as if the other fighting arms of the English army played no part at all. This was not so, for the archers did not completely stop the French attacks and some would get through to the English lines, as had been the case in other great battles of the Hundred Years War such as Crécy, Poitiers and Nájera. Here too, at Agincourt, the 'man-at-arms' would play his part.

Men-at-arms, or 'homines ad arma' as they were more eloquently called in Latin, was the collective name given to those present in full armour, by that time increasingly plate armour, who could range from a duke down to a humble member of the gentry. In other words it was not so much a social distinction as a military one, though there were some social overtones too.

Their armour had developed significantly in recent times. The best-armed (that is generally the wealthiest) of them were protected almost completely from head to foot. Underneath the armour they wore a padded jerkin to help absorb the shock of arrows. A man-at-arms would need an assistant to arm him. His armour was heavy, weighing in at about 50 lbs. It has been pointed out that this is close to the equipment weight of a modern infantryman but this takes no account of the extensive physical training regime that the latter are expected to endure which would not have been undertaken by medieval warriors in the main. However, pictures of a knight being raised via a hoist onto his horse (which have become to an extent a stereotypical image of knights at this time) seem well wide of the mark.[50]

Armour had changed dramatically in the past half-century in particular. There would have been a large range on display at Agincourt, with the rich nobles typically wearing the latest armorial fashions while the humbler men-at-arms would have made do with older armour. But a complete suit of 'white armour', that is undecorated with any textile covering, was now the norm for the best-equipped warrior. Beneath the man-at-arms' helmet, the former mail neck covering had often been replaced by a gorget, a steel-plate neck protector which provided much better cover.

Complete breast and back plates with a skirt of five or six overlapping plates reaching down below the thighs had also developed. Gauntlets (from the French *gant*, glove) had also become deeper, protecting the hands more effectively. Because of the improved armour, shields were getting smaller and indeed by the end of the fifteenth century would to all intents and purposes have disappeared altogether, partly because the wielding of large, cumbersome weapons like poleaxes required the use of two hands.[51] This all suggested an increasing invincibility for the man-at-arms. The next few hours were to prove that this was far from the reality in practice.

Weak points in his armour had gradually been allowed for in improved design features. For example, there had been plating added to protect a man-at-arms' armpits, which were vulnerable when he raised his arm to strike as clearly there needed to be manoeuvrability in his armour to enable him to do this. In addition, mail skirts had also been added to protect the upper legs and thighs; these were known as *taces*.

Helmets, though, were a problem. Two alternatives had evolved by this time. One was the bascinet, covering the face with only a visor for visibility. Those with a pointed snout were known as a 'dog-faced bascinet'. The drawback of this type of helmet was obvious. The narrow visor so limited visibility that often it was pulled up during battle, exposing the face to an arrow strike or other blow (much as 'Hotspur' had died at Shrewsbury). In fact, when trying on a medieval helmet of this type it is alarming how little one can see, with an extremely narrow field of sight and almost no peripheral vision at all. It would have been difficult to breathe inside one too, especially as exhaustion started to take its toll on a man who had been striking out with his sword or axe for a while. It has been noted that 'chronicle sources furnish a remarkable number of instances where nobles and knights were killed or injured by arrow wounds to the face'[52] and it does not take much imagination to see why when trying one of these helmets on.

The alternative type of helmet was the great helm, somewhat old-fashioned and cumbersome. On the other hand, it was a very solid form of protection and some suggestions have been made that Henry V was supposedly wearing one in the battle that was imminent.⁵³ However, this kind of helmet was by now mainly confined to the tournament field.⁵⁴ If Henry was indeed wearing such a helmet, it was another sign of his innate conservatism but it seems extremely unlikely.

In terms of weaponry, a man-at-arms would often carry a lance which, at approximately six feet long for a man fighting on foot, would be about half the length of that carried by mounted warriors. The poleaxe was a popular weapon too, a shaft four to six feet long with an axe head, ideal for smashing into an opponent's head or body at close quarters. At its tip was an axe blade with a spear point and a hammer at the rear. It was often used by men-at-arms when fighting on foot.⁵⁵ The sword was the ultimate symbol of chivalry and most men-at-arms would have one, most of these weapons being about three feet long. There were also some warriors who chose to carry longer swords than this, though there were repercussions for mobility.

There were several social sub-divisions to be noted under the generic heading of a 'man-at-arms'. For example, a knight would invariably be a man-at-arms but many men-at-arms would not be knights. A knight had been dubbed so and had gone through the ceremony of knighthood. Many others, the majority, would not be knights but esquires, which meant that they might hope for knighthood in the future but had not yet qualified for the privilege. Men-at-arms would own horses and be trained in their use in battle and the tournament, though these were often reserved for men with the right pedigree from the higher knightly echelons. But the majority of them would fight on foot during wartime.

The Duke of York was one prominent man-at-arms who had much to prove in the hours ahead. He was not alone. Another man in a very similar position was John Holland. Holland had been born in 1395 and was a cousin of the king. His father, the one-time Duke of Exeter, had been among the highest-ranking men in the land. That had changed due to the complicated power politics that followed the removal of Richard II. His father had plotted against Henry IV, had been discovered and subsequently executed. This left Holland without a title and with his future prospects much diminished. He had done much to prove himself to Henry V during the campaign so far; now here was a chance to seal his place in his good graces.

There were many other less socially significant men-at-arms present. One of them was Thomas Hostell, who was in the company of John Lumley, who had mustered with the Duke of Clarence at 'St Catherine's Hill, near the New Forest' (which could be the hill of that name near Winchester but is more probably another similarly named near Christchurch). Hostell was the man who had lost an eye to a crossbow bolt at Harfleur as well as having his cheekbone shattered. An experienced campaigner who had also fought for Henry IV, here he was just six weeks later waiting to fight the enemy. Fortunately he would survive the ordeal ahead, but fate had not quite finished with him even then.

The cream of French chivalry stared hard at their outnumbered opponents. Among them was one of the finest knights of his age, John le Meingre II de Boucicaut, the Marshal of France. Now about fifty years old and therefore in the twilight of his active career as a knight, he had immense experience around Europe and the Near East. He had been appointed by Charles VI as his lieutenant-general at the end of July 1415. He had been behind the strategy to stop the English from crossing the Somme but when that failed he argued that the best policy was to let the English army go. He was overruled.

Men such as Boucicaut and d'Albret, who fitted well into the category described by the Religieux as being 'knights who were worth listening to because of their age and experience',[56] found their advice did not count for very much now. Perhaps with his wise eye Boucicaut looked on the English in a different light than some of the hot-bloods around him and saw all too clearly what lay ahead.

What was about to happen contrasted rather starkly with the world of chivalry in which Boucicaut was one of the leading contemporary figures. He had played a part in the famous jousts of St Inglevert in 1390 and had formed his own chivalric order, 'The White Lady with the Green Shield', in 1399 with the aim, both noble and romantic, of defending defenceless, disinherited ladies against opportunistic lords who sought to take advantage of them.

His attitude to chivalry can be summed up by an incident when he was in Genoa, when he bade good morning to two prostitutes. His companions, knowing the nature of the ladies that he had addressed so politely, pointed out to him his error. Boucicaut replied that he would rather greet two prostitutes by mistake than omit to be courteous to one lady because he had misjudged her. These were noble and honourable sentiments but they did not fit well with a battle, as the marshal was about to discover.[57]

There was another issue that Boucicaut could never quite escape from. Despite his honours, he did not come from the highest ranks of French society and his father-in-law had noted of him disparagingly that he did not come from 'great lineage' and did not bring much money to his marriage.[58] Now he was to find himself overruled by socially superior but militarily inferior men like the dukes of Orléans and Bourbon.

Most of the chroniclers give the French an air of optimism in their demeanour, as if the battle would be a formality. There is one particular account that has the Constable d'Albret giving a long speech in which find him allegedly saying that 'you must understand, ere keep an Englishman one month from his warm bed, fat beef and stale ale, and let him taste that season cold and hunger, you then shall see his courage abated, his body wax lean and bare, and ever desirous to return into his own country'.[59] Rather disappointingly, this example of racial stereotyping concerning *les rosbifs* is not contemporary with Agincourt but came from the work of Edward Hall, written in 1542.

Le Fèvre and Waurin tell more about the French dispositions. The vanguard, they say, included 8,000 men-at-arms and an uncertain number of archers (Waurin gives numbers of 5,500 for the latter, but Le Fèvre just says 'few archers', which is a rather different picture). In the vanguard, led by d'Albret the Constable, were many of the great men of France including Orléans, Bourbon, Boucicaut, Lord Dampierre, Admiral of France, Guichard Dauphin and the counts of Eu and Richemont. The original plan had seemingly been to put the French archers on the flanks to engage their English counterparts but this was not put into practice.[60]

Cavalry forces were also in place on the flanks. One, led by the Count of Vêndome, was composed of 600–1,600 men (depending on whose account is believed) and the other, led by Clignet de Brabant and Sir Louis de Bourdon, had 800 men. Their collective task was to help break up the archers. If they were positioned on the flanks, it follows that here too they assumed the majority of the English archers would be, as their job was specifically to break them up. The chroniclers' accounts do not mention that Robert de Rambures was in command of the flanking cavalry, as was the original intention, so either they are mistaken or there had been a change of the original plan.

There are even suggestions that the French had some small field guns with them, as an Exchequer account notes the fact that one of the English archers was later killed by a 'gune'.[61] The use of handguns had become well-established practice during the fourteenth century. They required relatively little training to use. First appearing in Italy in large numbers, they had subsequently spread across Europe. They were even available to, and used by, rioters in England in 1375, suggesting that by this stage they were not even considered to be exotic anymore.[62] Given this, it is not surprising to see some references to their use by the French at least at Agincourt.

One man in particular was conspicuous by his absence from the French side. The Duke of Burgundy could have brought a large force with him but was nowhere in sight, being *persona non grata*. On the surface France may have appeared more united than she had for a while and certainly there were some prominent Burgundians present on the field of battle, but the duke himself was not one of them. Neither was his son, Philip, Count of Charolais. The count would later claim that he had been deliberately locked in his room in the castle at Aire so that he could not take part in the battle, as a result of which he would weep tears of frustration – or so he would say half a century later, at any rate.[63]

Time was moving on now. The sun was timidly rising higher in the grey autumn sky and still there was no sign of a start to the fighting. Le Fèvre and Waurin estimate that the time moved on to between nine and ten in the morning and still the battle had not commenced. Individual battle plans continued to develop, though. A group of eighteen French knights got together and resolved that their job in the looming battle was to challenge the English king directly and knock his crown off his head or die in the attempt. The English, on the other hand, seeing that there was no sign of action imminent, pragmatically took a bite of breakfast where they could find one. Some of them moved out to make their way towards the rear of the village of Agincourt, hoping to remain unseen in the attempt so that they could take the French by surprise.

Despite their numerical advantage, the French army still did not move. They realised that they held the upper hand and were in no rush to hand over the strong advantages that they had. If the English wished to fight, let them come across the boggy field, weighed down with their weapons. After all, it was they who needed to force their way through so that they could travel on to Calais and safety. The English were hungry, tired and probably scared; as the day drew on their position was hardly likely to improve.

As the day advanced, Henry realised that the French were not going to attack. It was perhaps not clear to him why the French were prevaricating. Possibly they were waiting for reinforcements or even trying to starve the English into submission; at any rate the delay was doing his cause no good.

So Henry resolved to seize the initiative and took yet another massive gamble. He had already ordered the baggage to be placed in the rear in front of Maisoncelle along with the priests with the army. Among these was the *Gesta* chronicler, who watched on from horseback from the back of the English line, though this would leave him in a good position to see what was going on along the front line. Most of the horses with the English army were also posted to the rear according to Monstrelet.

There is an interesting detail mentioned by the 'Pseudo-Elmham' chronicler that Henry did not take the decision about what to do next unilaterally. Instead he called a hurried council of war to ask his commanders what they thought the next move should be. Whatever reservations they had had earlier in the campaign, they now said that the best decision was to fight, perhaps thinking that their situation would only get worse rather than better the longer things went on. Interestingly, the chronicler suggested that Henry himself was now not convinced at this course of action, considering it 'difficult and hazardous to depart from his position'. But he ultimately decided that going on to the offensive and forcing a battle was the lesser of two evils.[64]

Once most of the baggage was safely in position, calling on the Virgin and St George to aid him Henry advanced towards the French. He ordered his standards to be raised and extolled his men to fight. This was no 'England expects' message, no Nelsonian battle cry that would stir the souls of modern men. It was rather a plea to the hearts of God-fearing soldiers who believed implicitly in the power of the saints to intervene in the affairs of humanity if properly and conscientiously extolled to do so, an approach much more in keeping with the mores of the time. The king told his men 'because the enemy are unjustly trying to keep us from our journey, let us advance against them in the name of the Trinity'.[65]

The king also, according to Le Fèvre, reminded his men that he was in France to reclaim his rightful inheritance and that his cause was just. They were men of England and they should remember those they had left behind and fight to win such glory that would do their people proud. And just in case that did not do the trick, he also nudged their memories by recalling that the French had promised to cut off three fingers from the right hand of every archer so that they could no longer prove troublesome in the future.[66]

The French had organised themselves into three ranks: a vanguard, the main body and the rearguard. As noted, Monstrelet said that in the vanguard were 8,000 men-at-arms, 4,000 archers and 1,500 crossbowmen. This was a much higher ratio of men-at-arms to archers than in the English ranks. Records concerning the French forces raised, while less comprehensive than the English equivalents that survive, suggest that a two-to-one ratio of men-at-arms to archers was the norm. This meant that there were still thousands of archers available that could be called upon to counteract their English counterparts if they had been deployed. The main force was of a similar size to the vanguard according to the same writer, while he is very vague about the rearguard, merely noting that it was composed of the 'surplus men-at-arms'. In any event, he reckoned that the French had a six-to-one numerical advantage.

Monstrelet gives an interesting insight into the mood of the French army on the eve of battle. He tells of soldiers who had previously argued among themselves burying grudges given the perilous trial that lay before them so that they could if necessary face their Maker with a clear conscience, of the men sitting down in groups by their standards, of a general quiet confidence though with a suggestion that a few of them were apprehensive about the battle that loomed.

By now the decision to fight had been made. Henry knew that he could not just sit where he was and wait for the French to assemble yet more troops or let his starving, cold, wet and illness-wracked army deteriorate further. Short of bargaining for his freedom, something that would cost a king's ransom, risk his crown and would anyway have been unthinkable to a man of his temperament, nothing remained but to fight.

But Henry's actions and words were having an effect on those he led. His men were inspired by his presence to the point that they almost became angry at the extent of the challenge facing them, so that 'the glass-green bile rose up within their hearts and anger provided strength and courage'.[67]

The king ordered the banners of his army to be moved towards the enemy. In those days of limited communication, these played a crucial part in coordinating movements on the battlefield; an ordinance released a few years later in 1419 would explicitly state that there should be no raising of the flag of St George unless it was properly authorised.[68] Now his army, the cross of St George worn on the front and the back of the soldiers' clothing, moved towards the French to start a fight which would ordain whether they would live or die and whether or not their lord and king would leave the field of battle as a victor, as a corpse or, perhaps worse, as a captive with only years of captivity and a massive ransom to look forward to.

9

AGINCOURT: TO ARMS (10 A.M. TO MIDDAY, 25 OCTOBER 1415)

... a vast multitude is yielded up to death.

The Pseudo-Elmham chronicler

The moment of truth had arrived and death or glory now awaited the English army. The order was given by King Henry – 'banners advance'. Before they set off in what all must have known was a highly risky venture, which for some would be one of the last things they ever did on this earth, many of the English army knelt, crossed themselves, kissed the damp ground three times and put a few grains of soil in their mouths. The last of these rituals was a sign of a man's essential humility and his mortality, a token that he had come from dust and to dust would he return. Then, these symbolic but personally important acts completed, the English army set their faces towards the French lines and set determinedly off.

Today, it is not difficult to picture the scene. The fields still remain much as they were six centuries ago (even if we are not exactly sure which field the battle was fought on). The trees on either side of the inverted triangle were thicker back then but the battlefield itself is still farmland. It was a few minutes' march for the English army to advance from their night camp just in front of Maisoncelle until they reached the front-line position, from which they would fight the battle. The mud clung tenaciously to them as they trudged forward determinedly, grabbing hold of each heavy foot with each energy-sapping step.

They advanced methodically, keeping order as well as they could. The muddy ground did not make for quick progress and the armour worn by the men-at-arms was also not conducive of great speed. But there was no need to hurry. The French were not going anywhere fast, so the English took their time, taking a breather occasionally to ensure that they were not exhausted by the time that they reached the starting position for the battle. This also helped to keep some semblance of order in their line.

The measured advance begs a question. Although we cannot be sure of exactly how far they moved forward, an assumption that they were advancing for five to ten minutes in full view of the French suggests that their adversary had plenty of time to prepare for an increased likelihood of attack. Indeed, it would have been an ideal moment for them to do so for the English archers had stopped their march and were going through the awkward process of hammering their stakes with their mallets deep and firm enough to resist a charging horse with a heavily laden knight on its back. The subsequent unpreparedness of the French does not suggest that they did very much with this window of opportunity, which reveals further problems with their command structure. Their inactivity suggests a definite lack of decision-making ability or, more technically, an absence of clear command and control just when it was most needed.

Henry had disposed his forces well. What the French did not yet realise was that they were under threat not just from the front but also from the sides. English archers had been placed in the woods on either side to shoot into the heaving mass of Frenchmen that would soon be trying frantically to get at the English men-at-arms. Specific references were made in some accounts suggesting that Henry had sent men forward to a meadow near Tramecourt (on the right of the battlefield as the English looked). There were allegedly 200 of them on the mission and their task was to launch a surprise attack.

Some chroniclers denied that this was the case, perhaps as one modern historian has suggested because it has a hint of 'sneakiness' in it.[1] Yet it would be unwise to dismiss the suggestion so easily. Great military leaders like Alexander, Napoleon Bonaparte and Wellington do not make history by playing by the book; rather they rewrite it. Henry had so far acted unconventionally in his tactics and he had to do so to make the most of the limited resources he had. After all, he was outnumbered and his men were weakened with hunger and fatigue, not to mention dysentery; he had to adopt innovative tactics to make up for the disadvantages that he was faced with.

He showed this unconventionality by the way in which the battle started. To the amazement of the French, the outnumbered English army, noting the reluctance of their opponent to attack, had begun moving forward. This was not at all what was expected of them and it was a move that appears to have caught the French on the back foot; some of them had even gone off to get warm as the morning was damp, others to feed their horses.[2]

Again, where exactly this new English front line was is a matter of conjecture. Some historians (or at least their maps) show the repositioned English army to the south of the road between Agincourt and Tramecourt, while others show it to the north of it. If the latter, it is hard to believe they were very far north of it, if at all, as the village of Agincourt, still in French hands and at the time complete with castle, would be on their flank which would not have been a desirable military position for the English to be in.

The English army had adopted a good position from which to fight the battle. Although from a cursory glance the battlefield might appear to be fairly flat there are in fact subtle rises and dips that give distinctive twists and turns to the local topography. The battlefield was not quite all at a level along the English front line. At the right and centre of the English line (or the left and centre of the south-facing French line) it was fairly flat but on the English left (the French right), there is a marked depression in the ground between the two lines, certainly on that part of the field to the south of the road between Agincourt and Tramecourt. This would make it more difficult for an attacking French force to reach the English army if it were placed here. In light of this, it is perhaps significant that the toughest fighting that was about to take place was on the right and in the centre of the English line.

Some historians, otherwise cautious and sagacious in their approach, go weak at the knees at discussion of Agincourt (though fortunately research in recent decades has been much more objective in its approach). For example, James Wylie, who wrote a monumental and meticulously researched multi-volume life of Henry V about a century ago, approaches most of the Agincourt campaign with a sense of balance and proportion. Yet when he gets to Agincourt he insists that the battle cannot be understood without thinking of it as a vast tournament.[3] But in fact what was about to take place was a brutal slogging match with little quarter given.

Most of the focus on Agincourt is properly on the main battle yet there were apparently some diversionary attacks going on. Monstrelet tells of a foray by a small group of Englishmen to the rear of the small village of Agincourt itself. At the end of this raid, he said, the English, finding no resistance from French men-at-arms, set a barn and a house belonging to the Priory of St George at Hesdin ablaze; something of an irony given the identity of the patron saint of the English (the town of Hesdin is a few miles to the south of Agincourt).

The archers were under the command of the veteran fighter Sir Thomas Erpingham, the steward of the royal household, a grey-haired figurehead of stability and solidity for the men around him to look up to. He urged the English to give all they had in support of the king. He rode along the lines of the archers with a small escort with him, exhorting them all to fight to their last breath and give their all for the cause. He was an experienced warrior, having seen action in Spain and he had also been involved in Crusading action in Prussia, as well as possibly having taken part in campaigning in Ireland; but he would never have seen anything like this.

As the English advanced to a position where they were close enough to bring the fire of their archers to bear on the French ranks, the tension was ratcheted up by each forward step they took. The moment for the archers to begin their bombardment was now at hand. The men stopped, shuffled into line and hammered their stakes into the stodgy ground. Now the apprehension was almost tangible. The archers reached into their arrow bags and each took out a shaft. They pulled the bowstring back taut and tense, the muscles in their arms bulging as they exerted every ounce of pull that they could.

Then they took general aim towards the French lines a few hundred yards away and there was a pause pregnant with tension while the archers waited for the command to unleash hell on the enemy. Erpingham stopped and looked ahead defiantly at the masses of the enemy in front of him. Now was the time. According to some accounts, it was he who gave the command to shoot as the main French body moved into range. He had in his hand a baton, and when he felt the right moment had come he threw it high into the air, shouting the command 'nestroque' (probably, 'now strike').[4]

It is doubtful in the extreme that many people heard the command. Thousands of men were gathered together for an imminent attack; it is unlikely that the keyed-up English troops were standing quietly like men at church and that any save those close at hand heard what he said. The baton would have been a more useful and visible sign but even that would have been hard to see along the line. We must assume therefore that further commands rippled along to each flank. From then on, command would largely have to be local and with each passing minute it would become increasingly fragmented. When the French eventually responded, it would be very difficult, if not impossible, to maintain a cohesive response.

The French anyway had plans of their own. Although the Duke of Orléans was the notional commander, it is very likely that more experienced men like Marshal Boucicaut and the Constable of France, Charles d'Albret, had formulated the tactics developed in the original battle plan. These, as we have seen, envisaged sending in heavy cavalry on either flank with a mass attack in the centre, mainly of dismounted men-at-arms. The massed charge of mounted cavalry had been largely abandoned as a French battle tactic during the latter decades of the fourteenth century (the disaster at Nicopolis when they did use it was a salutary reminder of why they had changed their approach).[5] Thousands of French bowmen were to support the attack on the English lines. Such was the plan; it did not last five minutes.

The English archers took aim at their enemies, who were probably wondering at the nerve of their outnumbered opponents.[6] Their 'clout shooting' practice was about to prove its worth. They were aware that the French allegedly had stated that if they caught the archers they would cut the middle fingers off their right hands with which they drew back the bowstring. A story would later develop that this was the origin of the famous 'two-fingered salute' that would become so common in England though sadly there is no un-contestable evidence that this is so.

In this respect it is also noteworthy that the accounts of the time talk of the bowmen using three rather than two fingers and this appears to have been the preferred method, particularly given the massive drawing power required to use a medieval bow. Indeed the sixteenth century writer, Sir John Smythe, a strong defender of the merits of the bow, bemoaned the fact that by his time men were using the weaker two rather than the three-fingered draw.[7]

There were two main types of arrow available to the English archers. There was the bodkin, a sharply pointed arrow suitable for closer-range shooting and capable of penetrating most plate armour with its needle-like profile, though it should be noted that there could be an enormous variability in armour and that made of steel rather than iron was far more effective. There were several battles of the period, such as at Neville's Cross against the Scots in 1346 and at Poitiers ten years later, when the robustness of the enemy's armour proved a significant problem to the English archers.[8] And the chronicler Monstrelet had written that, at the Battle of Othée (fought between Burgundians and rebels from Liege) John the Fearless was so well protected by his armour that, although hit by many arrows and other missiles, he 'did not, on that day, lose a drop of blood'.[9]

The English bowmen also used a longer arrow, perhaps up to thirty-nine inches in length, with which to shoot across greater distances. Given the effective range of these longer arrows, the two armies were now perhaps 250 yards apart, towards the maximum effective distance for long-distance shooting. Following the commands given, whether or not instructed to do so by the sight of Erpingham's baton flying into the air, the archers drew back the bowstring as far as they could with their sinewy arms and then loosed their shafts high into the sky. Arrowheads by this stage in their evolution had become very sophisticated with steel tips and edges around a softer iron centre given them great penetration as the French were about to find out.[10]

There was an irony in the way that Agincourt was fought as the English were not the only force well-equipped with archers. There were also thousands of French bowmen and crossbowmen present, but they were all it appears in the rearguard by now though some French accounts suggest that the crossbows fired off a couple of bolts in return to the opening volleys of the English before retreating.[11] But as the English arrows filled the sky, the French could not respond with anything meaningful. Although the French archers may have been inferior in terms of skills and training to their opposite numbers, they were all that was available to respond, yet they were unable to do so.

There is a commonly held perception that the crossbow was the weapon of choice for the French army but this is not borne out by some of the surviving evidence. Monstrelet as noted talked of 4,000 archers and 1,500 crossbowmen in his account.[12] And the French king Charles V had done his utmost to build up the skills of French archers; a decree of 1367 ordered that a register of all the archers and crossbowmen in France should be set up, in terms that suggest that the bow as used by the English was in widespread use in his country.[13]

However many were present at Agincourt, the French bowmen played no real part in the battle. It is difficult to explain this inaction on the part of the French bowmen satisfactorily. Perhaps they were considered simply not good enough to be put into the fight, yet the fact that no serious attempt was made to deploy them still seems strange for if these men were anything, relatively speaking, they were expendable. Why not at least try them?

A sizeable number of the French archers were however equipped with crossbows rather than 'longbows'. These were cumbersome and sometimes in the wet the bowstrings were seriously compromised; this was the case at the Battle of Crécy when a downpour had made the strings of the French crossbowmen useless. Perhaps with the inclement weather, they had become problematic to use at Agincourt too and this may have ruled the crossbows out as a viable option. The knowledge of what had happened at Crécy may also have mitigated against their perceived usefulness.

The English archers in contrast, being well used to wet weather, had kept the bowstrings 'under their hat' to ensure that they stayed useable. And the cumbersome process required to load a crossbow bolt meant that only two to three bolts a minute could be shot against ten or more from the English bowmen. But on the other hand the stopping power of a crossbow was formidable and it was easier to train a crossbowman rather than a bowman with a 'longbow'. The *Gesta* chronicler talks of a 'first but over-hasty volley' from the French archers followed by a rapid retreat as the English arrows began to strike home.[14]

The most likely explanation for the confusion in the French response to this initial cloud-burst of missiles at Agincourt was that they were simply caught off guard when these massive English arrow-storms were unleashed, something which comes across from some of the chronicle accounts. The French army looked in horror as the air above them was filled with broken, barbed clouds heading directly for them. The sky was blackened with thousands of arrows, a hail-storm, arcing high into the air and then falling to earth with a frightening velocity.

The English were shouting a great war cry, relieved that the tension had now been released, that the time for thinking what lay ahead had passed and that the time for action had come. In the heat of battle there was little time to worry about what might happen in the next few hours. Now it was a case of living second by second.

As the English missiles began to play havoc with the French ranks, those on the receiving end were stung to respond at once, to attempt to strike back and swat away these troublesome pests whose arrows were starting to bring men down all around them. Those at the front were maddened by the damage that was being caused and wanted to strike back as soon as they could.

What must the impact of that first volley have been? Some of the Frenchmen there may have seen the English in action a few years before at St Cloud, but this was on an altogether different scale. As that whizzing sound of the arrows in the air was heard for the first time the French braced themselves to receive it. The effect was devastating, especially for those without armour. Men fell with arrows in their chests, in their arms, in their heads, as the terrible darts pierced skin and crunched into bone. The impact must have physically shattering and psychologically terrifying. Monstrelet's account includes the revealing detail that as the French stood there, the intensity of the arrow storm was so great that they bowed their heads as if they were being buffeted by a tempest.

There were few options open to the French. One was to stay where they were and do nothing – a suicidal policy unless they called their own archers forward to launch their own missile storms – but this was not by now in the French tactical manual. Another was to retreat out of range – retreat, when they had sworn to bring the English to their knees – an unthinkable slur to French pride and another death knell to the ruling regime. Monstrelet notes that despite this, for a short time, the army did actually move back a few paces, forced to do so by the intensity of the man-made tempest. But once retreat had been subsequently driven from their minds, just one option remained: attack.

And so they did. Their ire raised by the temerity of the English in attacking them and with losses already being sustained due to the arrow storm, they got themselves hurriedly ready to charge forward and wipe these arrogant Englishmen out. But they were not, unlike the English, subject to a unified command. There were far too many would-be commanders. And so the response when it came may initially have been fierce and intense but it was uncoordinated, spontaneous and undisciplined. Inspired only by thoughts of destroying their opponent, the pride of France charged forward into the killing zone, like a herd of elephants stung into action by a swarm of aggressive bees.

Before them, the English stood defiant, their flimsy palisades of stakes offering some protection for the archers and their banners flapping gently in the breeze.[15] There were a number of standards flying, including one of St George carried by Thomas Strickland, an esquire, who would later petition Henry VI for a reward for his services in the battle.[16] Also there were the banners of St Edmund, the martyr king, and St Edward the Confessor, whom many later medieval English kings aspired to emulate, as well as that of the Trinity. The latter was a reminder that Henry saw the campaign as being defined as one being fought in spiritual rather than secular terms. God would now adjudicate on who was right and who was not.

Erpingham had by now dismounted and braced himself to receive the shock of the French counter-attack. He had attached himself to the men around King Henry with his banner defiantly planted before him. The battle was underway; now it was time to see how the French would respond as the mass of their army advanced towards the English.[17]

When the French were first hit by the arrow storm, many of the lords and knights with their army were stung by the attack of the archers to retaliate at once. These well-armed men pushed their way to the front, even blocking the view of those behind them with their banners, which looked magnificent no doubt but were a very impractical accoutrement today. Time was lost while some of them were told to remove their standards from the front line and, their pride hurt, resisted the command for a while. The French bowmen, both those with conventional bows and crossbows, were forced to the rear, destined to play no meaningful part in the battle.

The French cavalry launched themselves into the attack against their impudent enemy. They moved first and the fact that they were mounted meant that they would hit the English some time before the dismounted bulk of the army did – provided that they survived that long. Their first targets were the squadrons of archers on either flank of the English army. This had always been in the plan but it is not clear that they were at this precise moment ready to put it into action.

But those that were prepared set their spurs into the flanks of their steeds, urging them into the fray. That, however, was easier said than done. The ploughed fields across which they charged were churned up further as the heavily laden cavalry did their best to close with the English; they may not have far to travel in terms of distance but today it seemed a long way indeed. The mud grabbed at the hooves of the horses, pulling them deeper down into its gripping embrace with each pace forward they took until the charge lost its momentum completely, lessening any potential impact that might be made when they eventually reached the English. As one nineteenth-century writer tellingly described it, the charge in fact took place at a 'funereal pace'.[18]

In contrast, the English were ready for them. The sturdy French steeds and their riders formed perfect targets for the archers, looming large against the autumn sky as they lumbered ponderously towards them. They did not miss their moment or their mark. Huge showers of arrows were shot off at them by the English, forcing the attack back before it had even threatened to get close in any meaningful numbers. Within a minute the charge had been broken, a barely noticeable wave repulsed by an immoveable sea wall.

A few of the cavalry managed to break out in small gaps between the archers and the woods but the majority, those who were not cut down, retreated in disorder back in the direction from which they had come. There were some French catapults that were being used early on in the battle but they did not have any sustained impact and were soon neutralised. Even the men firing these were afraid of the English archers and after initial limited successes their fire became desultory.[19]

Slowed by the effect of the cloying mud, the attack by the French cavalry on the flanks of the English army petered out, those who managed to make it as far as the line of stakes failing to break through them. Only a few of the cavalry were lucky or brave enough to survive the arrow storm that was aimed at them and those that did could easily be dealt with. The leader of the French attack, Sir William de Saveuses, was horrified when so few men followed him but in an impetuous and brave gesture he charged on regardless. He fell dead from his horse, shot with an arrow.

Gallantry was not an exclusive preserve of the English at this battle. Yet heroic though this gesture was, it was also futile; as a French general from a much later war when watching the doomed Charge of the Light Brigade would say, 'C'est magnifique mais ce n'est pas la guerre.' The death of Saveuses might also have been caused in part, as one historian has plausibly suggested, by the fact that he was a prominent Burgundian and in his force were several leading Armagnac supporters; these men had every reason to distrust each other, in some cases indeed to detest each other. It is noteworthy that Saveuses died while most of the leading Armagnacs with him survived, their very survival being something of a novelty in this battle that was just beginning.[20]

There was a major problem with the attack launched by the mounted Frenchmen from the start, and that was that the numbers that had been involved, just a few hundred, were much fewer than had been envisaged. In all probability the sudden and unexpected attack by the English archers had caught many of the horsemen off their guard and some may well have even have taken themselves off, not expecting to see action for some time. The shortfall in numbers inevitably reduced the potential impact of the attack. That said, the fatal combination of the mud and the skills of the English archers probably meant that any larger movement by the French cavalry would only have resulted in even higher loss of life from among their numbers and consequently greater confusion on the battlefield after the attack of the horse was driven back.

The first volleys of the archers aimed at the struggling cavalry was enough to stop the momentum of the charge. Many of the knights broke and fled at once, leaving their leaders stranded and fighting for their lives 'with only a small number of brave hearts'. The charge had come to absolutely nothing and it was now time for the great multitude of the foot soldiers to try their hand.[21] The opening moments of the Battle of Agincourt could hardly have gone worse for the French.

For the English archers, by contrast, the beginning of the battle could hardly have gone better. The sight of heavily armed cavalry charging in their general direction could well have been an extremely intimidating one. But the archers, men like Thomas Pokkeswell or the bowmen from Kendal, had once more proved their worth against better-armed opponents. If their confidence had needed strengthening before the battle began, it had certainly received a significant boost.

This, though, was just the beginning of the first phase of the battle. The opening gambit had been unsuccessful for the French but they had plenty of men to play with and it was now time for the bulk of the army, those who were dismounted, to prove their worth. With their vanguard packed with some of the most prominent and best armed men in the kingdom, the French juggernaut slowly moved towards the enemy. Packed into a closely confined space, their flanks hemmed in by the woods on either side, the great mass of the van started to trudge ponderously up towards the English lines.

The men-at-arms in the French centre had moved forward when the cavalry did, obviously at a slower pace than the mounted men could go. Before they set off to face up to the English they crossed themselves and embraced each other. They seem to have been well aware of the significance of the moment and some sought forgiveness of men who now stood alongside them that they had wronged in the past. It must have already been clear to them that the English were ready to take a murderous toll of their massed ranks as they moved forward.

It is impossible to describe exactly what it was like to be under that arrow storm. The rate of fire meant that at the height of the barrage, for such it was, 50,000 arrows a minute were raining down on the Frenchmen. No one alive would have faced anything like it before, for there had been nothing like it seen for half a century or more. Seeing the sky blacken with thousands of missiles, hearing the whizz of the arrow as it soared through the air and then plummeted to earth at high velocity would have had something of the effect that crossing no man's land would have on the Western Front 500 years later. Each Frenchman would have thought that one, or more, of those arrows was heading for him personally.

That walk across no man's land would have been hellish. Not only were those marching forward lowering their heads in a feeble attempt to protect themselves against the arrows as if they were pushing forward in the teeth of a hurricane – and as they got within 100 yards even the best plate armour would be at risk of being penetrated by a bodkin-pointed arrow – they were also moving through the mud of the newly ploughed field, churned up by maddened horses. Many of these had lost their riders and were out of control, inflamed by arrows shot into their flanks and trying desperately to get away from the deadly darts of the archers. Added to this, those men who tried to push forward were weighed down with heavy armour which did not make for a rapid advance to the English lines. It quickly turned into a heaving, surging mob and a scene of utter pandemonium.

This part of the assault saw a massive body of dismounted men moving slowly across the muddy field toward the English lines. The fighting area in the centre was constricted by the woods on either side so that it was soon packed to the extent of overflowing. The French army split into three columns, one each aiming for the three main English standards accompanying each 'battle'. They had already suffered from the arrow storm before they had gone very far, the missiles frequently piercing the sides and visors of their helmets, the sharp bodkin-headed arrows even piercing armour as at it struck home at relatively short distances.

Yet the blood of the French was up, an antidote to their fears. 'With terrifying shouts they charged over the field with the cavalry sent in front to knock down our archers with the iron-clad breasts of their warhorses and then to trample on them with the hooves of those same steeds.' However, those steeds and their riders had been repulsed and tried to batter their way back through the massed lines that were pushing forward.

With the foremost ranks of the French (or those of them who

had survived the hail of arrows anyway) now at a distance of just 100 metres from the English line, the target was so big that it was almost impossible for the archers to miss. With the French forces packed so closely together there was no need to aim other than in a general sense – 'each arrow in its target lodged, each strike a wound inflicted'.[22] The horses were protected by a chamfron, armour to protect the head, but their flanks and rumps were unprotected. If the English archers were shooting from the flanks, possibly from the woods on either side, then they would be able to hit home in the unprotected sides of the horses, causing them to stampede in panic.

As increasing numbers of Frenchmen started to fall to the ground, impaled by arrows, another problem was starting to manifest itself. A number of French soldiers already lay dead, dying or incapacitated in the front ranks where they had been struck down. Behind them large numbers of uncoordinated troops were doing what they could to enter the battle. A massive crowd of heaving humanity was formed as those pushing in from behind stumbled and fell on top of those lying at the front. Some men were starting to die, not of arrow wounds or the hacking of swords or axes, but suffocating slowly but surely as they gasped frantically for a precious breath of air, trapped under a pile of living, dying or dead bodies.

The confusion was made far worse by the fact that what remained of the French cavalry, seeing very clearly which way the battle was going, had naturally tried to retreat. This merely added to the chaos. The massed ranks of the dead and wounded obstructed the escape route of the horsemen who had survived. Even as they tried to ride away, thousands of infantry pushed forward in the opposite direction, compounding the already impossible situation.[23] Soon the scene in front of the English lines disintegrated into a vast, heaving scrum. It was not long before a new enemy appeared to assail the French: panic.

There were perhaps 8,000 men in the vanguard (Waurin and Le Fèvre suggest at least this, and perhaps considerably more), too tightly packed together in this cramped space to allow freedom of movement, making it difficult for the men there to even swing their swords freely. Their very numbers were now more of a hindrance than a help.

As those who survived the arrow storm bunched together near the English lines, it became a terrible case of crowd control gone horribly wrong. The press of the French in the narrow space was so great that men, weighed down by a fatal combination of the sticky mud and their sheer numbers, fell and struggled to get up again, not so much because their armour was ridiculously heavy (for modern tests suggest that tales claiming that armour made a man almost completely immobile are very exaggerated) but because others fell on top of them and they were pinned down. Already exhausted by their weary trudge across the field, hundreds of fallen Frenchmen struggled not so much to get up as to breathe.

Henry's tactics were simple enough: use his archers to decimate the French before they came close enough to enter into hand-to-hand combat with the men-at-arms. This was a tactic of attrition; to wear the enemy down before they could close with his foot soldiers or even cause so many losses that the enemy would break and run before they got that close. For if they managed to survive the tempest of arrows that rained down on them and survived in sufficient numbers then the French, with their huge numerical advantage in men-at-arms, could bring their superiority in this arm to bear. It was the battle philosophy of the Western Front half a millennium later.

It was a numbers game dependent for its success on the simple but chilling equation of how many Frenchmen survived the arrow storm by the time that they closed with the English, an attempt as a much later general would put it to 'bleed the enemy dry'.[24] But there were a large number of Frenchmen in that cramped field and some pushed determinedly forward through the storm.

Despite the thinning out of the ranks as a result of the shooting of the archers, some French soldiers clearly did manage to make it to the English lines, where the fighting became intense. There were only so many arrows to go around and the archers had shot many of them off in the opening exchanges, and although determined efforts were made to resupply them it was inevitable that there would be problems in keeping up with demand. As the French van pushed on, the press grew greatest around each of the three main standards. At close quarters the superior numbers of the French troops started to make a difference. Slowly but inexorably the English began to fall back.

The standards acted as a rallying point for the English army but they also served as a focal point for the French to aim for as they showed where the English commanders were placed; kill the commanders and you would lop off the head of the army. The English king was especially visible, wearing the quartered colours of England and France, the gold fleur-de-lys on a blue background on two of the four quarters, and three golden leopards on a red background on the other two, with a golden crown on his head making him even more prominent. He, and his leading supporters in the English army, also wore the tell-tale SS collar of the House of Lancaster around their necks.[25]

Having survived the arrow storm, the French soldiers who had pushed their way through to the English lines now crossed swords with their enemy at close quarters. The fighting was frenetic, chaotic, the noise of battle deafening. From their vantage point the priests at the rear of the English army cried to God asking that He would smile kindly on their king and 'deliver us from this iron furnace and the terrible death which menaced us'.[26] The fighting was desperate and there was little sign of quarter being given for 'at the mid-point [of the battle] the English were increasingly eager to kill, for it seemed that there was no hope of safety except in victory'.[27] It was, in other words, a case of kill or be killed.

It is clear from the fact that there were some losses sustained by the English that a number of French soldiers managed to get through to their lines after living through the arrow storm. There was certainly a hard fight in places. Thomas of Walsingham wrote that 'then, as the battle lines clashed, the loud war cries of our men struck the stars on high, and the vast sky was somehow filled with their shouts. Then again on all sides there flew a cloud of arrows. Sword rang on sword, while the javelins, which were constantly hurled, struck helmets, armour and breastplates. So the French fell in great numbers as the arrows pierced them, here fifty, there again sixty.'[28]

The battle reached its climax. The archers loosed torrents of arrows into the French flanks, not taking a breath between shooting one arrow and the next. But there was not an inexhaustible stock of arrows and the French were not shooting any back so the English archers eventually ran short of them. Significant numbers of the enemy had also managed to get to close range, where the arrows were of limited use. So now the archers seized any weapon that came to hand – axes, stakes, swords, spearheads and mallets – and charged into the fray; they struck down, hacked and stabbed the enemy. Spurred on by the king, who according to the chroniclers was an inspirational figure, the English charged into the battle as it seemed no army of their countrymen had ever done before.

It is easy to be cynical and assume that the chroniclers of the day talked up the role and courage of the king in the interests of propaganda. They had every reason to do such a thing. Yet the balance of evidence needs to be looked at too. There is plenty of evidence both before and after the Agincourt campaign that Henry was a soldier's king. He had, after all, received a serious arrow wound in the face at Shrewsbury over a decade before and fought on manfully even after this sickening injury. He would be in the front line of many sieges and would die from a soldier's greatest enemy, disease, caught on campaign. All of this suggests that he shared the hardships of war with his men and took his chances alongside them, or more pertinently in front of them, metaphorically speaking, as a leader.

So before dismissing the words of Thomas of Walsingham out of hand, we might like at least to keep an open mind as to whether or not they might just be true:

King Henry himself, fulfilling the role of soldier as well as of king, was the first to charge the enemy. He inflicted and received cruel blows, giving his men in his own person brave examples of doing so as he scattered the enemy ranks with his ready axe. And in the same way, the knights, emulating the acts of the king, strained with all their might to lay low with the sword that forest of shouting Frenchmen which opposed them, until at last force made a way and the French did not so much fall back as fall dead on the ground. And indeed when they saw those, whom they believed to be unconquerable, brought low in the clash of battle, at once 'their hearts were numbed; an icy tremor ran along the marrow of their bones'.[29]

It is an evocative depiction; the king laying about him not with the sword, the weapon of chivalry, but with an axe, felling his opponents with violent gusto in a hacking, pounding frenzy in the blood-red mist of battle.[30] His knights, inspired by his example, charged on foot headlong into the fray and started to get on top, bit by bit, man by man. The French, certain of victory at the outset, began to lose self-belief, their confidence began to evaporate and fear began to take over the vacuum that their fleeing courage had left behind. It may be the archers that are rightly credited with the victory first and foremost but other parts of the English army also had to play their part and at this crucial stage of the fight they played it to the full.

There were moments when the battle appeared to be in the balance, not least when at its height one of England's foremost nobles was struck down. At the fiercest point of the close-quarter combat, Edward, Duke of York, fell, 'overcome by the whirlwind of war' as Elmham put it. Although precise details are sketchy, it would probably have been now that the presence in his ranks of those crack troops, led by Cornwall, Umfraville and Holland, started to make a difference. Seasoned by the great deeds they had undertaken on the campaign already, they fought resolutely on, refusing to budge another inch.

It was here on the right that the struggle appeared to be greatest, perhaps reflecting the fact that the ground here was more conducive to a successful French attack. As well as the Duke of

York, from his original retinue of 400 no less than ninety appear to have died at Agincourt judging from post-campaign records.[31]

This tells of a hard-fought and bruising encounter. Few if any of the English lost here would be as a result of arrows shot from a distance, as the chronicles are consistent in saying that the French bowmen and crossbowmen played very little part in the fight. Therefore these losses speak of close-quarter confrontation, of swords slashing into flesh, of axes hammering down and shattering bone, of blood shed by men just a pace or two apart from each other. Men could peer into the eyes of those with whom they were in life-or-death hand-to-hand combat. For many the last thing they would see would be a dagger aimed into their eyes or a leaden mallet hurtling down towards their skull. This was not a long-distance war of archer against knight but a close-quarters slogging-match between men-at-arms and impromptu light infantry.

The fighting was also heavy in the centre, where the king too was in great danger. His brother Humphrey, the inexperienced Duke of Gloucester, was struck down near him and fell to the ground badly wounded in the groin. (Monstrelet suggests that the king tried in vain to come to York's rescue; unless he was capable of being in so many places at once this seems a conflation and probably refers to the Duke of Gloucester). Seeing Gloucester in trouble, Henry went at once to his aid, standing over his prone body to protect it so that no further harm would come to him. The fighting around the king grew frantic. Henry with his crown-topped helmet attracted the attention of the French as a prize target.

If legend be believed, this crown had some interesting connections, both exotic and historically appropriate. It was said that set in the crown was what was known as the Black Prince's Ruby. This was a gemstone that was probably mined in what is now Tajikistan but then made its way to Spain. An exiled Spanish prince, Don Pedro the Cruel, who came from Seville, sought the help of the Black Prince in war and offered the ruby in return. Now Henry was wearing it into battle and it was in grave danger of being lost.[32]

The battle hung in the balance, its decisive moment reached. The press was closing in on Henry and the fighting grew ever more ferocious; perhaps the suicide squad of eighteen young men who had resolved to take the king or die in the process were moving in on their target. Swords and other weapons smashed into armour and bone, causing terrible trauma to those unlucky enough to stop them. Then an axe came crashing down on the king's head, breaking a floret off his crown and leaving a dent in his helmet. Stunned, the king slumped to the ground.[33] His men rushed round him, determined to give their own lives in defence of his.

According to later legends that developed, one of those in the king's bodyguard was a Welshman by the name of Dafydd Gam, who was accompanied by his son-in-law Sir Roger Vaughan of Bredwardine. Gam had been a staunch supporter of the Lancastrian cause in the protracted campaign against Glendower in Wales. At one stage he had even been captured by him and was forced to raise a ransom for his release. His surname may be connected to the slang 'gammy', which means that he had some form of disability – perhaps, according to sources that are more anecdotal than contemporary, in the form of a squint.

The king's bodyguard, including Gam and his son-in-law, fought stoically around him, meaning to sell their lives dearly before the enemy could harm him. Inspired by the glorious prospect of capturing the English king and winning redounding glory as a result, the French fought frantically towards Henry. At the head of the French assault party that was closing in around the king was the Duke of Alençon, one of the foremost men in their army. His very being possessed by the prospect of the fame and fortune that was now close enough to touch, the duke had thrown himself headlong into the melee.

But Henry's bodyguard formed an impenetrable wall against which chivalry could make little impression. They closed ranks around Henry and hit out at the advancing French, refusing to concede an inch. Eventually the scrap started to go their way. The chroniclers tell us that sword struck sword, axes hammered down into armour, the screams of the wounded and dying and the clash of steel on steel, the visceral war cries of the cream of English and French soldiery, a veritable cacophony filled the air.

The French were either cut down where they stood or started to fall back. The Duke of Alençon realised that his attempt to take the king had failed; it was time to concede defeat. He took off his gauntlet and moved to hand it to Henry, a sign of surrender. It was a move prompted by the conventions of chivalry, as if the duke was taking part in some ceremonial of the tournament. But this was no tourney, this was war. In the heat of the battle the gesture was either not seen, misinterpreted or ignored.

One of Henry's bodyguard struck out at the duke and he fell to the ground, the life ebbing out of him.[34] In later times it would be said that it was Davy Gam himself who struck the fatal blow that brought the duke down, only to be cut down himself shortly afterwards. In the nineteenth century the Welsh historian George Borrow would talk of Gam at Agincourt, 'where he achieved that glory which will for ever [sic] bloom, dying, covered with wounds, on the field of Agincourt after saving the life of the king, to whom in the dreadest and most critical moment of the fight he stuck closer than a brother'.[35]

The legend also told how both Gam and his son-in-law Roger Vaughan were knighted by their grateful king even as they lay dying of their wounds. There is no definitive substantiating evidence to confirm the truth of this tale but it is a fine example of how such snippets of family history help to perpetuate the memory of battles such as Agincourt.[36]

Whether true in every detail or not, this vignette epitomises, among other things, just how the bloodlust of the English was up, or perhaps how concerned they were for the king's safety, that such a valuable potential prisoner as the Duke of Alençon should be killed rather than held for later ransom. The duke's dreams of chivalric glory were dashed to pieces in the mud and blood of the battlefield.

The conflict around the main 'battle', led by the king, at last turned after the bitter fight that had taken place around him was finally won. The Duke of Gloucester was dragged, badly wounded, from the front line and to safety. Seeing that the French before him were in retreat, Henry then turned his attention to the vanguard (or more accurately the English right), which seemed to be in need of help now that the Duke of York was down. Eventually, all along the close-packed line the English gradually assumed the ascendancy.[37]

This was bitter and fierce fighting with no quarter. It was noted by the Religieux that the English 'kept themselves with advantage in the middle of this bloody melee, not without losing many of their own men but fighting with so much passion, for they knew that for them it was a matter of life or death'.[38]

The melee was fought with brutal ferocity until around midday. It was a fierce slogging match, which should have favoured the superior numbers of the French in most circumstances. But the agility of the lightly armed English archers allowed them to strike and withdraw freely from the fray, making them invaluable light infantrymen as well as deadly bowmen.

The French, on the other hand, were badly affected by the large numbers that had been lost in that terrible trudge across no man's land. The march itself had drained them of energy too and by now they were approaching the point of exhaustion with every leaden footstep, sucking life and energy from them as they tramped slowly through the clinging, cloying mud. The stubbornness of the English was proving to be an unwelcome surprise after their initial optimism.

With the benefit of hindsight, and knowing the way that the battle would turn out, it is easy to skirt over this period of the battle. It is of course impossible to reconstruct every detail but we can get a sense from many of the chroniclers that this was a pivotal moment. This was visceral violence, almost primeval in intensity, and a Roman centurion would have recognised the push and thrust, the hack and stab, of the hand-to-hand fighting even if the weapons would have seemed strange.

It also suggests that the battle was a closer-run thing than glib patriotic commentators may have intimated in the past (though Shakespeare should be forgiven – he was a playwright, not a historian, and he was rather good at his chosen occupation too). Enough Frenchmen got close enough to kill the Duke of York, take down and threaten the life of the Duke of Gloucester and were near enough to the king to be within one lucky thrust or stab of bringing him down too. If the king had been lost, then so too would the battle.

Therefore, the traditional view of Agincourt as a one-sided victory where the archers brought down any Frenchman foolish enough to brave their arrows does not ring true. Sufficient numbers of Frenchmen, whose own bravery has perhaps not been given enough credit by commentators either English or French, put their heads down against the wind of arrows that blew in their faces, ignored the cuts and the bruises that must have been inflicted even if their armour had protected them from worse, and got into a hand-to-hand fight with the English men-at-arms and threatened to strike down Henry himself. Some of their actions and tactics may have been unwise; this does not mean that they were not courageous.

But the English stood their ground defiantly. The English soldiers in the front line at last sensed an atmosphere of fear now overwhelming the French. Now it was their turn for the blood-red mist to descend. They seized the weapons from out of the hands of their opponents and hacked them down like cattle. The hand-to-hand fighting was now at such a level that there was no pattern left in the battle anymore. Tactics were pointless by this stage; the battle was a succession of close-quarter personal fights for survival. In most cases it seems that it was the English combatant who came out on top. The killing only stopped when the English had no energy left to kill their opponents.[39]

It was as if a monster had been released from within the English army. Weeks of terror and deprivation as they marched aimlessly across northern France was now being compensated for in this orgy of blood. The French, having marched across the ploughed field and been eviscerated by the arrows of the archers, were now approaching the point of collapse while the English found new energy from the unbelievable fact that the battle appeared to be going their way. Nothing gives a soldier a new lease of life like the prospect of survival when not long before all had seemed lost.

To the writer of the *Gesta*, too, the French were terrified at the ferocity of the attack that was launched on them; 'fear and trembling seized them', and never before had such a body of fine knights 'offered opposition so lacking in vigour, and so confused, or so unmanly'. A number of them offered to surrender but in the heat of battle few were taken prisoner but were put to death there and then.

A great mound of the dead lay heaped across the battlefield. The English climbed over the piled-up cadavers and struck out at the French in front of them with swords, axes and any other weapons they could find including the lead-covered mallets with which the archers had hammered in their protective stakes. After two hours of this intense fighting the French were at last broken. The vanguard and the second wave was to all intents and purposes wiped out. Seeing the French running off, the English at last took time out to look for French survivors whom they could hold for ransom. They pulled at the mounds of the dead, occasionally finding a man alive in the heap and putting him to one side, intending to let him live so that they could profit fully from him.

The terror of the French soldiers trapped in that confined space defies imagination. From the euphoria of certain victory, they were now faced with the almost inevitable prospect of a harrowing, painful death. The French tactics may be subject to criticism, and so too their command structure. What could not be doubted, though, was the heavy price they paid. The Master of the Crossbowmen, David de Rambures, should have been leading the charge against the archers on the flanks but instead found himself in that vast press in the vanguard along with all four of his sons. Of this family group only one son, Andre, emerged with his life. European history might have been rather different if he had not, for many of the royal families of Europe including those of Britain, the Netherlands, Spain and Belgium as well as Kaiser Wilhelm II of Germany were descended from his bloodline.[40]

Thomas of Walsingham, who was not present at the battle, may have lifted some of his account from the *Gesta* chronicler, who was (though he was not on the front line), and his account speaks vividly of the slaughter. The collective writings of the chroniclers tell of a battle that was brutal and bloody and finally descended into a killing spree.

Shakespeare was not the only man who could wax lyrical on these tumultuous events. The unknown writer of the Pseudo-Elmham chronicle was almost poetic in his words, which nevertheless also convey something of the sheer horror of the situation:

The air thunders with dreadful crashes, clouds rain missiles, the earth absorbs blood, breath flies from bodies, half-dead bodies roll in their own blood, the surface of the earth is covered with the corpses of the dead, this man charges, that one falls, this one attacks, that one dies, this one recovers, that one vomits forth his soul in blood, the killer is enraged, the dead crashed in grief; the living desires to surrender, the charge of the victors does not allow time for withdrawal, cruelty reigns, piety exults, the brave and the strong are crashed, and mountains of corpses are piled up, a vast multitude is yielded up to death, princes and magnates are led off as captives.[41]

But in the end it was done. Penned in by the men behind and barely able to move their arms in the press, those Frenchmen in the constricted killing zone at last collapsed, dead, dying, wounded or merely exhausted. The English looked on, exhausted too, but this was the exhaustion of the victor, their elation at this precise moment causing the adrenaline to course through their veins before they passed to the next phase, of relief at survival and more than one murmured prayer of thanks that they had done so. Against all the odds, they had won. Or so, at least, it seemed.

10

AGINCOURT: THE MASSACRE (MIDDAY TO 1 P.M., 25 OCTOBER 1415)

... burn and slay.

Lord Stanley's reply at the Battle of Shrewsbury
when asked what should be done with the prisoners

It was the greatest moment of Henry's still young life, a remarkable victory. With the tide now turned against the French, the English looked to the problem of what to do with their prisoners. There were still a considerable number of French troops not yet committed to the battle, but it was far from clear that they had any stomach to become involved in a battle that had been so disastrous for their compatriots. For the English, an unbelievable triumph had been won. For the French, there was a sense of deep shame, not least because some of their greatest knights had been overcome by common foot soldiers of no social standing – at least if some of the chroniclers are to be believed.[1]

Both the French vanguard and the second wave had by now been committed, though in the chaos they had both merged into one 'fellowship of death' as Shakespeare described it. The French troops that remained as yet uninvolved and to the rear had given no hint that they wished to take any part in the battle. If the cream of French chivalry had been so badly cut up, what then could be hoped for from them, many of whom were much less well-equipped and who were now largely without leadership?

It is perhaps significant that one French chronicler, Pierre Cochon, wrote that 'the French thought that they would carry the day given their great numbers, and in their arrogance had proclaimed that only those who were noble should go into battle. So all the men of the lower ranks, who were enough to have beaten the English, were pushed to the rear.'[2] It appeared unlikely that they wanted to get involved in the fight.

It seemed to the English that the battle was over and they therefore set to their task of taking captive those left alive with enthusiasm; after all, this was the profitable part of a battle. There were many such prizes lying around on this bloody field. Among those taken prisoner were the Duke of Orléans, the erstwhile leader of the French army, and the Duke of Bourbon. The former was allegedly captured by Sir Richard Waller, found by King Henry under a walnut tree with his prisoner and promptly knighted, though the chroniclers do not mention this and the roll drawn up by Sir Nicholas Harris Nicolas in the nineteenth century from records that he came across did not mention him.[3] These were rich prizes, and the English found themselves in a position that would have seemed unthinkable just a few hours before.

But the sense of triumphant euphoria was to evaporate in an instant. The French still had large numbers of troops scattered around the edges of the field and, even as the English were helping themselves to captives, a shout went up that these men were about to enter the battle. The *Gesta* chronicler wrote that 'but then, all at once ... a shout went up that the enemy's mounted rearguard (in incomparable number and still fresh) were re-establishing their position and line of battle in order to launch an attack on us, few and weary as we were'.[4] In an instant the scenario and the mood changed.

Up to this point, some prisoners had been taken but this was a time-consuming process. There were rituals to be gone through if a knight were to surrender to his foe during a battle. He would offer his right glove and, once this was accepted, he had effectively handed himself over to his captor. Of course he could not just stay there on the field of battle and prisoners would be escorted to the rear. He might even receive medical treatment if he had been injured, not so much for chivalric reasons but for the fact that he was now a valuable asset that needed to be looked after even though medical science was limited in what it could do. It is interesting to note in this respect that there are many references in medieval accounts of fragments of arrows being left in the bodies of those wounded in battle because it was too difficult to extract them, rather as soldiers in much more recent times would continue to carry around shrapnel from shells in their bodies.[5]

In this battle, with the English outnumbered and a number of prisoners already taken, there were practical problems with finding enough spare men to look after the French who had surrendered. The *Gesta* chronicler noted that there was simply not enough time for the English to accept surrenders in the heat of battle and the rate of deaths to total casualties was already in all probability unusually high as the English put their opponents out of their misery with swords, knives, mallets or poleaxes before setting out on the next bout of hand-to-hand combat. According to some accounts, some men had surrendered no less than ten times during the course of the battle, suggesting that it was difficult to firmly secure a prisoner in the melee. But they were in the minority, as many were despatched as they were taken.

Now the situation from an English perspective was to suddenly get alarming, with attacks from the rear now also being reported alongside the possibility of a renewed assault from the front (some accounts suggest that the latter was to be led by Clignet de Brabant, though he did not have a large number of men with him).[6] And so followed the most controversial moments of the battle. The fight, just minutes before seemingly won, now appeared to be in the balance. Now the English king took a terrible decision; except for a few of the more prominent nobles who had been captured, Henry now ordered that all those Frenchmen held prisoner should be put to death.

It was not a popular order among the English army. The men-at-arms seem to have refused absolutely to do it. There were several possible reasons for this. One was that they were unhappy with the ethical implications of such an act which was against the theoretical code of chivalry. But then there were more pragmatic reasons too. What if they one day were taken prisoner in such a situation? Could they then expect the same rough justice to be meted out to them? Tit-for-tat killings were a feature of some aspects of medieval warfare and mass slaughter ordered in the heat of battle could have very unfortunate repercussions in the future.

The execution of the prisoners could set a dangerous precedent for the rest of the campaign and there were previous examples of knights being unhappy in committing such mass killings of prisoners. For example, when Calais fell to Edward III in 1347 he was not inclined to show mercy to his captives, the famous

'Burghers of Calais' later immortalised by the sculptor Rodin. In contrast to one version of the story that it was the injunctions of his queen, Philippa, who changed his mind there is another much more pragmatic tale which suggests that it was a knight, Sir Walter Manu, who convinced him to do so in case the roles were reversed in the future and the English happened to become French prisoners.

When King John took Rochester castle in 1215 he was of a mind to hang the garrison. He was talked out of it by a knight who told him,

> My lord king, our war is not yet over, therefore, you ought carefully to consider how the fortunes of war may turn; for if you now order us to hang these men, the barons, our enemies, will perhaps by a similar event take me or other nobles of your army, and, following your example, hang us; therefore do not let this happen, for in such a case no one will fight in your cause.[7]

There were therefore precedents for resisting such commands. Now despite Henry's formidable personality some of his men had apparently disobeyed his orders. To resist the king's will, as appears to have been the case in this instance, was not only a brave move but a potentially reckless one. It was also one of doubtful moral stance given the conventions of the time. The medieval monarch was deemed to have been given his position and his power direct from God; the role was, in technical terms, a sacred one.

Some medieval rulers such as the Holy Roman Emperor Frederick II – who was admittedly extreme in many of his views – even considered that to go against a monarch's orders equated to blasphemy.[8] In other words, two rulebooks were in conflict;

one regulation concerning the code of chivalry, the other on compliance with the orders of an anointed monarch.

There was of course also the fact that by killing the prisoners the men-at-arms were saying farewell to the prospect of potentially lucrative ransom payments. A battle was a tremendous and infrequent opportunity for men to come into great wealth. The men who had been captured were prized tradable commodities and it no doubt seemed foolish to forego the rich ransoms that might be available in return for their later release. At any event the men-at-arms were not at all happy at the king's orders. To carry them out, instead the king had to instruct a body of archers about two hundred strong led by a squire to do so.[9]

But in any case this was no time for an argument, moral or otherwise, right in the middle of a battle. Given the apparent reluctance of the men-at-arms to slaughter the prisoners, whether through solidarity with fellow soldiers, a sense of shame at breaking with convention, a pragmatic concern for their own future or pique at the loss of a healthy ransom payment, Henry got together the esquire and two hundred archers to carry out the task.

The loss of ransom payments would be a blow to the English army. The chronicler Froissart tells of one example when the famous fourteenth-century English commander Sir John Chandos was prevailed on by his men not to avoid battle so that they would duly have the prospect of making some money from the fight.[10] Now Henry's men were faced with the same prospect of losing out on a lucrative and possibly never-repeated opportunity after all that they had been through.

The archers too would also be faced by the possibility of financial loss as a result of the killing of potentially valuable prisoners, but in other ways they had less to lose than the nobility.

Archers taken in arms were frequently put to the sword so the thought of what might happen to them in the future if captured was less relevant. That paragon of Muslim virtue Saladin ordered that all crossbowmen taken after the fall of the Crusader castle at Bait al-Hazan should be killed. Henry II, King John and Henry III of England had all singled out bowmen for similarly harsh treatment[11] (though crossbowmen as opposed to archers using the 'long bow' seem to have been given the sternest treatment of all, as in some ways their weapon was seen to be 'unsporting' and the church may even sought to ban it at the Second Lateran Council of 1139).

The men delegated to carry out this butchery started to fulfil their instructions. Some terrible scenes were subsequently played out once the order to begin the slaughter was given. One group of prisoners were massacred in Maisoncelle (it was just a few minutes' walk back from the front line), burned to death; hardly a glorious mark on Henry's record.

One man was particularly unfortunate to die in all this carnage. Duke Anthony of Brabant had ridden hell-for-leather to reach Agincourt in time to fight, travelling many miles to get to the field only to find that the battle was already nearly over when he got there. He had ridden so hard that he arrived on the field in advance of his heraldic accoutrements. This proved fatal.

When he reached the battlefield, the duke assembled with the small party of men that had managed to keep up with him in a thicket near the battlefield (a purely speculative detail this, but the copse of trees where the nineteenth century 'Calvarie' now stands would be an ideal spot for this). Even his armour was behind him, so he put on some owned by his chamberlain instead.

The duke put together an impromptu surcoat by seizing a flag from one of his trumpeters, cutting a hole in it and putting it over his head, which was unlikely to be a particularly convincing heraldic device to anyone. When he was taken, he was not recognised by his captors. And when the slaughter subsequently started none of his supporters was there to point out who he was. He was therefore butchered with other men of lower social standing.[12]

The actions of the Duke of Brabant were regarded by his contemporaries, even those largely sympathetic to him, as being impulsive and his death was deemed to have been caused by his 'imprudent haste'. His demise was one of the more pointless and avoidable given the fact that the battle was already lost by the time he threw himself into it. A battlefield was a million miles away from the chivalric romances of Arthurian literature. It is interesting and noteworthy that, even in France, long considered the heartland of chivalry, contemporary chroniclers, while recognising that the duke was chivalric in his actions, also considered them to be reckless.

Brabant's secretary Edmond de Dynter, who was not present at the battle but was in his service and would have been in an excellent position to verify some of the facts shortly afterwards, noted compelling circumstantial details that suggest that the duke was indeed killed as a prisoner. For one thing the men who later found his body told Dynter that it had been found a fair way from the battlefield. For another, his neck bore a wound (a throat cut was a plausible way for a quick despatch) and his face was stabbed, which would have been difficult if his helmet was still on. These marks confirm the writings of other chroniclers who gave details of how the captives were despatched.

It is worth bearing in mind that Dynter would have spoken

first-hand to men who found the body and may even have seen it himself before burial so he has the makings of a reliable witness who has little vested interest in making such details up. Yet the late arrival of Brabant poses another question mark about the massacres. His dash into the battle left little time to capture him and then take him off somewhere further away before slaughtering him as part of the final actions of the battle. A more plausible explanation is that he was not killed in the general massacre but was later despatched as being of insufficient value by an uninformed captor. This suggested a cold-blooded, casual attitude to slaughter as opposed to a snap decision in the heat of battle.

The Duke of Alençon was also singled out by chroniclers for criticism for his role in the battle for he 'stood out from all the other princes by virtue of his agreeable personality and by his immense wealth, and who until then had enjoyed a great reputation for wisdom. But carried away by a foolish passion and by an overwhelming desire to fight, he had left the main body of the army over which he had the command and had thrown himself boldly into the middle of the melee.'[13] Again, chivalry was considered in this case to be pointless. Even French chroniclers appeared to be getting tired of the concept.

These comments suggest that even in France chivalry was something to be confined to a significant extent to story books, courts and tournaments. Great wars had coloured the Middle Ages blood-red; the Hundred Years War, the Crusades, bitter civil conflicts across Europe, all had scarred the landscape of chivalry with an unattractive and utilitarian tint of pragmatism. Since the disastrous defeats at Crécy, Poitiers and elsewhere the French had managed to protect their country by avoiding pitched battles. The catastrophe at Agincourt was a reversion to old, outdated tactics which the French thought that they had left behind them.

Now Brabant, Alençon and other great men were dead, some struck down during the course of the battle and others slaughtered in cold blood. This controversial action placed a question mark over Henry's sense of honour. Modern historians tend to believe that Henry did this because he thought that the French were about to renew their attack and he did not want to run the risk of hundreds of captive enemy troops joining in.

However, Shakespeare suggests that his anger was fired up by reports of attacks on the baggage at the English rear. If this story is not true, the Bard is certainly not guilty of making all the details up himself. Both the *Gesta* chronicler and Walsingham refer to key details of the incident. The latter tells how 'certain French scum' attacked the rear, pillaged the baggage and ran off with the loot – suggesting that the moving of the baggage from the village of Maisoncelle had not been completed and that there was maybe a lack of haste that would have unfortunate consequences.

The loot so taken included a valuable crown and a fine sword belonging to Henry. Some of this treasure was lost forever though other items, such as Henry's crown and coronation orb as well as a gold cross containing a sacred relic of the True Cross, were recovered by Raoul de Gaucourt when on a mission to France in 1417. This was while he was attempting to meet the various conditions imposed by the English king in return for which the French lord would be formally released from captivity.[14]

Other French troops were ecstatic when the raiders on the English rear returned soon after, believing that the day was theirs. In some accounts, it was even said that as a result of this raid and the booty taken, rumours reached Paris that the French had won a crushing victory.[15] Shakespeare even has his man Gower describing Henry's actions in ordering the execution of the prisoners as being those of a 'gallant king'; whatever else they may have been, they were certainly not this.

Several men are named as being leaders of this attack on the rear of Henry's lines: Isambart d'Agincourt, Robinet de Bourneville and Rifklart de Clamace. They were all local men and it is very likely that the attack was part of a pre-planned French tactic. After all, the French had camped in the village and the surrounding area on the previous night and would have had many hours to hatch a plan. In addition the written French campaign tactics that have been discovered suggested exactly such a move would be made. Using men who knew the territory intimately was a logical and sensible move.

The road from Agincourt to Maisoncelle runs for a mile or so slightly to the west of the battlefield. It is in the nature of a sunken track and would have been difficult for the English to see from the left of their line. The deceiving dips and rises on the left of the English frontline would have hidden the road from view, especially with Henry's men focussing on the fight in front of them. With their attention distracted elsewhere it is not surprising that the flank attack had not been spotted until it hit home. That said the Chronicler of Ruisseauville, writing from an abbey just a couple of miles north of Agincourt, suggests that the raid came from the men of Hesdin some miles off to the south which is also militarily feasible.

Although for these local men the prospect of plunder may have been the greatest incentive, their motives did not particularly matter to Henry, especially as at the time he could not have known what they were. Their attack had caught him on his blindside and would have caused confusion in the mind of an English command structure that was already stretched. The king might be forced to despatch troops from his limited resources to deal with the problem whether it was a ploy or not. He simply could not afford to take the chance that this was not part of a more coordinated strategic movement on their enemy's part to enclose his army in some kind of pincer movement. And he could also see large numbers of French troops in front of him too. Given all this it seemed that the battle was in actuality very much still in the balance.

Not long before the massacre there had been a lull in the battle as the ferocity of the French attack had petered out. Prisoners had been collected and were starting to be moved from the battlefield. They had had their helmets removed. One of them, Gilbert de Lannoy, was wounded and taken off and locked up in a house with twelve other captives in a similar situation. This implies that the battle was regarded as over; men in the heat of battle would not have the luxury of the time to lock men up and then return to the fray. And yet, now this – attacks from the rear and more troops in front. Maybe the fight was not over after all.

Taking this account at face value and putting oneself in Henry's position, if he had received news of this attack on his rear before the outcome of the battle was clear, this was alarming especially when he could also see more men to his front. He could not be sure that the raiders at his rear were not just the vanguard of some larger French force attacking from behind the English; it was likely that frantic messages had been rushed up to him from the rear telling him that the army was under attack from that direction and for all he knew that assault might be being made with some force. If that were the case then it could mean that some of the enemy had managed to outflank him and, given the larger French numbers, he was in grave danger of being surrounded.

Even worse, there could be fresh French forces arriving late from elsewhere and threatening to surround his forces. With this came news that French forces were moving towards his rear, just the position where hundreds of French captives were most likely being held by now. In such a situation, the massacring of these men appears, if not honourable, at least understandable. This interpretation would make the slaughter not an act of hot anger as Shakespeare would have us believe, a violent kneejerk reaction to a breach of chivalric conventions, but a cold, calculating, rational if brutal action, much more in accord with what we know of the personality of the king.

Those responsible for launching the raid behind Henry's lines were later named and singled out for acting dishonourably or at least stupidly in what they did even by French commentators like Monstrelet. He suggests that their actions were responsible for the slaughter that followed even more than the king of England was. As we have seen, the men included Robinet de Bourneville and Isambart de Agincourt, the latter clearly a man with good local knowledge.

The Duke of Burgundy later captured them and locked them up for a considerable time. This was despite their best efforts to ingratiate themselves with the Count of Charolais by presenting him with a magnificent sword, ornamented with diamonds, which had belonged to Henry. This and other rich jewels had been looted from Henry's baggage. It also appears possible that a number of horses were looted by the French for the English would soon come to regret the apparent abduction of them soon after the battle when they renewed their march to Calais.[16]

Shakespeare has his Henry saying that 'I was not angry since I came to France until this instant'[17] and there may be some element of truth in this. However, rather than anger at a dishonourable break with convention it appears more likely that it was the anger of frustration that inflamed the king and led to his peremptory actions fuelled by his fury that the French still stubbornly refused to accept the judgment of the Almighty.

Yet the fact that Shakespeare chose to present Henry's actions as being in hot anger reveals the feeling that there was uncomfortableness in some circles about the massacre. Shakespeare's version of events is an attempt to explain and justify the actions of someone who has been unrealistically painted as a chivalric paragon. The playwright presents it as a hot-tempered response to what was effectively a breach of chivalric convention by the French, in other words the opponent broke the rules of chivalry first. But these rules anyway were often reserved for the realms of medieval literature and, it has been remarked that relying on these as a benchmark for what actually happened in battle is rather like forming a view of the First World War by reading Captain Johns' Biggles series.[18]

In the context of the times, Henry could not be seen to be acting in an unchivalrous manner without justification as this was not the desired image for the king to portray. The opening lines of the famous *Agincourt Carol*, an anonymous musical work from the early fifteenth century, state boldly that 'our king went forth to Normandy/with grace and might of chivalry'. With such sentiments being expressed no unjustified breaches of chivalric convention could be allowed to besmirch the idealised image of the English monarch. With Agincourt, appearances were everything.

In Monstrelet's account of the battle, Henry announced his orders to his troops to kill the captives by means of trumpet calls. This is significant as of course to mean anything to those in earshot there must have been some prior notification of what such a signal would sound like and represent. This suggests that the king must have had some perception that it might be necessary to kill his prisoners. Such perceptions add support to the theory that there was a big numerical disparity between the two armies and that the English did not have the luxury of being able to devote a large group of men to looking after captives. The king may also have been anxious that his own men would be so concerned about protecting the captives, and the large bounty that they represented, that they would take their minds off winning the battle.

Tito Livio says that Henry, fearing a renewed attack from the French, also sent heralds to them, asking if they planned to launch another assault and telling them unambiguously that if they did so the prisoners he already held were to be slaughtered. Other chroniclers say that he began to do so in plain sight of the enemy as a way perhaps of confirming that he intended to go through with his threat.[19]

The killing began in brutal earnest. Scores of captured and unarmed Frenchmen were put to the sword, 'their necks and their faces cut' as Le Fèvre and Waurin described it.[20] Only the most important captives were saved, the Duke of Brabant not among them as he was not recognised for who he was. Some men were luckier than others. Gilbert de Lannoy (who was a close friend of the Duke of Brabant), locked up in a house, was not run through but was left to burn to death when his prison was set alight.

He managed to haul himself out and escape though he appears to have been too badly injured to do more than crawl a few feet away from the blazing house. He was soon recaptured but rather than being killed was sold on to John Cornwall (who seems to have been adept at collecting valuable prisoners). The moment of immediate crisis for the English had presumably passed by this stage and the slaughtering of prisoners had therefore halted. De Lannoy was an experienced knight and may have been recognised for the important figure that he was.

It was good for Henry that de Lannoy did survive. He was an excellent example of a man caught up in the divided loyalties that split France at the time. He was very much in the camp of the Duke of Burgundy and would later become chamberlain to Philippe the Good, successor to John the Fearless. When Henry V later cemented his claim to France, de Lannoy would undertake a mission for the king of England and erstwhile king of France by travelling to the Holy Land to see if the now defunct Kingdom of Jerusalem could be resurrected; Henry developed that archetypal obsession of medieval monarchs, the desire to lead a successful Crusade. All these future events hung on a very thin thread as de Lannoy, the epitome of chivalric ideals and a member of the Order of the Golden Fleece, stood on the verge of an abyss but was pulled back from the edge of it at the last moment.

Henry's likely motives in ordering the slaughter of the prisoners are referred to in the slightly later account of Tito Livio, who suggests that there were still a large number of Frenchmen who had not yet entered the battle but were about to:

Meanwhile the most prudent king sent heralds to the French of the new army asking whether they would come to fight or would leave the field, informing them that if they did not withdraw, or if they came to battle, all of the prisoners and any of them who might be captured, would all be killed by the sword with no mercy.[21]

This account adds to others which suggest that Henry, believing that his men could not survive another assault on a large scale, sent a coldly calculated threat to the French warning them off launching one. It was in effect a form of blackmail; desist from attacking again or your brothers-in-arms will die. It fits well with what we know of the personality of the king who was fearful of what another attack might bring. As it happened most of the leadership of the French army were by now dead or captured and the men at the rear, most of them from lower social ranks who had witnessed the slaughter of their countrymen, were in no mood for a fight, with a few exceptions.

The alternative interpretation to this cold and calculating thought process is that Henry, suddenly faced with the prospect of an attack on several fronts, simply panicked or even lashed out blindly in angry frustration at the unwelcome prospect that defeat would be plucked from the jaws of victory at the last minute. Either is plausible but given the character and personality of Henry the most likely reason for the massacre was that it was a calculated move to discourage the French from attacking again; and if this was indeed the aim, then it worked.

The threat from the rearguard, which was not yet committed to the battle, never came to fruition in a large-scale way though there were some small attacks that were subsequently launched. Most of the remaining Frenchmen did not want to fight; as one chronicler, a French priest from Rouen called Pierre Cochon, put it, 'all the men of lower ranks, who were enough to have beaten the English, were pushed to the rear'.[22] If they were not considered good enough to fight earlier on, why then should they be willing to probably die now? The aristocrats of France had wanted the glory of battle for themselves; they were welcome to it.

Most of the rearguard therefore headed off. 'The enemy ranks, having experienced the bitter taste of our missiles and with our king advancing towards them, by God's will abandoned to us that field of blood together with their wagons and other baggage-carts, many of these loaded with provisions and missiles, spears and bows.'[23] The wording suggests that the English were on the march again and what remained of the French army was about to break.

Some French prisoners did survive the massacre and it gave their captors their fifteen minutes of fame and a sizeable share in ransom payments. A man-at-arms by the name of William Wolf, in the retinue of the Earl of Arundel, took no less a person than Marshal Boucicaut as his prisoner while Ralph Fowne, in the retinue of Sir Ralph Shirley, captured the Duke of Bourbon. But many others were slain in the slaughter, their throats cut or their eyes gouged by the inappropriately named *misericordia*.

So what are we to read into this controversial moment in the battle? One of the leading modern historians who has added much to our understanding of Henry suggests that an analysis of his official correspondence reveals much in terms of his style; 'abrupt, to the point, clear and unequivocal'.[24] If we apply that same analysis to his decision-making in battle then the same characteristics appear here, in this action, which is also abrupt, to the point, clear and unequivocal.

The stern treatment of those held captive sent a message to other Frenchmen who were not yet committed to the battle; attack at your peril. It would appear that the message was clearly received and understood by the majority of the enemy. There would be no further attacks from the French on the muddy, bloody field of Agincourt. If the slaughter of the prisoners was highly controversial (more it must be said to later commentators than to those who wrote of the battle at the time), it was also seemingly successful in achieving its clear if brutal objectives.

Suggestions that this was a war crime (which have emerged particularly in modern times)[25] are completely anachronistic. There was no Geneva Convention in 1415, no War Crimes Tribunals. There were few written rules to refer to and conventions were exactly that, custom and practice that was in practice flexible in its interpretation. These were violent times with little protection for anyone unfortunate enough to be caught on the wrong side. Just the year before Agincourt was fought, the city of Soissons in the Champagne region had been brutally sacked after being captured; captives were massacred, nuns raped, citizens slain by the score. Yet these were atrocities committed not by English troops but by Frenchmen against their own countrymen.

The famous French chronicler Froissart had written of the fierceness of the Flemish as another near-contemporary example. They refused stubbornly to be taken alive in battle and 'if they think none of their men are prisoners, they will certainly put all their prisoners to death'. So if Henry's actions were harsh, they were certainly not uniquely so in the annals of the time.[26] At Dupplin Moor in 1332 wounded Scots were remorselessly finished off; in this earlier battle the regent of Scotland and the son of the late Robert Bruce, two earls, eighteen bannerets and fifty-eight knights were slain.[27]

One modern historian has said of the medieval 'rules' about the treatment of battlefield prisoners as being 'so selectively and individually applied as to be meaningless on many occasions' and that there was a 'limited application of the laws of war in the Middle Ages' and that 'they always deferred to the military imperative'.[28] This was what Henry would have seen his actions now as doing: deferring to the military imperative, doing what was required to win the battle. Such harsh decisions are made in all wars in all times.

It is a nonsense to suggest that the Battle of Agincourt somehow brought an end to the Age of Chivalry, a concept that in the main only ever existed in the Arthurian romances of Chrétien de Troyes and others of his ilk – certainly by the fifteenth century. For every occasion when a man acted chivalrously in real life (often when it cost him little to do so) another could be found when a so-called defender of chivalric virtues acted contrary to their precepts. The roll-call of medieval atrocities is long and it is impossible sometimes to morally allocate blame to one party or another and the moralist is instead left to proclaim 'a plague on both your houses'. Prominent historians suggest that the contradictions of chivalry are not just a subject for modern comment but were also remarked on at the time.[29]

Take for example the siege of Richard I's famous castle of Château Gaillard in 1203–4. Here the castle was defended by an Englishman, Roger de Lacy, who expelled local non-combatants from inside its walls as he did not have enough food to feed both them and the garrison. The first batches were let go by the French besiegers but subsequently, on the orders of King Philip II, they were prevented from leaving. When the next party evicted by de Lacy tried to leave they were shot at by French archers. They therefore spent the next four months, in winter, huddled beneath the castle walls between the English defenders and the French attackers with no food, a terrible ordeal in which many of them died. It could be argued that neither side, English nor French, was acting particularly chivalrously in this particular case.

This brutal scenario was to be repeated on a larger scale by

Henry V himself when besieging the city of Rouen in 1418-9, an event that also saw a heavy use of large guns and became a byword for the brutality of the age. Soon after, at the siege of Montereau in 1420, Henry paraded captured prisoners before the town who exhorted those still holding out to surrender. The English king had threatened to hang the prisoners if the defenders did not give up the fight. When the town failed to respond, Henry had no compunction in executing the prisoners as threatened.[30] As one eminent historian remarked of the period, 'War was savage, and codes of chivalry did little to soften its impact.'[31]

The earlier years of the Hundred Years War saw an escalation in such violence. King Edward III and in particular his son the Black Prince introduced a concept of total war that reset the rules of fighting. While they espoused the concept of chivalry (after all, it was the king who established that ultimatum symbol of English chivalry, the Order of the Garter), it was chivalry on their terms. The prince would introduce a violence into his raiding activities in France that had nothing to do with chivalric virtue. In response, the French had adopted their own version of un-chivalric tactics, in particular through the efforts of the inspirational though lowborn (and therefore in the context of the time low-ranking in terms of chivalry) military leader Bertrand de Guesclin.

It was true that the era of the Lancastrian kings in England had already been marked by some harsh actions. The removal of Richard II, though not the first example of regicide in English history, was undoubtedly shocking. The execution of Archbishop Scrope was seen by some as an abhorrent act against a cleric. The burning of Lollards under the current king's rule was another example of a stern monarch in action as was the prompt execution of the Southampton plotters earlier in 1415. England was heading rapidly towards the bitter infighting of the romantically misnamed Wars of the Roses where battles were routinely followed by public executions of noblemen from the losing side.

To say that these were violent times seems something of a cliché; yet it is also the truth. It has been suggested that violent crimes in medieval England were recorded at a rate of twenty per 100,000, about ten times the rate in the nineteenth century. Ironically such offences went down in England during the period of the Hundred Years War as violence was deflected abroad and many potential criminals were busy fighting against the French rather than inflicting themselves on their fellow countrymen and women.[32]

There was a record of atrocities between French and English in the past. When Philip Augustus of France and Richard I of England had fought against each other, the French king executed a number of Welsh mercenaries taken in arms. In response Richard had directed that 300 prisoners be thrown to their deaths from the cliffs of Chateau Gaillard. He had also infamously ordered the slaughter of 4,000 unarmed prisoners after the capture of Acre on the Third Crusade, though in the eyes of contemporaries perhaps the horror of this had been diminished somewhat by the fact that the victims were Muslim rather than Christian.

One French writer, commenting later on Agincourt, suggested that the terrible losses there were a punishment from God for the sacrilegious actions of his countrymen at Soissons in 1414, saying that it was 'because of their acts of cruelty and impiety' that 'this disaster was divinely inflicted'.[33] It is perhaps appropriate in this respect that, when the English were about to take Harfleur earlier in the campaign, the Bishop of Bangor cried out, 'Fear not, the King of England has not come to waste your lands; we are good

Christians and Harfleur is not Soissons.' It was very appropriate that Saints Crispin and Crispinian hailed from the city.

There were supposed to be rules in place to protect knights in particular from slaughter in cold blood once they were prisoners. Knights went through deeply symbolic dubbing ceremonies which made them to an extent brothers in arms. This did not however mean that they were inevitably safe from death on the field of battle if they were captured. Several types of war were distinguished; in *guerre mortelle,* war to the death, mercy could not be expected even after capture, while in *bellum hostile* it could be. The latter made sense from a monetary perspective – a rich knight was worth far more alive than dead – but the French themselves sought to set the rules by unfurling the blood-red *Oriflamme* as they had done at Crécy and Poitiers though probably, some historians suggest, not at Agincourt even though King Charles had symbolically handed it over at St Denis earlier in the year.[34]

Contemporary commentators made little of Henry's actions in killing the prisoners, even those whose loyalties were towards France rather than England. Harsh though his actions were, they were not unique either before or after the battle. There had been a slaughter of prisoners on both sides at the Battle of Derval in 1373. The English would later massacre Armagnac prisoners in January 1420 even though they were marching under a safe conduct and in the same month the Duke of Alençon would do the same to English captives he had taken.[35]

Perhaps the latter massacres had something of a tit-for-tat element to them and herein was one of the dangers of Henry's actions. A ruler who had shown such pitilessness to men who had been taken in battle could expect his own soldiers to be treated in the same way if they fell into enemy hands.

Despite the fact that the concept of chivalry was at its peak, with some of its greatest advocates like the Duke of Berry alive at the time of Agincourt, the fifteenth century was to be as violent as any other in those tumultuous times. Within half a century, Englishmen would be slaughtering not French opponents but their fellow countrymen in their own civil war.

History, though, makes us what we are, and events that we have personally been involved with do so more than any other. Perhaps as the Battle of Agincourt reached its crucial moments another earlier confrontation played itself out in Henry's memory. Maybe his mind went back to that moment when as a young and inexperienced warrior he, then Prince of Wales, had been present at the Battle of Shrewsbury, an unforgettable experience not least because of the scar that disfigured him as a result of his arrow wound in the cheek. That had been a violent, brutal battle in which little quarter had been given. It had been hard-fought and at its conclusion one of the king's commanders, Sir John Stanley, had been asked what should be done with the prisoners that had been taken.

Stanley's reply had been unambiguous and chilling, just three words: 'Burn and slay.'[36] Perhaps twelve years later, this was the unequivocal message that replayed itself in Henry's mind. Shrewsbury had been a harsh proving ground, part of a whole process of growing up that had been an especially stern education. It had made the king what he was, determined to the point of ruthlessness, stern to the point of mercilessness and, above all else, convinced of his own rights, supported as he saw them by the Almighty Himself.

In the aftermath of the Battle of Shrewsbury those leading rebels who had been taken alive were executed in a precursor to what would become the norm in the Wars of the Roses half a century later. Their official crime was treason, rebellion against their rightful king, but their real crime was to resist the claims of Henry IV to the crown of England. If that king's son, now Henry V, truly believed that his claims to the throne of France reflected the will of God, then his enemies at Agincourt were also rebels, stubbornly refusing to acquiesce to what the Chinese would call the Mandate of Heaven. As such, their lives were forfeit.

Perhaps another lesson from earlier life also loomed large, that moment when Owen Glendower had come to the relief of Aberystwyth when its fall seemed certain. On that occasion defeat had been snatched from the jaws of victory. The king, older and wiser now, had clearly decided that there would be no repetition on the field of Agincourt.

In effect the king was employing a tactic that many commanders before or since would recognise: terror. The medieval period saw the excesses of Genghis Khan who unashamedly used it as a way of cowing those who were inclined to resist him into submission. Alexander the Great, that paragon from Antiquity, had all the defenders of the city of Tyre crucified once he took it. Richard I sent an unequivocal message to his opponents in the Holy Land by his massacre of prisoners at Acre. So did the largely French Crusade which sacked the city of Béziers in the south of France so thoroughly in 1209 that perhaps 20,000 people died, a number of them orthodox Catholic men, women and children slaughtered by their co-religionists even as they sought sanctuary in their churches.

Chivalry was only ever a very flimsy set of principles on which to rely. But if anything it was by now increasingly an anachronism anyway. The brutal nature of warfare during the Hundred Years

War and the rise of nationalistic fervour in both France and England had made it less and less relevant to the battlefield. The views of a French poet and political writer, Alain Chartier, writing soon after the battle were summarised by the modern historian Richard Barber in the following terms, noting that Chartier 'is not so convinced of the value of chivalry itself' and goes on to say that

> he sees it as a decoration for tournaments and feasts, best left to heralds and masters of ceremonies, and when in the *Livre des quatres dames* he attacks the French knights it is for their lack of martial virtues ... He sees love of luxury as the chief reason for the defeat of French knighthood, an accusation already made by Honoré Bonet in his *Tree of Battles*. Not only did the knights lead a life of ease, but they regarded war as a means of obtaining wealth, in which robbery and pillage were more important than fighting the enemy, and their mercenary nature is underlined. Besides this, he has no time for the international aspects of chivalry: a knight's job is to fight his country's foes, not fraternise with them, and patriotism is one of his greatest virtues. He sums up by blaming lack of loyalty, inadequate spending on military matters and lack of good counsel as the causes of the disaster.[37]

This analysis fits very well with the ruthlessness of Henry V on the battlefield of Agincourt. It was military expediency that dictated Henry's actions and they were successful in cementing his triumph. Whether or not the end justifies the means is an argument for ethicists; it is unlikely that the king felt many qualms about it.

Given his temperament, it is unlikely that the massacre of the prisoners bothered Henry very much at all. His pronouncements, or at least those of his sympathetic chroniclers after the battle, suggested that he considered that the French were to blame for their own losses as the battle had been fought because of their refusal to accept the will of God. The massacre of the prisoners worked as the battle stopped soon after. Whatever else might be said of it, his harsh actions at what was a decisive stage of the battle secured victory for Henry. As such the cold-blooded slaughter of the prisoners might not have been in keeping with the ideal of chivalry, though this hardly makes him unique in these paradoxical times. It may not have been right, but, whatever else might be said of it, it was certainly effective.

11

AGINCOURT: THE FINAL RECKONING
(1 P.M. TO 4 P.M., 25 OCTOBER 1415)

He hath bent his bow and made it ready, and in it He hath
prepared the instruments of death.

Psalm 7:12–17

Despite the understandable reticence of the rearguard to fight, there appears to have been one final assault by the French in an attempt to yet achieve something from the battle. Monstrelet noted that the counts of Marle and Fauquemberg and the lords of Louvroy and Chin still had about six hundred men-at-arms who had not yet been committed to the battle. With these 'they made a gallant charge on the English; but it availed nothing, for they were all killed or made prisoners'. Elsewhere the same chronicler noted that there were other small bodies of French still fighting; 'but they were soon routed, slain, or taken.' In other words, all these later attacks succeeded in doing was adding to the roll-call of the dead or those taken captive.

The battle was effectively over, this time definitively, and the rear-guard 'departed with great sadness at their shame',[1] though for the many common soldiers in those ranks the sense of relief would far outweigh any limited embarrassment; chivalry and glory had little to do with them after all. In Monstrelet's version of events, even now the sire de Longny drew near late on with 600 reinforcements. When still about a league off he met a number of wounded Frenchmen retreating who told him that the battle was lost and he therefore turned himself and his men around. Even to the great ~~and the good of~~ France, chivalry had its limits.

Throughout the battle the heralds of both England and France stood side by side in an unusual display of neutrality and camaraderie, looking on as their countrymen hacked the life out of each other (the Pseudo-Elmham chronicler states that the English king told them specifically not to bear arms in the battle but to concentrate on their heraldic role).[2]

They had an important part to play in events, one which went far beyond the ceremonial. At the start of the battle, they would help marshal the troops together. During it they could be used to relay messages to the opponent's commander. At its end they played a key role in identifying the dead and seriously wounded. It was then that heraldry came into its own as each noble wore his own specific badges of honour. The heralds were well versed in recognising these distinguishing features. Perhaps chivalry did have a kind of limited usefulness after all.

Heralds had a respected role which set them apart from other men around the battlefield. They were given a form of what we might now call 'diplomatic immunity',[3] even when the battle was in full swing. It was in many ways a privileged position given the extreme violence of battle and the general free-for-all of the melee that epitomised large-scale if relatively rare confrontations such as that at Agincourt. Primarily the heralds' role was a dual one, messenger and observer.

As the battle appeared to be drawing towards a close, one of the French heralds, Montjoie king of arms, was summoned by Henry to declare a winner of the battle. It was an interesting instruction capable of several interpretations; maybe Henry really was not clear or maybe he wished the French to concede defeat. Montjoie king of arms conceded that the battle was won by the English. Henry then asked him for the name of the nearby castle he could see. The reply came that it was named Agincourt. So, said the king, would the battle be called. The Battle of Agincourt was therefore given its name, one that has in the main stuck ever since.

This story does not ring wholly true, for the name did not take in England at once. For several years the English seemed unsure what to call it at all, for example naming it 'the battle in Picardy'. Even in France there was some confusion, with the battle given various names at first as well as 'Agincourt', for example that of 'Hesdin', 'Maisoncelle' (almost as close to the battlefield as the village of Agincourt) or 'Blagny',[4] though so humiliating was the defeat that many preferred to refer to it euphemistically as 'the accursed day'. 'Agincourt' later came into common usage in England but it would be some time before the name became synonymous with the glorious victory of Henry V on the muddy fields of north-west France.

These slightly surreal discussions on the field of battle between the herald and the king (and not every chronicler mentions them by any means, so they may not have taken place at all) could not detract from the horror of the carnage itself. The dead lay strewn thickly across the field though the large majority of them were not English. The English chroniclers typically failed to agree on a figure for their own losses, though none of them suggests that the total killed exceeded one hundred by very much. French chroniclers in contrast record a figure of up to six hundred for the English dead.

The very small numbers of the dead given by the English chroniclers were necessary to give the impression of a miraculous victory that owed more to divine intervention than any act of man. Shakespeare names four nobles and esquires slain and twenty-five others as being the sum total of the dead. He also picked up the theme of this being an Act of God rather than man, by having the English king say, when informed of the casualties, 'O God, thy arm was here; And not to us, but to thy arm alone, Ascribe we all! When, without stratagem, But in plain shock and even play of battle, Was ever known so great and little loss on one part and on the other? Take it, God, For it is none but thine!'[5]

The contrast in the scale of the losses therefore became part of the miracle of Agincourt. The small numbers of English dead juxtaposed to the massive number of the French as a result also became a core part of the English mythology of the battle. God's sanction needed to be apparent in the victory of Agincourt and the huge contrast in numbers lost was a perfect way of demonstrating it.

Stories of the miraculously low English losses developed quickly. Within a few weeks the Mayor and Aldermen of Salisbury were contrasting the large French losses with the tiny number of casualties the English army had suffered, mentioning just fifteen men lost.[6] The king, as commander of that army, knew better than anyone that this was not true; it would turn out that the Duke of York's contingent had lost nearly one hundred men on its own. But he also knew that presenting this as a miraculous triumph showed the battle to be nothing less than a judgement of God and a vindication of the king's right to rule in both England and France.

If the chroniclers would give varying estimates of the dead from Henry's army, there was more unanimity among them concerning the precise identity of some of those killed on the English side. The greatest of them, of course, was the Duke of York, who had (in some accounts) died a hero's death, falling beneath the 'whirlwind of war'.[7] There were alternative versions of his death, some saying that he had been killed by a head wound, others that he had suffocated.

The nineteenth-century writer Sir Charles Oman said of York that the duke was 'a man of forty-five years and corpulent' and that 'he died of exhaustion without receiving a wound', though accounts suggesting that he was overweight did not appear until the sixteenth century.[8] On the other hand, Monstrelet's account states that it was the Duke of Alençon who killed him shortly before taking on the King of England and losing his own life as a result. A ballad of 1443 said of the duke's death how 'his bascinet to his brain was bent',[9] suggesting either a heroic death or a desire to believe that he had had one. Perhaps we may be forgiven for hoping that the Duke of York died fighting as a gallant man-at-arms (as opposed to suffocating) on the field of Agincourt. We may no longer think that the nature of his end was important, but he most certainly would.

Like many of the more prominent warriors in Henry's ranks, York had made out his will before the campaign. He wished to be buried in the church of St Mary and All Saints at Fotheringay, of which he had been a sponsor and where a later monarch, Queen Elizabeth I, would erect a memorial in his honour (much to the queen's disgust the previous monument had been destroyed during the Reformation of Henry VIII). This was near to the castle which would become most famous as the place where Mary, Queen of Scots was executed. The duke gave orders that the cost of his funeral was not to exceed £100.[10] A sword and a dagger was left to the king for whose cause he had died. His wife, Philippa, was to have his bed (which was decorated with feathers and leopards), some tapestries, silver vessels and various other items of furniture.

Neither were his servants forgotten: £2 10s for each esquire, £1 to each of his lesser men and half a mark to each page. Masses were to be said for his soul to ease his passage through purgatory and from there to a glorious Life Everlasting; pragmatic and hedging his bets even in death, both Richard II and Henry IV were to be mentioned in these too, as well as his father Edmund of York. A horse was to be given to Sir John Popham, a man-at-arms in his entourage and the son of the keeper of Southampton Castle, in which his own brother had been condemned to death by the court of the king in whose service he had died.

York's will therefore contained several allusions to the complicated political times in which he lived, in which he had somehow managed to walk a tightrope from which Richard, Earl of Cambridge, had fallen spectacularly. Both men were now dead, one in circumstances of the greatest ignominy and the other with a halo of heroism and glory lighting up his reputation, but both dead nonetheless. They might have gone to their graves with a greater sense of pride if they only knew that within half a century a Yorkist relative would be King of England.[11] Ironically if the Earl of Cambridge had only bided his time for another few months, everything that he ever wanted would now have been his due to the death of his brother.

Also killed was the young Michael de la Pole, Earl of Suffolk, whose premature demise perhaps marked the most tragic loss on the English side as he had only inherited the title two months back when his father had died of dysentery at Harfleur. He was only twenty years old and by the conventions of the time still a minor. This was a sad campaign for the Suffolks and the title now passed to Michael's younger brother William. He in turn would meet a tragic end. In the build-up to the Wars of the Roses he became a deeply divisive figure and was captured while fleeing into exile and beheaded, and his decapitated corpse left on the sands near Dover. The first half of the fifteenth century was not a universally successful time for the Suffolks.

Two newly dubbed knights also died at Agincourt. They were Sir Richard Kyghley, a Lancashire knight, and David ap Llewelyn, Shakespeare's 'Davy Gamm'. The latter as we have seen was a long-time supporter of the Lancastrian cause in Wales and a prominent member of the gentry in the south-east Marches of the country (he hailed from Brecon).[12] Then there were an unknown number of others, including archers; we know the names of a few of them, such as Stephen Gerneyng, who was in Erpingham's company.[13] One archer, by the name of Roger Hunt, a member of James Harrington's company (the same group that had been involved in the riotous behaviour in Salisbury when four citizens were killed in a brawl), was killed by a field gun.[14]

Kyghley's men were certainly involved in something of a scrap. He had led two companies of men to France. From the first of these, composed of five men-at-arms and eighteen archers, one man-at-arms had died of disease, two had returned home sick and four archers as well as Kyghley had died in the battle. Of the second company of fifty, the picture had been more mixed. Six died of sickness at Harfleur and ten had been invalided home.

Eight remained in the garrison at Harfleur and all the others survived the battle, though seven had been taken prisoner on 24 October in the skirmishing that took place on that day.[15]

Others were of course injured. The king's brother, Humphrey, Duke of Gloucester, was in the thick of the fighting and was badly wounded. However, he would be taken to Calais and would recover and outlive Henry by several decades. He would later be Lord Protector for his infant nephew Henry VI when his brother died before his time in 1422.

Whatever their full extent, the English losses were small when compared to those of the French. With the fighting over, the *Gesta* chronicler tells us that 'we who had gained the victory came back through the masses, the mounds and the heaps of the slain'.[16] The milk of human kindness was sadly lacking from him, though. As he looked at the piles of the dead, he blamed their own actions for their fate. The English, he said, had no wish for a fight and it was the impetuous impulses of the French that had led to their doom. If this was a supposedly Christian writer, it was the God of the Old Testament rather than the New that inspired him.

Men had died horrible deaths. Battlefield victims recovered from graves in England from the medieval period show a disproportionate number of head wounds in evidence as swords or axes had come crashing down into the skull. There were also a surprising number of shinbone fractures, perhaps where legs had been hacked at to bring a man down and incapacitate him before finishing him off. But what took place on 25 October 1415 may not have been typical; as one writer has remarked, 'at Agincourt more men probably died by suffocation or by having their throats cut when lying on the ground than actually in battle'.[17]

The battlefield was not a pretty sight. Pillagers were now

stripping the dead, wounded and captured of everything of value. Many of the casualties, however illustrious or distinguished, were stripped of everything save the merest basics that would be enough to cover their modesty.

Nor was it apparently just the English who were responsible for the looting. The French chronicler Monstrelet wrote that peasants, both men and women, from the surrounding villages were helping themselves to what they could.[18] After all, it was likely that some of them had been on the wrong ending of looting and profiteering from their social superiors in France and they were merely returning in kind what had been meted out to them. They searched the hedges and the bushes and pulled out men still alive and struck the last breath of life out of them before taking away their horses, their armour, their money and anything else of value that they could lay their hands on.[19]

It was a terrible vision of devastation and destruction; there was 'not a man with heart of flesh or even of stone who, had he seen and pondered on the horrible deaths and bitter wounds of so many Christian men, would not have dissolved into tears, time and again, for grief'.[20] And back in those very different times, the fact that the slain were Christians really mattered. The letting of Christian blood was not to be taken lightly; killing Infidel Muslims on Crusader battlefields was completely acceptable; the taking of Christian lives, on the other hand, was a point of the gravest seriousness for which those responsible would one day be judged against the harshest of standards, not in this world but the next.

During the particularly violent days of the eleventh century, when the Church had been so upset at the levels of strife that rather than abolish violence it sought to direct it – a process that led among other things to the Crusades – much thought had been given to what was acceptable and what was not. The Council of Narbonne had decreed in 1054, 'Let no Christian kill another Christian, for there is no doubt that he who kills a Christian sheds the blood of Christ.' Such sentiments worried Henry and he and his supporting chroniclers were keen to emphasise that the French were responsible for the battle being fought and not him. The king was probably trying to convince himself of the justice of his cause as much as he was trying to convince Christendom.

However, what was also in evidence here was that the nature of warfare in Western Europe had changed out of all recognition in the past century. Typically battles in the region in earlier times had seen much lower levels of casualties. In the twelfth-century wars in France involving English troops, noble casualties in particular had been very slight. Only when an enemy regarded as 'savage' and therefore not worthy of concern was involved, such as at the Battle of the Standard, had the number of men killed been high. But the Hundred Years War had changed all that. The battlefields of Crécy and Poitiers had been littered with French dead. This was total war, nasty, brutal and with little quarter given. Edward III had thrown down the gauntlet and Henry had picked it up.

But for a pious monarch such as Henry V, the killing of fellow Christians was a matter of no little significance. The *Gesta* chronicler specifically alluded to this conundrum: 'Our England therefore has reason to rejoice at the victory gained and the deliverance of her men, and reason to grieve for the suffering and destruction wrought in the deaths of Christians.' As a pious and orthodox Christian, the chronicler also hoped that the people of England would ponder on the lessons to be learned from the battle and stamp out heresy once and for all.[21] Henry, though, duly gave thanks to God for his triumph and ordered that from this moment on the two saints Crispin and Crispinian should be included in the Masses he heard every single day.[22]

Among the dead on the other side was the flower of French chivalry, including the dukes of Bar, Alençon and Brabant, who had made such frantic efforts to reach the battle and paid for it with his life. Brabant was a brother of John the Fearless, the Duke of Burgundy, as was Philip, the Count of Nevers, who was also killed, destined to fight just one disastrous battle in his short life. This emphasises the fact that, however divided France might be because of the internecine struggle between Armagnacs and Burgundians, for one day at least they had to some extent come together. It was a brief and fragile reunion. In the aftermath of this infamous defeat, chroniclers supporting one party or the other would try frantically hard to deflect blame for it on to their opponents.

The roll call of the French dead was overwhelming. There were four other counts and ninety barons and bannerets slain as well as Charles d'Albret, the Constable of France.[23] There were also allegedly 1,500 knights dead and 5,000 other French gentlemen along with them.[24] It was a hammer blow to France, not just to the Armagnacs but to the Burgundians too. It would take decades to recover the losses. Also among the slain was the Archbishop of Sens, who had played a full and active part in the hand-to-hand fighting, 'dealing blows on the enemy to right and left' before he too was struck down.[25]

How large the death toll of the French actually was will probably never be known. If grave pits were discovered that would help approximate a scale of the losses but not exact numbers. Unfortunately, no substantial remains have ever been found to suggest that the grave pits have been discovered, even leading to some suggestions that the battle was not actually fought at the traditional site at all.[26]

On the French side, though, accounts of at least 4,000 dead appeared early on and a figure in this vicinity may be in the right area. If the French really had an army of about 12,000 there, some of which would not have been engaged, this is an extraordinary casualty rate. However, it may be possible because of the restricted size of the battle area and also the ferocity of the fighting, not to mention any alleged massacre of prisoners. We have many details of the French nobles killed but not much attention was paid at the time to the hundreds and thousands of others who lay dead for the simple fact that no one really bothered about them.

The English on the other hand suffered – if we believe the chroniclers already quoted – a handful of deaths. The most common figure is around thirty, though some push it up to just over a hundred. We do not have accounts or other records which give more reliable numbers to back up the chroniclers in total but we do have records of those killed in the Duke of York's retinue of ninety. This is a 10 per cent death rate as a proportion of the men he had with him. It was probably not replicated everywhere as the duke's men were quite possibly under greater pressure than anyone else; after all, their leader was killed in the fight.

But York's retinue would not be the only company under pressure. Some French chroniclers give much higher figures for the English dead, some suggesting around six hundred killed. This is a 7.5 per cent death rate and not out of kilter with the Duke of York's losses. This is more consistent with the accounts of closely fought hand-to-hand fighting that have survived. Such a situation does not accord very well with the picture of the miraculous victory of Agincourt that some of the chroniclers try to portray but is probably much closer to reality nevertheless.

It appears certain that, taken as a whole, thousands of lives were lost by both sides combined. One thing most chroniclers agree about was that this was a particularly bloody battle. Corpses lay strewn in heaps in the confines of the battlefield and here and there wounded men struggled to catch a breath or to get away from the hands of the enemy, usually without success.

These were stomach-churning scenes for most people to witness but to some this was a very profitable day indeed. A number of important members of the French aristocracy had been taken prisoner and William Wolf, as we have seen, had obtained custody of no less a man than John de Boucicaut, the Marshal of France. Boucicaut would join the ranks of those lucky enough to survive the battle but unlucky enough to be faced with the prospect of obtaining a large ransom before he would taste freedom again. In fact, Agincourt would mark the effective end of his military career as he would die, still captive, in Methley, Yorkshire, on 29 June 1421.[27]

There were a number of other important Frenchmen taken prisoner too. As well as Marshal Boucicaut there were the dukes of Orléans and Bourbon and the counts of Richemont (the second son of the Duke of Brittany), Vendôme and Eu. Richemont was lucky; perhaps because of the position of the Duke of Brittany, whom Henry had attempted to woo in advance of the Agincourt campaign, as well as family connections with Henry through his mother, he was the only one of the important prisoners to be ransomed before Henry's death in 1422.

On the other hand, the Count of Eu had been marked out as a potential troublemaker and he was 'bought' by Henry from the man who had captured him, Sir John Grey of Ruthin, for the substantial sum of 1,000 marks.[28] Henry then ordered that on no account was the count (who had succeeded to his title when only three years old) to be released before Henry's son, the future Henry VI of England, had come of age. The count would not taste freedom again until 1438, nearly a quarter of a century later.[29] He returned home to Eu, where he lived on for over three more decades before he finally died in 1472, marrying twice but not having any children to succeed him. His magnificent effigy can still be seen in the family vault in the collegiate church at Eu, a special place which is a veritable treasure trove of his dynasty's history during these dramatic years.

Richemont was perhaps lucky to survive as he had clearly been in the thick of the fighting. He was found buried but alive beneath a pile of corpses, his coat of arms being splattered in blood but recognisable enough still to identify him. He was taken to Henry, who was delighted to see that he had survived the battle; he would have had some explaining to do to his stepmother if this had not been so. The fate of Richemont's brother, the Duke of Brittany, was in some respects kinder. According to some accounts he was still at Amiens, some miles to the south, when the battle was fought and therefore avoided Henry's army. On the other hand, some of those in a different faction to him inevitably suggested that his actions (or inactions) that day were rather inglorious and entirely deliberate; given the time he had had to get to Agincourt, they are probably right.

The prisoners included a fair number of the leading men of France, though so did the roll call of the dead. However, the *Gesta* records that there were few other men of gentle birth among the captives other than those named above.[30] This almost certainly reflects the ruthless efficiency with which many of the prisoners had been killed on the king's orders. Walsingham records a figure of seven hundred Frenchmen taken prisoner; French chroniclers go up to 1,500, but either way there was a huge bias towards the number of the dead as opposed to those taken captive.[31]

Much ink has been spilt discussing the size of the casualty lists at the battle. Chroniclers are notorious for understating or overstating numbers in the interests of making a point or two. However, it is one thing to argue about numbers of largely faceless casualties in the hundreds and thousands, quite another to play fast and loose with the truth about named individuals. When we are told that a significant number of leading men of France were dead after the battle and they are named then at least we can be confident that this is broadly right. The death toll was very large indeed, but to give it some context it is perhaps worth bearing in mind that the Battle of Towton, fought in 1461, was probably the bloodiest in British history with a remarkable 28,000 assumed dead.

The number of the dead was nevertheless proportionately very high indeed, and perhaps here we can get a sharper insight into what happened in the battle. Imagine the scene before it was fought. There stood a great French army faced with something that looked little different from a rabble in much of its parts. For decades the French had studiously avoided open battle with English invasion forces, chastened by the hammer blows of Crécy and Poitiers. When the English came to France, the French largely fought on the retreat, hoping that the gale blowing across their country would blow itself out – and it usually did.

For a proud race like the French, especially a nation that prided itself on being the epitome of all that was chivalrous and glorious, fighting on the back foot like this would sting and call into question their sense of honour. But they saw Agincourt as the chance for retribution, for redemption, for a resurrection of all that was glorious in France, especially when they seemed to hold so many advantages.

It seemed too good a chance to miss, and the flower of French chivalry, smelling the prospect of such glory, almost fought each other to get at the English. In the process the humbler men, not real fighting men as perhaps the French nobles would see it, were pushed to the back. It was the cream of France that rushed forward, that fell pierced by English arrows or collapsed exhausted under the weight of an avalanche of blows from swords, from axes, from mallets, from anything hard and heavy that came to the hands of the English.

Divided under the weak leadership of an inexperienced and impetuous command structure, the numerical supremacy of the French forces had fuelled hubris and overconfidence. Seeing the size of their advantage, the French army had believed that the prize was there for the taking. But an astute Scottish chronicler, Andrew Wyntoun, who produced a history of Scotland in the 1420s, wrote that men should not be overconfident if they are wise, 'for underrating [the enemy] and overconfidence leads to defeat'.[32] Although he was referring to Scottish defeats against English archers such as that at Dupplin Moor it is tempting to speculate that his work and observations, coming just a few years after Agincourt, had been partly inspired by the outcome of that more recent battle.

In the meantime the undervalued hoi polloi of the French army watched on, in one sense horrified, in another relieved to be out of it. There was little remaining French leadership to tell them what to do anyway and they had no desire to expose themselves to slaughter. Why should they? They had seen their betters struck down by the score and they themselves were indeed in comparison a 'rabble'; only a terrible fate seemed to await them. So probably the majority of the rank and file wisely stayed out of it and lived to fight – or more probably to farm – another day, for these were not men trained for war but little better in too many cases than poorly trained conscripts.

The major difference between the armies was the proportion of men-at-arms to archers on either side. The French relied on the 'great ~~and the good~~' of the military and social establishment and it was they who provided the bulk of the French fighting forces, which was a tactic that played into the hands of the enemy. The bowmen and crossbowmen of the French army played virtually no part in the battle and therefore for whatever reason did not appear to have been highly rated by those in command.

In contrast, the English common man was valued for his military skills by his social superiors. Encouraged, or rather virtually forced, to train with the bow, he was a very different proposition. His skills were lethal in a battlefield environment. Strangely, later writers would in some ways undervalue their part. Finding a mention of the archers in Shakespeare's *Henry V* is a very difficult task indeed. The Bard played up the role of the nobles in the English army; it is the Earl of Westmorland who asks the king did he not wish for 10,000 extra men, not the much humbler Hungerford. The archers are almost entirely conspicuous by their absence.[33]

Perhaps this reflected the reputation of English archers by the time that Shakespeare wrote the play, for by then the 'longbow' was a thing of the past. Those who fought to maintain the old prominence of the weapon during the sixteenth century had by now lost the battle. Repeated attempts to make the yeomen of England practice their archery had not worked.

Another sixteenth-century writer, William Harrison, complained that French and German opponents now mocked the English because of the decline of their archers, presenting their posteriors to them when faced by them in battle; in immortal words, Harrison protested that, in Edward III's time, 'the breech of such a varlet should have been nailed to his bum with one arrow, and another feathered in his bowels before he should have turned round about to see who had shot the first'.[34].

But however much the English people loved the works of their country's greatest literary genius, in the longer run they were not so prepared to forget the role of humbler men. Among the strongest memories of the modern film versions of Shakespeare's great play, the most striking are the battle scenes with the clouds of arrows sweeping across the field. Shakespeare did not pen this in his drama; it was the spoken lines that mattered for him, not the battle scenes. But modern cinema in some ways righted a wrong by emphasising the role of the humble archer, the yeomen of England, to whom much of the glory of victory belonged.

It has become fashionable to ascribe our view of Agincourt to Shakespeare, but this is somewhat unfair on him. His play impacts our view of Henry V far more than it does of Agincourt itself. For the clouds of arrows blackening the sky or the serried ranks of French cavalry charging rather stupidly at the English archers, safe and sound behind their hedge of stakes, we should blame not him but Laurence Olivier, not just as actor but more crucially as director of the 1944 epic film production of the play.

Shakespeare did not leave stage directions for how the fight should be presented and what we see is Olivier's view of the battlefield and the course of events there. Context naturally accounts for much, and the depiction of the common men of England winning an unlikely triumph against a much bigger enemy, albeit one that was somewhat awkwardly by this stage an English ally, fitted the mood music of 1944 – with its D-Day invasion and ongoing heavy fighting in Europe afterwards – rather well.

It is interesting to note that Henry's pre-Agincourt speech in the play was printed in full in some British newspapers during the Battle of Loos in 1915, the 500th anniversary of the battle though it was in the Second World War that the play was really milked for all it was worth [35]. Of course, when Olivier's Henry V led his archers into battle in the film version of that year, the world which he was playing to was very different from that of the man he was portraying. The Second World War is no doubt an anachronistic comparator for the Hundred Years War. Though there is a large amount of evidence that Henry V was successful in selling the expedition to France as a great patriotic enterprise – and these were times when such emotions were definitely on the increase in the country – the 'yeomen' of England were not really comparable with their fellows half a millennium later.

For although there was real change following the economic downturn that post-dated the Black Death, it was an evolutionary process that would take centuries to come to fruition as a result of critical events such as the great civil wars of the seventeenth century or the reform movements of the nineteenth. There were light years rather than half a millennium between the world of 1415 and 1944.

It is also necessary to remind ourselves that Henry V was a man of his time and not ours. He was driven by piety, or at least a sense of the righteousness of his cause, as the foundation of his great ambition. He was also a man with a ruthless inner core, capable of taking decisive but brutal action, far removed from any liberal tendencies which would be widely considered as desirable attributes in modern times.

The technology of war was very different too, of course, when we compare the two periods. But there is certainly one comparator of sorts with the conflicts of the twentieth century, for there was an insurmountable opponent that impacted greatly on the outcome of both Agincourt in 1415 and the terrible battles that tore the Somme region apart almost exactly five hundred years later – cloying, sucking, glutinous mud. It slowed the French down to a virtual standstill, sapped the energy out of them, held them in a tentacle-like grip and slowed them down to a ponderous crablike crawl. The weather, the teeming rain that soaked the English to the skin and started to squeeze the life out of them, in the final analysis turned out to be one of their greatest allies.

Here was an opponent that made the challenges facing the French too great to overcome and played into the hands of their foe. It would take some minutes for the French to cross the killing zone, through that hail of arrows, dodging the bodies of fallen comrades, before they could come face to face with the English. By the time that they had completed this harrowing journey they would have been tired and frightened and morale must have been starting to plummet.

Enter then the English at close quarters, especially the archers, now assuming their role as light infantry, tired themselves no doubt but not weighed down with heavy armour, nimbler than their opponents, able to dart around much more quickly. It had been then that the archers, alongside their own relatively heavily armoured men-at-arms, who had not had to march cross the field to enter the fray through a cloudburst of arrows, administered the coup-de-grace to their outfought and outthought opponents, this time through close-quarter hacking and slashing weapons rather than their long-distance arrows.

In 1415 the outcome of the battle was by anyone's measure a stunning success, and the hand of God was inevitably seen to be present in the judgment of victory at Agincourt. The *Gesta* chronicler saw it as the French getting their just desserts; 'except you will be converted, He will brandish his sword; He hath bent his bow and made it ready, and in it He hath prepared the instruments of death'.[36] The instruments of death? King David's psalm could have been written for an archer. The English, the *Gesta* writer averred, had justice on their side and the French had, as he put it, been 'delivered up, indiscriminately, to flight, to capture, or to the sword'. Such was the stern judgement of God and of his instrument, Henry V, King of England and France.

Just how great this triumph was in terms of the numbers involved will remain a closed book. Some outstanding modern research of the record books has revealed that the English army was probably larger than it has been imagined to be in the past; perhaps some 8,000–9,000 men rather than the 5,000–6,000 men often touted around. However, what does not appear to have been exaggerated by the chroniclers was the state of that army; tired, hungry, ravaged by disease and in all probability terrified, and wondering first and foremost just what their king and leader had brought them to, even if they did not have the courage to express such thoughts out loud.

How large the French army was, on the other hand, is a source of much greater uncertainty. The estimates of chroniclers like

Thomas of Walsingham that there were 140,000 French soldiers available is incredible and other suggestions of an army 200,000 strong are simply preposterous, particularly given the size of the battlefield.[37] However, to a large extent they represent a common numerical device of the times with figures like 200,000 not to be taken literally but rather medieval shorthand for a very large number indeed. Some modern historians assert it was probably closer to 12,000, a much smaller numerical disparity which would of course completely downplay the scale of the English victory when compared to normal perceptions.

Yet it is perhaps slightly too pessimistic, and even to an extent lazy, to say we will never know these details for certain without at least trying to make a little more sense of what information is available. There are a number of accounts written by both English and French chroniclers (and indeed some such as the Venetian Morisini who were neither). Many of them quote numbers. While accepting that there are indeed lies, damned lies and statistics (especially in the world of the medieval battle chronicler), something of a big picture can be developed.

Modern historians such as Professor Anne Curry have undertaken a good deal of detailed analysis of the Battle of Agincourt and have helpfully summarised what the chronicles tell us.[38] If we exclude a small number of what statisticians call 'outliers' we can form, based at least on a balance of probabilities, several sensible hypotheses with a reasonable degree of confidence.

Firstly, the English army was probably around 8,000 strong. Of the twenty-seven accounts analysed by Curry, twenty-four give a numerical estimate of the English army. One by the Venetian Morisini stands alone by giving what must be called a ridiculous figure of 100,000; known to be ridiculous because the Agincourt

Muster Rolls, based on the very prosaic basis of who was actually listed as complying with the muster (and even more prosaically qualifying for payment), list around 12,000 men.

If we allow for 2,000 men being invalided home, a garrison at Harfleur of just over 1,000, and an as yet unattested number of reinforcements coming over from England, 8,000 seems about right, including probably just over 6,000 archers (around 80 per cent of the total figure). This does not include camp followers and other non-combatants. Of the twenty-three versions analysed by Curry that remain, sixteen fall within the range of 6,000–12,000 as an estimate. Two more have between 12,000 and 20,000 as an estimate. One other account, that of the French de Cagny, also appears to be an outlier with again a grossly inflated figure of 80,000–100,000. Statistically this would suggest that a figure of 8,000 for the English army appears sensible.

Looking at numbers for the French side we have a much bigger statistical range involved. Nineteen different estimates have been listed by Professor Curry. Four of these give numbers close to the English side at around 10,000 (the Count of Richemont, who took part in the battle, estimated that there were 10,000 Frenchmen against 11,000–12,000 on the opposite side). The remaining accounts, both English and French, range from 50,000 to 140,000 on the French side. The latter group falls into two approximate halves, with a number opting for a figure around 60,000 and a number around 100,000 or more.

Some figures may be overstated because we lack the same statistical database that is available for the English side. They may also include non-combatants who were present but not involved, nor meant to be involved, in the fighting. But allowing for this and accepting that there is less consistency about absolute numbers for the French, nevertheless the overwhelming majority of the accounts suggest a significant numerical superiority, perhaps five to one to six to one for the French army over their opponents, and that picture has not yet been definitively disproved by any subsequent research though doubts have certainly been expressed about it in some quarters.

In the end, it is more a matter of faith than fact. French historical records (many of which were lost in the French Revolution) are sparse compared to those available to English historians, who have one of the world's great treasure troves of archival material to tap into. The French were of course metaphorically speaking in their own backyard and had more men readily available to coerce into their makeshift army. But we know that they were not well coordinated and that parties of men were arriving in dribs and drabs even during the course of the battle.

However, the accounts of the chroniclers do suggest that there was a significant numerical French advantage (though some writers of course were heavily influenced by the accounts of others and may just be copying their statistics). Offset against this, as well as their poor and uncoordinated leadership, they were a scratch force. So too a couple of months before had been the English, but they had had time since to learn how to work together, march together, fight together. The French had the advantage of superior numbers on their part, but in other respects had several serious deficiencies to contend with.

Allied to this, the course of the battle meant that large numbers of French troops had been unable to get into the front line. This would have the effect of diminishing the numerical disparity; perhaps in the 'killing zone' immediately to the front of the English lines there was no disparity at all. But whatever the various arguments on numbers, there was no doubting that the outcome was seen as a crushing triumph for the English nation, and for their young king in particular.

Perhaps in the way the battle was fought lies the secret to explaining the confusion over numbers. The French may well have heavily outnumbered the English. However, a significant number would have been there in support of the army as servants to the men-at-arms or as other non-combatants. A higher proportion of men-at-arms meant a larger number in the collective entourage as these men required significant support staff. When the English looked at the French from a distance it may not have been obvious who were potential combatants and who were not.

Then the way that the battle had been fought evened up the numbers even more. The constricted size of the battlefield meant that only so many of the French could engage at once. Several chroniclers mention a French vanguard of about 8,000, excluding the archers, who did not seem to get involved in the battle at all. This would mean approximate numerical comparability with the English. Of course the second wave added to this number but the rearguard was barely involved in the battle at all. Therefore when we look at comparisons between the effective fighting forces of the English and French armies at Agincourt then the disparity in numbers was nothing like as large as a blunt assessment of total numbers would suggest.

There was one other factor that led to the French defeat and this is one that is not often remarked upon, though historians like Professor Curry have emphasised the fact that not all the potential French forces were present in time at the start of the battle. A little gem of information can be found in the words of Le Fèvre and Waurin, who state that 'if the battle had been fought on the

Saturday [i.e. the following day] there would have been an even greater number [of French dead] as on all sides men were flooding in as if they were going to a festival of jousting, joust or to a tournament'.[39]

They may well, as these chroniclers suggest, just have added to the death toll or they may have made a difference; we will never know. But this picture of men still arriving to reinforce the French numbers evidences well enough just how difficult they found it to marshal their forces in time to get their army together before the English had marched out of reach.

But in this age very different to our own, the victory of Agincourt was to be marked by strange portents and supernatural events in places far distant from northern France. While this great slaughter was taking place, hundreds of miles to the north in Beverley, Yorkshire, holy oil was seen oozing out of the tomb of St John of Beverley, an event taken to be a supernatural sign of approval for the bloodletting that was taking place at the same time in France as the saint sweated because of his great exertions on behalf of the English. John was the bishop of first Hexham and then York in the late seventh and early eighth centuries and a very apt saint to be connected to the battle.

His banner had later been carried into battle at the great English triumph over the Scots at the so-called Battle of the Standard in 1138. It had subsequently been used by great warrior kings like Edward I and Edward III, those formidable ancestors of Henry V. 25 October was the anniversary of John's translation (the removal of a saint's remains from one place to another, more high-status, location) and Henry V would later do homage for the debt he felt he owed the saint and make him a patron of the royal household.

Henry would order that his feast day should be celebrated

throughout England and in 1420 would visit his shrine at Beverley with his then queen, Catherine of Valois. It was to him, rather than the French saints Crispin and Crispinian, that the triumphant King of England first and foremost gave thanks, second only of course to the Almighty Himself, who had worked in his own mysterious ways on the muddy ploughed field of Agincourt.

St John of Beverley was a warrior saint, very appropriate to a pious fighting king like Henry. Crispin and Crispinian on the other hand were saints of the working man, of cobblers, tanners and leatherworkers. In some accounts they had met their end as fourth-century martyrs after travelling to Faversham in England. Perhaps after all they were appropriate enough saints to be associated with the victory given the relatively humble social origins of many of the victors. Certainly Robert Tanner, present in the Duke of Gloucester's company during the expedition and one of the 'yeomen' (or in the Latin *valletus*) of England, would probably have thought so.

12

AGINCOURT: AFTER THE BATTLE (EVENING, 25 OCTOBER – NOVEMBER 1415)

Let your sharp arrows pierce the hearts of the king's enemies;
let the nations fall beneath your feet.

Psalm 45:5

The English spent some time on the field of battle after the fighting was over,[1] drinking in the heady sensation of winning such a success against the odds. Also, more prosaically we can be very confident they were patrolling the scene of their triumph to pick up as much loot as they could. Then, as the shadows of night started to draw on, they withdrew after rounding up horses to carry both their own dead and pilfered armour from the bloody field. It was still raining as the sun quit the scene, nature adding her own tears, weeping freely over the blood-soaked field of battle, triumph and death. There was a certain aptness in the way the day ended as the English owed their victory almost as much to the rainclouds as they did to their arrow storms.

The darkness would be of great benefit for the small number of French wounded who yet remained alive on the battlefield. Rather as the badly wounded English soldiers who had been injured on the first day of the Somme on 1 July about five hundred years later would do (and not so many miles away either), they crawled as best they could to safety behind their own lines, taking shelter either in nearby villages or even in the woods. Technology may change the character of war hugely; the basic actions of the men involved in conflict vary much less significantly over time. Unfortunately, just like many of those Englishmen in the First World War, a number of the wounded who managed to crawl away would nevertheless eventually die of their injuries.

As they settled down to rest, the English reflected on what they had seen that day, of the terror that had assailed them when they had comprehended the size of the task before them, of the noise of battle, of the intensity of the fighting, of the screams of the dying and the panicked whinnying of the horses of the enemy, of the great fellowship of death that now lay across the battlefield. It was – at least in the way that the story was told – miraculous.

And it could not have been won just through the strength of men alone. Some gave thanks to God and the Virgin for the victory but others said that there had been very direct intervention by the saints. Some said that they had seen a mysterious figure fighting alongside them in the battle, a knight so great and powerful that he could not be of this world. It could be none other than St George himself who had lent his invincible might to the English cause and fought alongside them as they triumphed against the odds.[2]

In Maisoncelle, the victorious English stripped the armour off the dead to gain some useful trophy from their triumph. In the process several men who were thought to have expired were seen to be very much alive, including the Duke of Orléans, who could now look forward to a long period as a captive. He would not be released until 28 October 1440, when a ceremony to mark his release was held in Westminster Abbey.

The duke, still legally a minor when captured at Agincourt, only finally returned to France as a man in advanced middle age by the norms of the time (though he would later become the father of the future King Louis XII). Despite the inordinate amount of time he had spent away from France there was no tangible benefit accruing to the English from his incarceration. That said, we know that he spent much of his time in conditions that were far from harsh.[3]

Henry, however, was still nervous and cautious, almost afraid that even now his miraculous triumph might be stolen from him. He warned his men to be on their guard as there was still the possibility that more French troops might arrive and there may therefore be a renewed attack on the morrow. He also told his men not to take more armour than they needed, perhaps reasoning that it would be an unnecessary burden if a further fight was to follow. Any captured armour deemed surplus to requirements was put into a barn the next day along with the bodies of some of the English dead, and the building was then set alight. This is interesting as the lack of respect shown to the bodies suggests that Henry was indeed still concerned to make good his escape and wanted to dispose of them as quickly as possible.

Henry spent the night after the battle once more at Maisoncelle, with very different emotions presumably in his mind than those of the night before. The English who had lived through this incredible battle gave thanks for their survival and no doubt celebrated and quite probably slept too, having perhaps not expected to see any but the longest of all sleeps when the day began. They carried their wounded back to Maisoncelle to receive the extremely basic battlefield surgery and medical assistance that was then available to them.

The king would have appreciated his meal that evening more than he had for a while, though the release of stress after the battle would not necessarily have aided his digestion and neither would concern over whether or not the French would rejoin battle the next day. That evening he was waited on by the more illustrious of his captives, a further humiliation heaped on them. He told them the catastrophe that the French had suffered was a just rebuke from Heaven for their own sins, a sanctimonious comment that has a strongly credible ring to it coming as it did from the pious Henry.

But the dead, too, must be considered. The body of the Duke of York was recovered and 'the king washed his body for burial with royal care', a sign perhaps of the high regard in which Henry held his service during the campaign.[4] It was then presumably boiled in that gruesome ritual in the cauldron to which the bodies of dead nobles were subjected. The corpse of the Earl of Suffolk, that young, tragic figure, presumably went through the same procedure.

On the English side, such rituals were reserved for the nobility only. For the common man, there would be just hastily dug holes in the ground, a few last priestly ministrations and that was it or, if they were unlucky, being burned to a cinder in a barn. For many of the dead, vast grave pits would be the last resting place. It was not quite 'the dead with charity enclosed in clay' as Shakespeare would have his audience believe.[5]

The Bishop of Thérouanne was soon after given permission to consecrate the ground so that it would be made spiritually fit for this purpose; Agincourt was in his bishopric. There was no differentiation of the troops in death and French and English were buried side by side close to the ground over which they had fought so violently just a few hours before. The bishop, accompanied by the Abbot of Blagny, supervised the inhumation of the dead in five massive grave pits, each holding about 1,200 men. A great cross of wood was erected over each of them, the last resting place of some 6,000 souls.[6]

By tradition one of the main burial pits was at a spot now marked by a nineteenth-century Calvarie – a statue of Christ Crucified – just a hundred yards from a crossroads where the road from Agincourt meets that from Tramecourt, very much part of the battlefield. In the midst of a copse of distinctive trees, it is certainly an atmospheric and appropriate location.

However, battlefield archaeology around the Calvarie in 2007 did not succeed in finding any bodies. The only signs of warfare were bullets from the two world wars. There was some excitement when equipment detected significant signs of metal buried below the surface, but this soon dwindled when digging showed that this was not medieval armour or arms but part of a pipe that was all that was left of a drilling rig that had been used in exploration in the area in the 1960s.

There are accounts that some bodies were found much later on the battlefield by a British archaeologist, Lieutenant-Colonel John Woodford, at the end of the second decade of the 1800s. Woodford was quite a character and had fought at the Battle of Waterloo. Soon after, he made the most of the opportunities afforded by being part of the army of occupation in France by digging around the battlefield at Agincourt. Tragically, his dig diaries were later lost, possibly incinerated in a fire in the building where they were stored. It would be quite a coup if those diaries were to be found after all, but that is probably too much to hope for.

It was said that Woodford found bodies during his activities. These remains were later (the story goes) reinterred respectfully in the churchyard of the eighteenth-century church in the village of Azincourt. This allegedly took place in 1838, and walking around the church today this date can still be seen scratched on the wall, supposedly indicating the nearby location of the reinterred dead of a few of those who died at Agincourt.

Not all bodies were interred respectfully or otherwise on or near the battlefield; for example, that of Duke Anthony of Brabant was found on 27 October by a party of his retainers looking for him.[7] His remains were taken in state to his lands in Flanders where he was given appropriately respectful treatment for a number of days and in a number of different places before the brave but impetuous duke was laid to rest on 3 November in the church of St John at Fure. There are records of other prominent French nobles being transported back to their homes for burial locally.

A few of the more significant men among the French dead were identified and taken away to various churches and abbeys for dignified burial, but they were in a very small minority. One problem was that only a few of the bodies could be identified, so badly cut up were many of them. Where men were given their own burial spots rather than being thrown into a grave pit with hundreds of other cadavers, room soon ran out. The churchyards of the local churches such as that at Ruisseauville were soon filled and closed to further burials.

The next day Henry led his triumphant army 'past that mound of pity and blood where had fallen the might of the French'. They did not merely walk on by, though. Anyone found there still alive was either made captive or killed according to Monstrelet. Elmham on the other hand says that 'he [King Henry] passed the battlefield with a great show of pious compassion', a somewhat different perspective. Given the savagery of the battle on the previous day, on this occasion one is more inclined to believe the Frenchman. Such slaughter in cold blood was again not unique to Agincourt; a similar fate had awaited wounded Frenchmen after the earlier English triumph of Crécy.[8]

As they marched across that forlorn field, the bodies of all the dead still there were often by now naked and despoiled, one chronicler's account describing them as being 'all naked just like those new born'.[9] By this stage, Monstrelet says, three-quarters of the English army were on foot, so the attrition had clearly taken its toll on the horses too (though there is contradictory evidence from the records to show that a number of horses returned to England after the campaign).[10]

The English were still battling against that powerful adversary of hunger and in addition were understandably fatigued by their exertions in the battle. But they trudged on, buoyed by the knowledge of their astounding victory and there, marching disconsolately between the vanguard and the rest of the army, were the French prisoners to prove it. The step of men like Thomas Pokkeswell, assuming he had survived, may have been slow but it had more of a spring in it now. Even now, the records of Boulogne surviving from the time suggest that the men of that town managed to capture a few English stragglers[11] but by and large the will to fight on the part of the men of France had been completely subdued by the size of the French defeat.

It would seem that most men did not take great booty from the battle (though a few did, as we shall see). Any significant prizes (valued at over £10) should be reported and would then be divided, a third each to the captor, his captain and the Crown – this included both inanimate booty and prisoners. There are few surviving records to note any large amounts being handed over in this way. Of course, valuables might have been hidden by those who had taken them but they would have been difficult to hide. More likely, other than armour there were few valuables of note to worry about. The French were, after all, an army on the move and neither the king nor the dauphin were there; they might have brought expensive royal regalia with them if they had been.

When a party from Amiens appeared on the battlefield just a couple of days later they found little of note. The sum total of the results of their expedition were two large cannon (also adding confirmatory evidence to accounts that talk of some French guns at the battle), a couple of pavises – large wooden shields commonly used by crossbowmen that would give some shelter against arrows – and fragments of a few tents.[12]

The English had, against the odds, survived and triumphed and that undoubtedly made a great deal of difference to their morale. By 29 October, after passing by the king's castle at Guines, Henry and his men were at Calais.[13] The body of the army had gone in to the town in advance of the king, bringing the majority of the prisoners with them, though the more illustrious captives stayed with Henry.

Henry and his army had therefore moved to Calais quickly and this suggests an intriguing possibility when allied to other information. When the collective evidence of his killing of his prisoners on the field of Agincourt, the hurried burial of some of the English dead and Henry's cryptic alleged question to Montjoie Herald about whether or not the battle was won are looked at as a whole, there is a suggestion that Henry was still not sure that the final victory was his. After all, he could see numbers of Frenchmen still milling about in the region of the battlefield on 25 October and he probably knew that more French reinforcements were on their way to the area.

Given this, the king may not have been completely confident that the French might not yet launch another attack on his weakened army, still dealing with the impact of hunger and disease and now tired after a major battle. All of which evidence, when combined, suggests that Henry's cautious instincts told him to make his way to safety as soon as possible after Agincourt.

When the English army reached Calais, it was said that many of the army were not welcome, as the townsfolk were worried about a shortage of supplies to feed this newly arrived host of mouths. A number of them were forced to sell their equipment to find enough money to get back to England as quickly as possible as well as buy a morsel of bread to eat;[14] heroes are not long remembered after many wars, especially when a requirement to hand over some money to them raises its unwelcome head.

Henry waited at Calais for several weeks after he arrived there (twenty days according to Elmham), a leisurely halt that was in marked contrast to his journey immediately after Agincourt. There was a very good reason for this – those captured at Harfleur who had been released to arrange their ransoms were due to present themselves in the port. A large number of them had not yet managed to sort out their ransom payments and could only look forward to several years (or more) in an English prison.

There was no doubt that a great victory had been won. All in all, it was indeed, as the *Gesta* chronicler said, an outstanding achievement:

Nor do our older men remember any prince having commanded his people on the march with more effort, bravery, or consideration, or having, with his own hand, performed greater feats of strength in the field. Nor, indeed, is evidence to be found in the chronicles or annals of kings of which our long history makes mention, that any king of England ever achieved so much in so short a time and returned home with so great and so glorious a triumph.[15]

Of course this could just be the words of a hagiographer waxing lyrical but it is hard to avoid the conclusion that Henry's performance had indeed been magnificent in the past few days.

There were a few exceptions to the general rule that the triumphant English did not make much material gain from their victory. Even after handing over their prizes and sharing the proceeds with their captains and the Crown, some of the humble archers did extraordinarily well out of ransoms. Robert Sadler, who was in the retinue of Sir Thomas Chaworth, received over £32 for his capture of Edrad de Droyle, more than one years' wage for an archer. There was even a market for ransom payments, with some men selling on their right to ransom payments at a discount. This was because in practice there could be a delay before ransom money was finally received and sometimes it never arrived at all. It was an interesting exercise in forward selling that was rather different than the commodity trading that takes place in the modern world.[16]

Henry discussed with his council whether they should stay in France or return home. They argued that after two great victories and with the men still badly affected by 'the bloody flux' they should go back to England to recuperate before coming back again at a later date.[17] The king agreed and duly set out for home. He had other reasons to do so. He had faced enormous problems in finding the funds to pay for the first two quarters' service of his men and returning home now would save the problem of finding another two quarters' worth from an already empty treasury. Hopefully over time ransom payments would help to swell the coffers to some extent, though these might take several years or more to arrive.

Henry arrived at Dover on 16 November, the occasion marked once again by a heavy snowstorm, just as his coronation day had been. There had been bad weather during the short crossing from France and one French chronicler wrote that several English ships belonging to Sir John Cornwall were lost as a result. Some of the French prisoners aboard allegedly said that their sufferings while crossing the Channel were worse than those that they had endured during the Battle of Agincourt.[18]

By now, Waurin and Le Fèvre's words suggest that the English army was already starting to disintegrate of its own accord. They add that when Henry found out that some of his men were in dire straits he intervened personally and ordered that ships be found to relay them on the short but sometimes rough crossing back to Dover and Sandwich. And so the heroes of Agincourt returned home and, we hope, Thomas the archer made the not insignificant journey (about two hundred miles) back from the Kent coast to his small hamlet home at Poxwell in West Dorset. For him, it might not have been quite so bad – he may have been one of the lucky ones who managed to get shipped back to Southampton or Portsmouth, considerably closer to home.

The men from Kendal had a rather longer journey of 350 miles to look forward to. Given the fact that some of the men had lost their horses this could have been a rather long trek, especially as winter was approaching. Although a considerable number of horses were shipped back, the evidence is not entirely conclusive. One record that has survived shows that the retinue of the Earl of Oxford returned with thirty-nine men-at-arms, most of them with pages and with seventy-seven horses in total. On the other hand, his eighty-four archers only had thirty-seven horses with them.[19]

But the king had indeed returned safely to his kingdom, his position now a very different one than when he had left it. That was only just a few months before but in many ways it seemed a lifetime. Blood had been spilt, lives had been lost, much hardship and suffering endured. Above all these trials, Henry had emerged victorious. As one much more recent writer might have written, the king had faced both triumph and disaster and treated both those two impostors just the same.

It was now time for the triumphant king to milk the moment. Such great victories came along once in a lifetime – if such a man were lucky. It was above all else a magnificent propaganda opportunity and it was certainly not missed. Henry stopped off for two days in Canterbury where he met with Archbishop Henry Chichele; the support of the Church had been crucial in the king's great enterprise and it was an appropriate mark of respect to recognise the fact. Perhaps they discussed what to do with the feast day of St George, the patron warrior saint of England, because soon after Chichele declared that its celebration on 23 April should be a 'double feast day'.[20]

This meant that special services were held and church attendance was compulsory, much as if it were Christmas Day. The Battle of Agincourt helped cement the importance of St George's Day in the English psyche, aided not a little by the later exertions of William Shakespeare, a man who supposedly was both born and died on the celebration of that special festival.[21] It was that other great foe of France, Edward III, who had first adopted George as the official patron saint of England at some time in the 1340s, but his position had been well and truly upgraded as a result of the Battle of Agincourt.

While at Canterbury, the king paid his respects at the tomb of St Thomas à Becket, victim of an earlier king Henry's wrath. The current King Henry then made his way to his manor at Eltham, close to the city of London. The news of the victory had come out of the blue when the city first heard of it at the end of October. On 25 October, the very day of the battle, a rumour had reached the city that a 'lamentable report' had been received stating that a disastrous reverse had been suffered. It was only four days later that these inaccurate details were corrected, a day of much significance for Londoners for on this day they also elected a new mayor.[22]

On that morning, 29 October 1415, the church bells had rung out across London and *Te Deums* were sung in thanksgiving for the great victory. It was the morrow of the feast of St Simon and St Jude and even as the new mayor rode to Westminster to take his oath the news filtered through via the Chancellor, Henry Beaufort. The amazing tidings were announced to the public from the great cathedral church of St Paul's. The queen mother and all the bishops then made their way to the sacred shrine of St Edward the Confessor in Westminster Abbey to mark the victory. London, then as now, knew how to put on a show.

This gave the city a further month to prepare a suitable welcome for the conquering hero returning home and they would not disappoint. The city enjoyed a special relationship with the king, and given the economic dominance of London in these times that was crucial. In fact it has been suggested that during the reign of Henry V the citizens of London contributed five times as much to his cause as the rest of England added together.[23]

On the morning of 23 November, as soon as the wintry sun was up, the people of London moved out in large numbers to Blackheath in preparation to meet their king.[24] The Mayor of London was there with twenty-four aldermen dressed in scarlet. They were accompanied by a massive host of people, which the *Gesta* chronicler estimated as being 20,000 strong. Many of them were dressed in the livery of their craft guilds to distinguish them from their fellows.

It was about ten o'clock in the morning when the king arrived among them. He did not have a large entourage with him, though some of the more prominent prisoners were there, in echo of an ancient Roman triumph. He was met by the abbot of Bermondsey and later by other leading London clerics. The king wanted to appear humble in victory, giving all the praise to God.

As Henry prepared to cross into London over a bridge, remarkable scenes met his eyes. A tower had been erected, made with great skill of timber and adorned with linen cloth painted to look like white marble and green jasper, looking to all intents and purposes as if they were made of bricks pieced together by the most gifted of masons.

To the right of the tower was a pillar topped with an antelope with the royal coat of arms draped about its neck. Opposite it was another pillar, this time with a lion placed on it, standing erect, in its right paw a staff holding a royal standard unfurled. Another tower held a figure of St George dressed in a complete suit of armour except for his head, which was uncovered and adorned with laurel with sparkling gemstones attached. Behind him was a tapestry of crimson with a large number of shields festooned across it.

St George's triumphal helmet was to his right and a shield to his left. In his right hand was his sword and in his left a flowing scroll, on which were inscribed the words *soli deo honor et Gloria*; 'to God alone be honour and glory'. This sentiment matched well with those that Henry wished to have linked with the battle, for if God was to have the honour it also followed that He had approved and indeed facilitated the result, reinforcing the righteousness of the king's claim to France.

The tower itself was fronted with another message: *Fluminus impetus letificat civitatem dei*, an abbreviated form of Psalm 45:5, which stated, 'Let your sharp arrows pierce the hearts of the king's enemies; let the nations fall beneath your feet.' The allusion to arrows was once again poetically perfect as it was to his archers that the king owed his great victory in many respects. The tower was topped by spears carrying the unfurled arms of the monarch.

Next to the tower a number of boys had been grouped. They represented the hierarchy of angels, dressed in purest white, their faces glowing gold with gleaming wings and with sprigs of laurel, of which in ancient times the victor's wreath had been made. As Henry moved near they sang out, accompanied by organs, the words *Benedictus qui venit in nomine Domini*; 'blessed is he who cometh in the name of the Lord'. This was to be in every way portrayed as a holy triumph, an expression of the will of God made manifest upon the Earth.

Another tower had been erected by the conduit (fountain) at Cornhill. Here the arms of St George, St Edward and St Edmund, the martyr king, along with the royal arms of England, were encircled in the middle of the tower. The expression of the divine will was again alluded to with the text *Quoniam Rex sperat in domino et in misericordia altissimi non commovebitur* displayed. It meant 'For the King hopes in the Lord and in the mercy of the Most High he will not be shaken'.[25] Once more the king's special relationship with his creator was emphasised and the divine nature of his kingship reinforced.

Nearby was a company of prophets, with 'venerable white hair' and turbans of gold and crimson. As the king passed near, the 'prophets' released sparrows and other small birds. According to the *Gesta* chronicler some landed on his shoulders and some on his breast and some circled around his head in twisting flight as if even nature was in awe of Henry. The prophets added their voices to the holy cacophony; *Cantati domino camticum novum, Alleluia. Quia mirabilia fecit, Alleluia*; 'Sing unto the Lord a new song, Alleluia. Because he has done marvellous things. Alleluia.' Again this was a reference taken directly from the Psalms, written by that poet king David.

And so the sacred theme was taken up throughout the day. The Apostles, too, made an appearance, along with English kings and martyrs. More hymns rang out, utilising the poignant language of many of the Psalms. Fairy-tale castles had also been constructed, a secular antidote to these exaggerated allusions to divine approval. The king's arms were displayed everywhere, as were representations of St George, the warrior saint and protector of England whose cross had been displayed on the armour and clothing of much of the English army.

From the fairy-tale castle a gatehouse jutted out, made of wood yet firmly secured against make-believe intruders. From this a bridge, about waist-high, extended. Across the bridge a choir of beautiful young maidens processed dressed in virginal white.

They danced and played the timbrel, as the maidens of Israel had done when David had killed Goliath, another apt reference to the unbelievable triumph of the English against impossible odds. Their message, though, was much more earthly than heavenly as they sang, 'Welcome Henry the Fifth, King of England and of France.'

Behind them on the castle were ranks of boys, 'like a host of archangels and angels, beautiful in heavenly splendour, in pure white raiment, with gleaming wings, their youthful locks entwined with jewels and other resplendent and exquisite ornaments; and they let fall upon the king's head as he passed beneath golden coins and leaves of laurel, singing together in perfect time, to the honour of God and as a token of victory, this angelic hymn, following their texts; *Te deum laudamus, te dominum confitetur* [we praise thee Oh Lord, we acknowledge thee to be the Lord]'.[26]

This was a fantasy presentation of heaven on earth, one mined shortly after by the mix of the secular and the divine in what would become the famous *Agincourt Carol*, with its very worldly verses and the far more sacred chorus of *Deo Gracias*. Here the secular and the sacred met; this was no victory for the might of men alone but one sanctioned by the authority of God Himself.[27] No opportunity to emphasise the divine nature of the outcome of Agincourt was missed. This was a quite deliberate theme and it is unthinkable that Henry was not integral to the stage management. Not by nature an extrovert, he nevertheless saw the potential for propaganda that the battle gave him and he determined to exploit it to the maximum.

The streets were thronged with crowds eager to be vicariously associated with the incredible triumph against the odds; the legend of Agincourt was becoming well established within just a few weeks of the battle. So vast was the crowd that the horses carrying the notables in the procession could barely get through. From every window overlooking the route eager faces peered out, adding their own voices to the cacophony of noise. Anyone who was anyone, male or female, wished to be there to join in what would be a once-in-a-lifetime event – if that. They were dressed in their best, in cloth of gold, in fine linen, in robes of scarlet. No one could recall ever seeing anything else like it.

Agincourt would cement the relationship between the king and his capital. The city was the trading powerhouse of the country and was dominated by its guilds. The majority of MPs came from these, including those of the grocers (with eighteen MPs between 1386 and 1421), mercers, drapers, fishmongers (who were deeply unpopular because of their monopoly on the sale of fish) and vintners. Goldsmiths and ironmongers had also been well represented.

It is highly likely that one of those prominent in London during these celebrations was its famous 'thrice Lord Mayor' Richard ('Dick') Whittington. He was a mercer and had famously made his way from his birthplace in Gloucestershire to make his fortune in London. He was so successful that at one stage he became simultaneously mayor of London and Calais. He would be chosen as a London MP in 1416. He epitomised the fact that even in those class-conscious times a man of humble birth could rise high in London.[28]

The city had fallen out so much with Richard II that he had seized their liberties from them, a dangerous move. As a result the city had supported Henry IV when he claimed the throne of England. Its ongoing support for his son was crucial. On the eve of his departure for France the king ordered that all the aldermen of London who also held estates in the country (and there were a number of them) should return to the city to ensure it stayed secure.

Now on this day England (and London in particular) was demonstrating its love of a great show, for which in some ways it is still renowned, a public ceremonial in which all could take part and offer due adulation to the great and the good while also displaying ostentation on a large scale. It was a time of 'gorgeous and extravagant fashions' for the upper classes in particular, which they could show off in 'the cut of their garments and in the furs, velvets, silks, and other costly materials of which they were made'.[29]

One man alone seemed above the adulation. Just as he had entered Harfleur with great humility, so too was the king now a picture of understatement, seemingly anxious to give the glory to God rather than accept the accolades for himself. He was dressed in purple, the imperial colour of the emperors of Ancient Rome, yet in every other sense his demeanour was humble and undemonstrative. He was not followed by a huge retinue but a small number of chosen men from his household in his escort. Behind him, once more echoing a Roman triumph, trudged some of his more important prisoners, including Marshal Boucicaut, for whom the pain of this moment must have been overwhelming and the sense of disgrace complete.

Henry's pace was gentle and stately and he made little outward sign of excitement. Perhaps this pious man really was trying to ensure that all the praise for his great victory went to his God rather than to him. Maybe, though, it was an act, calculated to create such an impression. Possibly there were other reasons for his sombre demeanour, a feeling of loss at those who had died, a sense of guilt for the alleged massacre committed during the battle or the massive shedding of Christian blood. Or maybe he was just overwhelmed at the magnitude of the victory he had won. More than likely, it was a combination of some or all of these paradoxical emotions.

Agincourt had instigated a bout of national rejoicing; it was seen as 'a proof of England's strength, her monarch's talent, and divine favour'.[30] It was as if God Himself was an Englishman. The king processed with all the humility he could present to the two great churches of his capital, those of St Paul and St Peter, St Paul's Church and Westminster Abbey respectively (though of course as Londoners would be keen to point out London and Westminster were different cities). After reaching the threshold of the latter and paying his respects, he then retired to his palace at Westminster, on the site of the modern Houses of Parliament in London. While he was here, he was visited by a delegation led by the Mayor of London, along with two hundred leading citizens. Their praise was very welcome but perhaps the £1,000 gift (approaching £500,000 in modern terms) was even more so.

It was a critical moment in the reign of this still-young king, the moment in which it was mythologised. And so it was for others, too. For some men there was redemption in this life as a result of Agincourt. John Holland's efforts during the campaign would not go unrewarded. In 1416 he was made the Earl of Huntingdon, a title once held by his executed father. He would also be made a Knight of the Garter, one of the greatest honours that could be bestowed on a man. He would later be captured by the French and imprisoned for four years, but after his release he would eventually be made the Admiral of England, Ireland and

Aquitaine and ultimately Duke of Exeter. This was redemption indeed.

For men such as Holland the outcome of Agincourt was overwhelmingly positive. Others benefited too; Thomas, Lord Camoys, who had probably commanded the rearguard at Agincourt, was well into his sixties but was also made a Knight of the Garter in 1416, a great mark of distinction and honour. The scenes in London that day were ones of great joy for all except Frenchmen. A remarkable triumph had been won.

Yet the victory, though overwhelming in its magnitude and one-sided in terms of its casualties, was not without its cost to the English. Amid the euphoria, there were personal tragedies to be dealt with. This was an age when in the midst of life death was an ever-present companion. The ravages of disease were a constant threat. The Black Death as one example was only the greatest attack of pestilence upon the country; there were many other smaller-scale onslaughts made by nature during the Middle Ages. Death in any age is never a glorious experience but in the context of the Middle Ages it could be particularly nasty. The walls of churches around the country were adorned with wall paintings that showed skeletons walking side by side with kings, a reminder that even the great were not immune to Death, the constant companion.

But in the context of the times there was a particular poignancy marking the death of a warrior in battle. While of course it was an unavoidable reality of all war, death in a winning cause added a lustre of heroism. There was an importance in enduring a 'good' death and there were few better than dying as a quasi-martyr for a righteous cause. The victorious dead must be duly honoured.

The deeply pious king wanted to do all he could to honour their sacrifice. Very practically, he eased their way into the Hereafter (at least for the more noble of them) by ensuring that the proper rituals of remembrance and prayer were observed. In this non-secular world, the intoning of prayers for the souls of the departed was not some empty, superstitious mumbo-jumbo but a crucial act to be undertaken for the benefit of the lost for all of Eternity. We may mock such sentiments from the superiority of our supposedly more knowledgeable world, but we are not those men. If we do not at least try to understand them, then neither will we understand the world in which they lived or the events such as the Battle of Agincourt, which took place during these very different times.

To give them the honour due, funeral services were held for the noble dead on 1 December in London. There were a host of important people there. The leading bishops and archbishops of the realm were present; so too were some of the great nobles, including the Earl of Dorset, who had made his way back from Harfleur for the occasion.

This was a poignant day indeed. The tragic Earl of Suffolk was remembered, as were all of the dead, both English and French, for the taking of any Christian life was an act of the deepest gravity. After the triumphal entry into the capital, it was time for reflection and contemplation.

But there was one man above all who would be honoured in this sombre service of thanksgiving and remembrance for the lives of the dead: Edward of Langley, Duke of York, the man who just a few months before had happened to be a bystander when his brother was tried for, and lost, his life for plotting to murder the king. His heroic actions had brought redemption to a tarnished family name but at the cost of life itself; a heavy toll to exact for such an honour. The records of the time tell of the provision of banners and pennons for the solemn occasion.[31]

The successor to his dukedom was his young nephew Richard, the son of his recently executed brother the Earl of Cambridge. Given his tender years (he was only four years old at the time) it is highly unlikely that Richard was present at the funeral, yet maybe he was aware that something had changed significantly in his life. He was now destined for a great and wealthy future. One day his son would become Edward IV, King of England (as well as the self-proclaimed King of France), at the expense of the heir to that monarch, Henry V, who today watched over these melancholy rituals in London. Such are the strange machinations of history.

In the midst of the grief there was one particularly bittersweet moment. One of the French prisoners was the Count of Richemont, and it was arranged that he should be taken to see his mother, Joan of Navarre, who was also the king's stepmother. She had not seen him for ten years. When he entered the room where she was, there were a number of her ladies there with her to greet him. One was sent forward to welcome the count.

He embraced her, thinking her to be his mother. Then the dowager queen stepped forward and tearfully took hold of her son, reflecting on the sadness of a mother whose own child did not recognise her. The count, too, was reduced to tears by the poignancy of the moment; a touching moment indeed.[32] But Richemont at least had a long life and freedom to look forward to, something that could not be said for thousands of his compatriots, though the scars of battle would remain with him for the rest of his days.

For a few fighting alongside Henry V, Agincourt was the day that *Fortuna, Imperatrix Mundi* ('Fortune, the Empress of the World') smiled on them and their lives changed forever. For some, such as John Holland, who found himself as a close confidante of the king, the effects were obvious. For others the benefits were more indirect and came only in the longer term. William ap Thomas was a member of the minor Welsh gentry who fought at Agincourt. There were many other Welshmen there, including Dafydd Gam and Sir Roger Vaughan.

Gam left a daughter and Sir Roger a widow, Gwladys ferch Dafydd Gam, whom William ap Thomas later married. This was Thomas's second marriage. As the first had also been to a well-off heiress, his fortune seemed assured. By assuming the vacancy left by Vaughan's untimely death, Thomas made his fortune. The splendid effigies of Thomas and Gwladys in St Mary's parish church in Abergavenny still bear eloquent testimony to their status nearly six hundred years after their death.[33]

There were of course many others, even on the English side, for whom no such luck accrued. Perhaps it is fitting to remember even more than these members of the aristocracy and gentry a humbler man, Thomas Hostell, who had survived losing an eye to a crossbow bolt and a broken cheek at Harfleur yet had manfully pushed himself on to Agincourt. He continued to serve after this and saw further actions at sea (surviving records show a man of this name involved in the 'Keeping of the Sea' in 1420) and was as a result 'sorely hurt, maimed and wounded'.

He was subsequently 'much enfeebled and weakened' and had fallen into poverty, 'being much in debt and unable to help himself' and was compelled to write to Henry VI in later life, 'now being of great age', to ask for charity, having not yet received any reward or recompense for his heroic actions. Thomas was, like a soldier in many ages, a forgotten hero once the war was over. He for one gained little from his valiant service, a very poignant counterbalance to the visions of glorious victory summoned up by recollections of Agincourt.[34] But it was because of men such as Hostell that the battle was won.

13

EPILOGUE

Gentlemen in England now abed shall think themselves accursed
they were not here.

William Shakespeare, *Henry V*, Act 4, Scene 3

What did Agincourt mean? Symbolically, to England, especially at the time, it meant an awful lot. The euphoria which accompanied the triumphal return of Henry V to London showed as much. To the English, it represented a divine judgement. Henry Beaufort, Bishop of Winchester and Chancellor of England, said as much when opening Parliament in the following year. In his speech, 'he referred to the triumphs of our king which God had afforded him against the obstinacy of the rebellious French'.[1] The word 'rebellious' was significant; it meant that God had decreed that the French were truly Henry's subjects and their 'obstinacy' represented resistance against not just the English king but also against the will of the Almighty.

But despite this, Agincourt did not mark a major long-term strategic turning point, and it is hard to disagree with the

387

assessment of a twentieth-century historian that 'the political results of the battle were more important than the military'.[2] In the short term, it really started rather than ended a renewed bout of aggressive activity in France. This revealed even greater levels of ruthlessness and harshness from Henry than he had shown at Agincourt. By the end of the campaign that followed over the next seven years, Henry had fought a dogged, determined series of sieges that had forced the French to the negotiating table and Catherine of Valois to the marriage bed. Henry allowed himself precisely one day as a honeymoon after the wedding.[3]

Henry was helped in his victory no end by the disunity of the French. On 10 September 1419 John the Fearless made his way to Montereau on the Seine to parley with another dauphin named Charles (not Henry's opponent in the build-up to Agincourt; he was now dead). This followed negotiations which appeared to be progressing well to heal the breach in France between the Armagnacs and Burgundians. Despite warnings to beware, the meeting went ahead and the duke made his way across the river with the dauphin heading towards him from the opposite bank.

They met in the middle of a bridge and the atmosphere was extremely tense. Suddenly there was an altercation; an axe swung through the air and daggers went flying. At the end of it all, the duke lay dead. The deathblow was also dealt to all hopes of French unity. From now on, for the next decade and more, Burgundy was in open alliance with England. A French monk said to his king a century later when showing him the wound in the skull of the duke that this was the hole through which England entered France.

Henry V's final triumph was all made possible by this dramatic turn of events, which was suicidal from a French perspective. There followed his campaign in Normandy and the subsequent Treaty of

Troyes which, in 1421, seemed to secure the kingdom of France for Henry and his successors. France, worn out by civil strife and war against the English, conceded that the future government of the country should be in the hands of the English king and future generations that came after him. But just months later, the hero of Agincourt died; as Shakespeare incomparably put it, 'small time, but in that time most greatly lived this star of England'.[4]

From the union of Henry and Catherine there came a son, Henry VI. When he succeeded as King of England in 1422, he was just nine months old and incapable of ruling. When he became a man he proved equally unable to do so and lost his throne to the great-nephew of Edward Langley, Duke of York, in the civil war 'that made his England bleed'.[5] By the end of his reign, Henry VI had far too much to worry about at home to be distracted with France, though ironically the losses sustained there during the early part of his reign were fundamental to undermining him later in England. He, like Charles VI, would also lose his sanity. Then England would be the country with the mad king.

In another ironic twist, Charles VI, whose heir Henry V was, died a few months after the victor of Agincourt. Henry VI was duly crowned king of England and France in 1429 and 1431 respectively, the only man in history to receive such honours, though his latter coronation was held in Paris rather than Rheims, the traditional home of such ceremonies and where in fact a rival French king had been enthroned just two years earlier.

Henry V's death had taken from him the title he so coveted. In the meantime other prominent French figures also passed on to face that daunting interview with the Almighty. One of them was the imprisoned Marshal Boucicaut, whose body was transported to the cathedral at Tours to be interred with full chivalric honours.

This paragon of chivalry had been the subject of a number of attempts to negotiate his release, including approaches from the papacy itself. Henry, though, remained ruthlessly determined to resist all these efforts while he was still alive. He was simply too great a prize to let go.

The decline of English fortunes in France was not in any way instantaneous following Henry V's death. For the remainder of the 1420s, English advances continued largely unabated. It was not until the famous siege of Orléans and the less well-remembered defeat at the Battle of Patay in 1429 that the war started to turn decisively in favour of the French cause (though there would be reverses like the Battle of Baugé in 1421, where the Duke of Clarence, Henry's brother, lost his life as a result of his rash leadership and impetuosity).[6]

Patay, which took place soon after the siege of Orléans had been raised by Joan of Arc, saw the English archers overrun by the French before they could get into position, with hundreds of them slain. It was an example of what might have happened at Agincourt if the battle had been fought differently.

Ironically, at Joan's side when the siege was raised was a familiar name, none other than Raoul de Gaucourt, the defender of Harfleur. He had spent a number of years after Agincourt undertaking various journeys at the behest of Henry V as part of what was required of him if he were to be released from captivity. During that time he could easily have broken his parole and avoided returning to England after his various missions but he never did so, showing his strong sense of honour. Despite this, he was never freed by Henry and was only released several years after the king's death, exchanged as part of a deal that saw the captured John Holland returned to England. Henry's treatment of de Gaucourt was shabby, and in return when the Frenchman at last returned home he proved a strong and energetic warrior fighting in the cause of France's freedom from the English.

Henry at least left a sound infrastructure on which to build, and it would take a number of years to dissipate it. Not until 1444 would there be a truce and Agincourt therefore marked the start of the longest period of continuous fighting of the entire Hundred Years War, lasting nearly three decades. Despite its incredible and auspicious beginning at Agincourt, the end result of this extended period of fighting was an England that was exhausted, utterly defeated and on the verge of war with itself. It was a period of vicious warfare that took the lives of tens of thousands of Englishmen and Frenchmen, including King Henry V himself. But by 1450 the end was nigh. The defeat of an English army at Formigny marked the finish of English rule in Normandy. In command of the French that day was Arthur, Count of Richemont, survivor of Agincourt and son of Henry V's stepmother.

The final act came on the field of Castillon in Guienne in 1453. Here a heavily outnumbered English army led by the veteran John Talbot, a close supporter of Henry V who had been his Lord Lieutenant in Ireland in 1415, took on a large French force. Believing that their enemy was retreating, the English charged ecstatically in a determined effort to repeat the great triumphs of Crécy, Poitiers and Agincourt, only to be shot to pieces by the newfangled heavy guns of the French. That same year the massive walls of Constantinople, inviolable for a thousand years against the attacks of all comers, were blown apart by Turkish guns. A new world had met the old, and the archers and their great triumphs were slowly being consigned to the pages of fading history and the shadowy realms of legend. And with the passing of an age, France was lost to England, this time for good.

All this was perhaps inevitable. France had greater resources than England and anyway, to quote Sigmund Freud again, 'the results of conquest are as a rule short-lived; the newly created units fall apart once again, usually owing to a lack of cohesion between the portions that have been united by violence'.[7] It is not quite true in every case – think, for example, England and the invasion of the Normans in 1066 – but it is true more often than not.

By 1435, a leading English commander in France named Sir John Falstolf was devising a strategy that avoided sieges, considering them a waste of time. Instead the English, he suggested, should raid through France, harshly pillaging any in their way as punishment for their treasonable abandonment of the English cause in the country. It was a plea for a return to the brutal ways of the *chevauchée*. The world had gone full circle and Henry V's original plan, akin to something we might call a 'hearts and minds campaign' – albeit one with a steel edge – had been abandoned as a failure.[8]

France was a headache now for the English. Within a week of the news of the final defeat at Castillon, Henry VI collapsed into a catatonic stupor which effectively left England without a king. It was a condition possibly inherited from his maternal grandfather, Charles VI of France. If so, it was an ironic reversal of fortune; by his attempts to conquer France through the wooing of Catharine of Valois, Henry V had introduced a fatal strain of madness into the bloodline of the Plantagenet monarchs of England. In the long-term scheme of things, Agincourt had helped destroy the very dynasty that Henry V had sought to make triumphantly permanent.

Ironically, it was from Catherine of Valois's later relationship with Owen Tudor and its resultant bloodline that a future King of England, Henry VII (her grandson), would also eventually emanate. He would be part of the Lancastrian bloodline, though only peripherally. He would bring an end to the dynastic infighting between the two main factions in England by marrying Elizabeth of York, the leading survivor of the Yorkist dynasty. But by that time the Wars of the Roses had reshaped England, and France had to all intents and purposes disappeared off the agenda. Occasionally the issue would resurface, such as during the reign of Henry VIII, but France would never again be within England's reach. Despite this, the claim to France would not be dropped by monarchs of England until 1801.

It is very doubtful that England was ever in a position to conquer France and hold it. There was also something of a vicious circle apparent. Edward I had spent a fortune securing Wales and trying to conquer Scotland; he had failed to achieve the latter objective and his son, Edward II, was left with a challenge that was simply too big for him, with the end result that he was forced to abdicate and was subsequently killed.

The same happened to Richard II, left to pick up the pieces after his grandfather Edward III had saddled England with a parlous financial situation and a war in France that showed no sign of a resolution in his country's favour. And the wheel would turn full circle again with Henry VI, the son of the victor of Agincourt, who would simply be incapable of dealing with the almost impossible hand that he was dealt.

But the writing was on the wall even before this. Henry V's treasurer presented an alarming report to his council in May 1421 (that is while the victor of Agincourt was still alive). Every department of his government was heavily in debt and a huge deficit loomed. In other words, England was living beyond her means – and the principal cause of this unhappy situation was the war in France.

The destruction in France meant that even as new lands were conquered, the decimation that had attended their conquest destroyed the means to pay for the war in terms of wealthy territories added to the king's domains. In other words, the English were winning a Pyrrhic victory in this latest phase of the Hundred Years War.[9] The situation would only deteriorate after this until, when what remained of France was mostly lost in 1450, the national debt was £400,000. With the Crown's net revenues at only £30,000 per annum, this was a precarious situation.[10]

Strategically, then, Agincourt did not change very much for England in the long term, though in the short term it gave Henry V a strong foundation on which to build as he sought to cement his claim to the French throne. Indeed in some ways the victory was a mixed blessing for the country, as it encouraged an ongoing investment in the war that simply exhausted England and its finances in the end. However, tactically it was an undoubted triumph.

The English were well aware of the power of archers even before this great victory, and the crushing defeat of the arch-rebel (or freedom fighter, depending on one's perspective) William Wallace at Falkirk in 1298 was largely attributable to them. But the architect of that victory, the redoubtable English king Edward I, had died and his son, Edward II, who led the English army at Bannockburn, was in comparison a military dunderhead. But his son and successor, Edward III, was altogether of a different stamp.

It was Edward III who had recognised anew the full power of

the archer, and it was he who had utilised their power at Halidon Hill and Crécy in conjunction with the dismounted men-at-arms. In the process, he had established a benchmark against which all future English kings in the medieval period would be judged. Many of them would aspire to emulate him, to establish afresh the glorious supremacy (however fleeting or ephemeral) of the English, especially over their near (and better-resourced) neighbours in France. No English sovereign would model himself more closely on the late, great Edward III than Henry V. However, Edward would prove to be a very hard act to follow.

His career gave plenty of evidence of the power of the 'longbow'. At Halidon Hill in 1333 he had led an outnumbered English army against the Scots. But he utilised the ability of his archers' to the full:

Each division of the English army had two wings of fine archers. When the armies came into contact they fired their arrows as thickly as the rays of the sun, striking the Scots so that they fell in their thousands and they started to flee from the English in fear of their lives.[11]

The French had had a chance to learn their lessons too, and much more recently than Bannockburn or Halidon Hill. The early fifteenth century saw the concept of French chivalry at something near its zenith. But there was a paradox; chivalry might be a grand idea to espouse and an uplifting concept to aspire to (though as already noted it was underpinned by hypocrisy), but it was not a good way to win battles, especially if the enemy was not obliging enough to adopt the same chivalric principles that the French did. So, for example, the French had found out on the field of Crécy.

So, much more recently, had they discovered in another disaster at Nicopolis (in what is now Bulgaria) on 25 September 1396 when a crusading army composed substantially of Frenchmen charged to its doom against well-prepared Ottoman Turk positions.

Much could have been learned by the French from Nicopolis, with its massed frontal attack against well-prepared positions, let alone the more distant defeat at Crécy. Yet the evidence to emerge from the Battle of Agincourt was that precisely nothing had been learned. A bitter new lesson had been delivered, and yet another humiliation had been suffered. It was, in the words of the French chronicler Pierre Cochon, 'the ugliest and most wretched event that happened in France over the last 1,000 years'.[12] In contrast (it may be coincidence but it may be more than that that), there was a contingent of English archers and men-at-arms also present at Nicopolis (fighting this time on the same side as the French) and perhaps they had noted how effective the Turkish tactic of lining their men up behind stakes had been.[13]

The English had certainly learned from history. A century before Agincourt, an English army had been badly beaten by a smaller Scottish force at Bannockburn. There the archers had been driven off by Scottish cavalry, a lesson that showed that bowmen unsupported by other arms were very vulnerable. They had pondered on the lesson and had put it into practice first of all at smaller-scale battles like Dupplin Moor. They had developed tactics through engagements like Crécy and Poitiers. At Agincourt, through the simple expedient of combining archers, dismounted men-at-arms and stakes, allied to a good position in which to fight, they had delivered the ultimate victory.

The men that had delivered this latest reminder that chivalric idealism was a poor basis for fighting a battle were composed of those who are now mostly lost to us as far as their lives are concerned. But this does not mean that we know nothing at all about them. We know where they came from – the archers from the south of Wales, from Cheshire and from Lancashire, for example, not to mention our friend Thomas Pokkeswell. We can at least find out something of what their lives would most likely have been like, of the places that they came from and of their part in the battle and the campaign that preceded it.

And we can be confident too of the emotions that they experienced, some of which are recorded by the chroniclers of the time. No doubt they were a mix, for in all ages no two men are exactly alike. For some men going into battle, it is a time to prove themselves. For others, it is a time to fear. In the medieval period, it was also an opportunity to make some personal gain, a reward for the cripplingly hard work they provided on campaign, sleeping in rain-sodden clothes and exposed to the elements, worn down by hunger, by fatigue, by dysentery.

Many would have prepared themselves on the eve of battle for the prospect of an imminent meeting with God, for there were few atheists in Henry's army, certainly next to none who would have admitted so openly, for their king was a stern defender of orthodox Catholicism who had sent more than one condemned heretic to an excruciating death, burned alive with the smell of their own scorched flesh filling their nostrils.[14]

For these men, as far as we can tell (for few of them could write and, if they could, nothing has survived to tell us what they were thinking of such matters), God was real, and so were Heaven, Purgatory and Hell. And how they died on the field of battle could make a huge difference to where they might spend eternity.

The real significance of Agincourt was at the symbolic level.

English national mythology happily embraced the story of the outnumbered few fighting as underdogs against overwhelming odds and winning. It was a tale that would be taken up and used and strengthened again, further reinforcing the myth; against the Spanish Armada in 1588, against Napoleon Bonaparte at Trafalgar in 1805 or in battle with the Luftwaffe in the Battle of Britain in 1940.

Indeed, during the early dark days of the First World War, 499 years on from the Battle of Agincourt, the legend was revived when during the retreat from Mons it was said that a heavily outnumbered British force fought a gallant rearguard action against overwhelming odds with the aid of St George. This tale was well told by a writer called Arthur Machen, who wrote a short story which was incorporated into his book *The Bowmen*, which was released the following year after first appearing in the press. It is a short and simple story, but one that appeared to tap brilliantly into the psychological needs of the British people at this particular moment.

In his tale, Machen told how a well-educated British soldier, in desperate need of help and faced with imminent death, uttered the phrase *Adsit Anglis Sanctus Georgius* – 'May St George be a present help to the English'. Barely had he finished when thousands of ghostly archers appeared, the victors of Agincourt, bringing down the Germans in large numbers. In his introduction to the book, Machen went out of his way to emphasise that this was fiction but the damage, if such it was, had been done when the story had first appeared in the press the year before. So strong was public belief in the re-emergence of the Agincourt bowmen in Britain's hour of need that Machen was virtually questioned as to his patriotism for saying he had made the story up.

Ironically, Agincourt was not completely representative of the realities of war at the time. Most medieval commanders fought few battles in their career. Medieval warfare was about longer, less glamorous, campaigns. As one writer has remarked, 'the battle of Crécy in 1346 was dramatic, but it was the subsequent siege of Calais that brought lasting gains to the English. It was the hard, long grind of sieges that gave Normandy to Henry V, not the single dramatic victory at Agincourt.'[15] The clue is in the adjective 'dramatic'; it is the colour of battle that captures the attention and few are more vivid than the fight on St Crispin's Day 1415. This, first and foremost, is why the battle lives on.

Many years after Agincourt, of course, an English writer by the name of William Shakespeare would take the tale of the battle and mould it into something even more wonderful. In the immortal words of the Bard, 'Gentlemen in England now abed shall think themselves accursed they were not here.' The king and his 'Band of Brothers' would fight gloriously and gallantly against their chivalric foe with Henry motivated, first and last, by the thought that at the end of it all the prize on offer was not so much France but 'Fair Catherine', princess of that country.

It is fair to point out, though, that Shakespeare did not mine the writings of the fifteenth-century chroniclers who wrote of Agincourt, accurately or otherwise, within a few years or decades of the battle. He based his play much more on the works of sixteenth-century writers, in particular the second edition of *Holinshed's Chronicles*, published in 1587, a compendium of writings from a number of authors written over 160 years after the event and as such a very second-hand version of events.

It is a brave or foolish man who dares criticise Shakespeare, yet as previously noted, the great man was a playwright, not a historian. In recent times increasing doubt has been placed on his interpretation of that (so-called) arch-villain Richard III. That is right and proper, but it is harder to question his portrayal of a national hero such as Henry V, whose incredible qualities have been used to inspire the entire nation even in recent times (think Olivier, Shakespeare's play and the Second World War). Yet there is much in Shakespeare's 'history' that just does not ring true, either of the battle itself or of the man who more than any other was responsible for its ultimate outcome.

It is the job of historians to question, not for the sake of revisionism but to make their subjects real, to bring them to life in ways that are unexpected, to enable caricatured individuals to be reborn as human beings, warts and all, as opposed to unrealistic paragons that only exist in the imagination. What emerges, unsurprisingly, are the images of men and women with strengths and weaknesses, of virtues and vices, of vast shades of grey, sometimes as impenetrable as a thick layer of clouds, rather than black or white. In the search for the truth, there will be casualties and one of them will inevitably be the mythology that attaches itself to a national hero.

This might seem to imply that in peeling away the layers of myth there is something of a diminishing going on. In fact, often the reverse is true; for in removing the varnish of legend and stripping back history to its core, sometimes a story even more gripping emerges. Such is the case with the story of 'King Harry' and the field of Agincourt.

What makes the story of such great interest is that the stunning triumph of Agincourt was far away from being one of the decisive strategic battles in history. In the short term, little changed in the state of France as a result and the country did not obligingly fall into the lap of the English king within weeks of the victory. It would be years, and only after further long, hard campaigning, until the English blood spilt in the battle would look as if it was to bear fruit for Henry V, and that after a war of sieges rather than pitched battles. And then, in a cruel twist of fate (or was it, in the context of the times, the hand of God?), the prize would be snatched away again before he had had time to even begin to enjoy it.

Neither would the tedious but unavoidable problem of paying for the war go away. As late as 1427, the Duke of Gloucester and the Earl of Salisbury were petitioning Parliament for reimbursement for the wages of their retinues that they had picked up the tab for during the Agincourt campaign (though Gloucester received other compensations such as Llanstephan Castle, which had formerly been in the hands of Henry Gwyn, a Welshman killed fighting for the French at Agincourt).[16] The campaign and its aftermath in the latter years of Henry's short reign had stretched the treasury to the limits, and quite probably beyond.

In the longer term, Agincourt seemed to matter even less in terms of its impact on the course of history. Within half a century the last English soldier (bar those in a small enclave around Calais) had been driven out of France. The French, divided in 1415, had since found a unity of sorts, one brought about to a significant extent by a common fight against the English and a hero/heroine of their own, this time a peasant (and a woman to boot) by the name of Joan of Arc.

The English, on the other hand, had travelled in the opposite direction over the same period. In the warm afterglow of Agincourt they had for a short while found a cohesion and a common vision that had not been there before. It would not last. By 1455

Englishmen would be far too busy fighting each other to worry about another war with the French; indeed we know of one man, Sir Bertram Entwhistle, who survived Agincourt (he was nineteen at the time) only to die at St Albans in the first battle of the Wars of the Roses, slain at the hands of his own countrymen.[17]

By this time, the lessons learned from a trail of almost unmitigated disaster in the preceding two decades of Anglo-French warfare suggested that only pain and disappointment would come from continuing the war in France. Indeed, Henry's premature demise perhaps only served to remind the piously pretentious monarch of the essential transience of earthly glory.

It could even be argued that the triumph at Agincourt, and the victories won in the Hundred Years War as a whole, were not positive militarily for the English in the long run. England, at heart often a conservative nation, was slow to adapt when the power of the longbow was overtaken by other military developments. The French were the ones who became adept later in the fifteenth century at more modern styles of warfare and were able to expel the English from almost all of France. Bowmen might be effective against massed ranks of lumbering men-at-arms, but they were less so against guns.

Even in the sixteenth century the 'longbow' was regarded with almost sacred reverence by the English. The presence of so many on the doomed *Mary Rose* evidences a clinging on to what was increasingly an anachronism. Henry VIII, inspired by legends of Crécy and Agincourt, sought to recreate those triumphs in his own time with no success but huge expense when it could not be afforded. Agincourt had created a dangerous illusion. But it was not sustainable. Armour had improved significantly, while skills with the bow had declined; repeated edicts from the government to insist that the sixteenth-century Englishman kept up his archery practice suggest that they were by now fighting a lost cause. By this time the hand gunner had a massive advantage in penetrative power compared to the archer.

So in the long term, at least, Agincourt changed next to nothing other than on a symbolic level. And yet for one man and his legacy, it was everything. For Agincourt was the battle that wrote Henry V into history.

This is a book about Agincourt, not Henry V. But in the legend of Henry V, the two are inseparable. Agincourt, in the eyes of his people and the eyes of history, lifted Henry above the ordinary to a place few other English monarchs have reached. If in any sense the battle was decisive it was in securing the reign and the reputation of King Henry V. If Henry's war aim was to cement his place as King of England then he was spectacularly successful; there were no serious attempts to unseat him after Agincourt.

Even the king seems to have realised that there was something extraordinary about Agincourt. Just two years later, he was about to return to France with another army to finish what he had started. At the time he was concerned that too many of his army were assuming airs and graces above their station. Some men, it was said, had started to bear coats of arms (or *cote armours*) that they were not entitled to wear. On the eve of his departure from Southampton in 1417 he sent writs out to the sheriff of the port, as well as those of Dorset, Wiltshire and Sussex, that they should carefully check the evidence by which men claimed the right to wear such honourable accoutrements. Men who had fought with the king at Agincourt were specifically exempted from such interrogation, though; they had done more than enough to merit the right to carry such status symbols.[18]

To the king, at least, the implications of the stunning victory were profound. A medieval monarch was supposed to excel as a warrior king and in this respect Henry's achievement was monumental. It is important to remember that since William I came to the throne of England in 1066 barely a reign had passed without a rebellion against the king's authority of some sort. Several kings, including Stephen and Henry III, had had to fight long civil wars for their throne against their own subjects. Two kings, Edward II and Richard II, had been deposed and subsequently murdered. William II had also died in a hunting accident that was, to say the least, suspicious.

Henry's own father had had to fight to retain the crown as well, and on the very eve of his departure for France there had been a plot to depose Henry V himself. But the triumph of Agincourt was a decisive blow in support of his own legitimacy. God had spoken on the field of battle and woe betide any who dared argue against His arbitration. It is noticeable that soon after returning to England Henry was granted access to the country's excise duties for life; there were few stronger signals of support that could be given than this. The Church joined in too, with generous grants from the convocation of the southern ecclesiastical province of England, held at St Paul's between 18 November and 2 December 1415, and the northern, held at York between 16 December 1415 and 16 January 1416.

Yet to immortalise Henry entirely is also to make him something he was not. He was a man, more famous and more talented than many men but flesh and bone nonetheless. Undoubtedly he saw his triumph in his own pious way as a reflection as the will of God, but he had human emotions too. His relationship with his late father had been strained. There were signs that the Duke of Clarence,

Henry's younger brother, was Henry IV's favourite. Perhaps the young king had now proved himself after all, in Hamlet-like fashion, to his deceased father by his astounding achievements. Rather like another great warrior from an earlier era, this more modern version of Alexander had taken Philip of Macedon's not insignificant achievements to a new level.[19]

Historians often argue that an assessment of a monarch should involve a review of their whole reign, and of course they are right. They often assert that a monarch's contribution to society should be measured more by their actions outside of war rather than in it, and again they may well be right. But for many people it is the human side of history that resonates the strongest. And rightly or wrongly, it is how men and women act at the time of greatest personal challenge to which we can most relate, to see how they can reach deep inside themselves and find something extraordinary. That is what interests many people the most, and that is what makes the story of Agincourt a timeless one.

Most of us are not outstanding individuals. We will be unlikely to get close to greatness ourselves and we seek our inspiration from those tiny handful of individuals who do. Henry V had a number of qualities; he was a very efficient administrator, a driven individual with great reserves of energy (though not without an associated personal cost), an extremely pious man even by the standards of the time. All of these may be considered admirable; it is doubtful, however, if any of them suggest greatness. And Henry, like us all, was also a man with weaknesses; capable of coldness, of brutality even, selfish, proud and ambitious to the point of absolute ruthlessness. He was far from being a perfect man or a perfect king.

Aspects of these qualities and weaknesses were evident at

Agincourt but that is not really the point. In the battle, context is all. Taken as a whole, if we pretend for a minute that Agincourt did not happen but everything else in his life did, Henry would still be seen as an effective and competent monarch, a good soldier and a capable administrator but probably, in most people's eyes, nothing much more than that. Agincourt took him to a different plane. On the morning of 25 October 1415, something extraordinary happened. At this precise moment, Henry V soared to heights of greatness that few other English kings could aspire to, before or since.

No doubt the chroniclers talked the story up for all it was worth. The religious elements in particular were milked to the maximum by men like Thomas of Walsingham and the anonymous writer of the *Gesta*. In those religious days, when God was still regarded as both real and omnipotent, His divine judgement as supposedly expressed on the field of Agincourt counted for much. The king's personal bravery and self-sacrificing patriotism were also emphasised and no doubt exaggerated. But there were important kernels of truth in some of this that seized the imagination and the picture of victory over overwhelming odds was not just painted by sympathetic English chroniclers but also by some potentially hostile French ones.

The Agincourt campaign lasted less than three months. The war in France would go on for much longer. Within two years, Henry was back with another large army to finish his conquest. The effort was to consume the rest of his life and in the end effectively took it. He was then, as he was in this campaign, energetic, indefatigable, determined, capable of inspirational leadership. And yet like another great military commander, perhaps the greatest, namely Alexander, he was dead in his thirties.

To die before one's time is part of the story of many prominent figures in history: Alexander, Henry V, Nelson, in our own time Kennedy or Princess Diana. In some ways it is a key part of cementing a legend. It means that the ravages of time, the disappointments of inevitable failure as mistakes are made, are avoided. The great often die young; it means that the veneer of greatness is never questioned as it inevitably would be had they lived on.

Henry falls firmly into such a category; his reputation, built on the muddy fields of Agincourt, was never exposed to the debilitating impact of failure. For an individual, to die before one's time is a personal tragedy; for the sake of an immortal legacy for those who have achieved great things in their brief lives, it is a priceless gift. As one historian has remarked, Henry 'was fortunate in the hour of his death, for he reaped the renown from his policy of war but not the inevitable bitter harvest of it. Like Edward III, he won unity for his realm and glory for himself at the price of immediate misery for France and eventual confusion for England.'[20]

But Agincourt was not just about Henry V. As the story unfolds, we see greatness emerge in unexpected ways, rather differently than if we stuck to the traditional image of the battle, of those brave archers standing firm against the French horsemen obligingly charging like mounted idiots against the impenetrable wall of stakes. As we have seen, it was not quite like that; but what emerges at the end of it all is one day in history that, six hundred years on, still bears the hallmarks of one man's morning of greatness as well as, more prosaically, the combined efforts of his archers, his men-at-arms and the mud, allied to the frailties of his enemy.

The story may not be remembered forever; few historical events will. The echoes of St Crispin's Day 1415 may not be recalled 'from this day to the ending of the world' as Shakespeare said they would, certainly not for the Thomas Hostells of this world. But the memories of that day on the mud-cloaked fields of northern France will resonate for longer than most.

NOTES

2 England and France: The Road to Agincourt

1. Barber 37. Barber's work is a valuable study on the concept of chivalry as a whole and its evolution.
2. Juniper/Gideon/Arte France, 2007
3. The Hundred Years War started in 1337 and did not end until 1453, although the fighting was not continuous – in 1415 France and England had been at peace for most of the past twenty-six years, though that did not stop raids taking place during that period.
4. Although it is interesting that Henry actually linked his claim to that of Edward I, Edward III's grandfather. See Cooper 69
5. See Pugh 12
6. Priestley 12
7. Strickland/Hardy 284. The detailed description of the surgery involving probes and tongs suggests that this was an absolutely excruciating operation.
8. Walsingham 329
9. Strickland/Hardy 284. The scar across his cheek being responsible for the portrait being in profile has become one of the emerging minor modern myths about the king. See Brown 35
10. Priestley 6
11. Ibid 8
12. Allmand 39
13. Quoted in Barker 31
14. *Gesta* 3

15. Walsingham 389
16. That said, it is interesting that the writer of the *First English Life of Henry V*, writing in 1513, says that Henry was 'in his youth ... most mutable and void of all spiritual virtues'; see *Sources & Interpretations* 206. The legends about Henry's wilder younger days, if they were indeed legends, clearly developed quite early.
17. Mortimer 12
18. Sigmund Freud letter; *Why War, Response,* September 1932
19. Sleeve notes to *Music for Henry V and the House of Lancaster*; CD by the Binchois Consort, Phillip Weller, Hyperion, 2011
20. The king's biographer J. J. Scarisbrick (43) states that Henry VIII modelled himself on Edward I, Edward III and Henry V. The first English life of Henry V appeared in 1513, early in Henry VIII's reign.
21. Walsingham 397
22. Mortimer 41
23. Beaufort was one of the king's greatest supporters and loaned £35,630 to him during his reign. See Jacob 136. He lent even more to Henry VI but it was not all one-way traffic as he was granted income and revenues from Southampton in return, a very sizeable amount.
24. Footnote 2 in Walsingham 399
25. Prestwich 267
26. Ibid 273–4
27. Ibid 273
28. Barker 99
29. Nicolas xxxiv–xl
30. See Prestwich 75. Edward I had provided an early example of using paid rather than feudal troops in the Welsh War of 1277, though this was not the end of feudal service, which would continue to some extent for some time thereafter; see Armstrong 22–3
31. Mortimer 124
32. Nicolas xii
33. Mortimer 131
34. Quoted in Nicolas, viii–ix; originally in Middle English, this has been slightly adapted into more modern English.

35. Dated 8 April 1415, Mortimer 143
36. Reproduced in Nicolas xix
37. Letter reproduced in Nicolas xvi
38. Mortimer 154
39. So too had the fortress at Guines, which had had its moat cleared of rubbish in 1413 and also had a watchtower added to its defences. See Barker
40. Mortimer 155
41. Ibid 156
42. Ibid 158
43. Ibid 172
44. Curry in ... *The Archers' Story* 66
45. See Nicolas xxxi
46. Ibid, xlvi–liii, gives a long list of such items.
47. See Cooper 85
48. In Nicolas xxxiv
29. Jacob 143
50. Nicolas lxi
51. Prestwich 88

3 Southampton: The Coup Attempt

1. Prestwich 101
2. Mortimer 198
3. Nicolas lxiv
4. See Pugh 13
5. For further information see http://englishhistoryauthors.blogspot.co.uk/2011/12/richard-ii-and-his-double.html by Brian Wainwright.
6. Pugh, 79
7. Mortimer 150
8. Jacob 136
9. See Daniell 6
10. See Pugh 109
11. Mortimer 253

12. *Gesta* 19
13. In Mortimer 302
14. Goodall, *Portchester Castle*
15. See Pugh 105
16. Argued for example by both Pugh and Mortimer
17. The confessions, some of them very fragmentary, are reproduced in Pugh Appendix II.
18. *Gesta* 19
19. Walsingham 403
20. Nicolas lxxvi. The allusion to sharing a bed should not be misinterpreted; it was a sign of his alleged closeness as an adviser and a confidante of the king.
21. Walsingham 405
22. Mortimer 320
23. Jacob 147
24. *Gesta* 19
25. These were changed days. Oldcastle had fought alongside Henry not long before and in return the king had reacted to Oldcastle's perceived heresies initially with a great deal of restraint. It was on the vexed issue of religion that the two men fell out.
26. *Gesta* 21

4 Southampton and France: The Invasion Begins

1. Curry ... *A New History* 68
2. Ibid 69
3. Reproduced in *Sources & Interpretations* 448
4. According to the twelfth-century chronicler Gerald of Wales, the warriors of the north of that country were famed for their skill with the spear while it was from the south that most of the best archers came; he talks of the archers of Gwent with their 'bows of wild elm, unpolished, rude and uncouth'; see Armstrong 24. Strickland/ Hardy 207 talk of the three named Welsh counties providing twenty men-at-arms, twenty-three mounted archers and 473 foot-archers,

the latter figure and its proportion evidencing the relative poverty of Wales as compared to England at the time.

5. Curry ... *The Archers' Story* 66

6. From the Muster Rolls; see http://www.medievalsoldier.org/search_musterdb.php

7. Cooper 82

8. There are substantial details provided in Curry *The Archers' Story* – chapter 4 is devoted entirely to Erpingham.

9. Suggested by Rothero 36

10. Mortimer 283

11. Ibid 288

12. According to the chronicler Walter of Guisborough, most of the archers at Falkirk were Welsh, though there must be some doubt about this as on the eve of battle many of them were on the point of mutiny against Edward I, a situation partly brought on it would seem by an absence of food compensated for by a supposedly excessive consumption of wine; see Armstrong 24. He also says that in the half-century following the battle the skills of English archers increased enormously.

13. Mortimer 135

14. Bradbury *Medieval Siege* 164

15. *Sources and Interpretations* 192

16. Cooper 84

17. Curry ... *The Archers' Story* 74

18. *Gesta* 25

19. On some campaigns in Britain the rate of desertion could be enormous. On Edward I's campaign into Scotland in 1300, of 9,093 foot soldiers present in July the number had dropped alarmingly to only 5,150 by the following month despite the absence of any major battle or other cause of attrition. See Armstrong 22

20. Richard CL Jones in Keen 182

21. McGlynn 146

22. Mortimer 331

23. Nicolas ix

24. McGlynn 88

5 Harfleur: The Obstinate Defence

1. Mortimer 330
2. Prestwich 166
3. *Gesta* 27
4. See the Medieval Soldiers' Database at http://www.medievalsoldier. org/search_musterdb.php – there are two entries for Thomas Pokkeswell which show that he was present both during the first and second quarter of the campaign; this suggests that he remained with the army throughout most or all of the campaign.
5. Prestwich 125
6. Bradbury *Medieval Siege* 163
7. Ibid 164. *Messenger* had previously been in use at the siege of Aberystwyth: records from that event note that it weighed in at an impressive 4,480 lbs or approximately two tons: see Prestwich 293
8. The chronicler known as the Berry Herald suggests that this is exactly what the English did; see *Sources and Interpretations* 179
9. In Mortimer 344
10. The adoption of the red cross for English warriors and white for the French can be traced back to a meeting before Henry II of England and Phillip II of France who met at Gisors in France in preparation for the Third Crusade in the late twelfth century, though Henry would be dead by the time that it set out.
11. Quoted in Nicolas cx
12. See Prestwich 287
13. Walsingham 406
14. Mortimer 352
15. Ibid 354
16. In Wylie, 43
17. His tomb was rediscovered in the Chapel of St Edward the Confessor, showing a man about six feet in height and buried with a gold ring and an opal set in it; see http://www.westminster-abbey.org/ our-history/people/richard-courtenay
18. *Gesta* 45
19. Ibid 47

20. See Deuteronomy 20:10
21. Starkey *Music and Monarchy*
22. Nicolas Appendix 101
23. Details from Jacob 144
24. Monstrelet's account has been reproduced in a translation by Thomas Johnes in London (1840). It has been reproduced on the internet at http://www.deremilitari.org/RESOURCES/SOURCES/agincourt.htm. It may also be found, along with all the other major chronicle accounts, in *Sources and Interpretations*.
25. The *Gesta* chronicler mentions 66; 53
26. Mortimer 370
27. From Froissart's chronicles quoted in Prestwich 219
28. *Gesta* 53
29. Barker 206
30. This was stated to be the case for example in the *Chronique de Ruisseauville* by an unknown author. Although there are some certain errors in this account, on the other hand it was written in the area local to Agincourt and contains snippets of information that are not revealed elsewhere. This makes it an intriguing though not necessarily totally trustworthy account. See *Sources and Interpretations* 122–3.

6 Northern France: The Long March

1. Mortimer 377
2. I am grateful to advice from Dr Jonathon Snook on the causes and impact of dysentery. A recent example of an outbreak was when poor water supplies in Haiti led to a serious outbreak of dysentery following the earthquake of 2010.
3. Wylie 45
4. Ibid
5. Byrne *Encyclopedia of Pestilence, Pandemics, and Plagues: A-M* 175–6
6. *Sources and Interpretations* 42

7. *Sources and Interpretations* 42–3
8. Figures from Mortimer 380–1. The Muster Rolls, meticulously researched and available online at http://www.medievalsoldier.org/search_musterdb.php, list 11,285 records of those who took part in the expedition to France, a small number of whom were meant for duty in the standing force in Aquitaine and the Keeping of the Seas. The *Gesta* chronicler suggests that 5,000 were invalided home from Harfleur though Taylor and Roskell, who translated this, feel this is a suspiciously round number and 'probably excessive' – see 59.
9. Many writers talk of 2,000 dead at Harfleur; see for example Bradbury *Medieval Siege* 164. The documentary records that survive suggest a much lower figure. It is possible that numbers of dead may have become confused with numbers of casualties as a whole. Curry (… *A New History*), notes that the documented figure according to surviving records is very low, quoting fifteen men-at-arms, twenty-one archers and one other man, a tailor by the name of William Tropenell. The contention that the number of dead is vastly overstated is supported by Jacob, 150.
10. Curry … *The Archers' Story* 74
11. The process is graphically described in Mortimer 365
12. Daniell 87
13. There was an interesting and not altogether fortunate family connection involved in all this; Mary de Bohun, King Henry's mother, was a descendant of the lord killed in the single combat at Bannockburn.
14. Extract: the letter is quoted in full in Mortimer 378
15. In *Sources and Interpretations* 56
16. Curry … *A New History* 109
17. So called because at one time it was thought to have been authored by Thomas Elmham, though this is no longer believed to be so – but it is unclear who actually did write it if he did not.
18. In *Sources and Interpretations* 65
19. Curry … *A New History* 113
20. Wylie 64. The *Holy Ghost* was a new ship that had not quite been ready in time for the initial invasion.

21. Walsingham 409
22. This is one of the main theses of Mortimer's *1415*
23. Mortimer 392
24. Curry ... *A New History* 99
25. In *Sources and Interpretations* 65
26. Tito Livio in *Sources and Interpretations* 57. Also, Pseudo-Elmham, ibid, 66.
27. Based on Prestwich 248
28. Barker 228
29. See Prestwich 260
30. Pseudo-Elmham in *Sources and Interpretations* 66
31. The Constable of France – *connétable* in French – was in theory the commander-in-chief of the army, second only to the king in terms of the military establishment.
32. Bennett 16
33. Pseudo-Elmham in *Sources & Interpretations* 66
34. *Gesta* 65
35. Wylie 111
36. A small cemetery for the British Army was established near Pont Rémy in the First World War.
37. *Sources and Interpretations* 117
38. Walsingham 409
39. Not all modern historians accept this story as Bromley's name does not appear on the pay records for the Agincourt campaign; see Curry *New History* 140
40. *Gesta* 69
41. In Curry ... *Sources and Interpretations* 44. Elmham's work is called the *Liber Metricus*. He was once thought to have been the writer of the *Gesta* but most historians now think that this was not the case.
42. Christopher Allmand in Keen 268
43. In Prestwich 240
44. *Gesta* 71
45. Footnote in *Gesta* 70
46. Ibid, quoting the French chronicler Le Fèvre

47. Elmham in Curry ... *Sources and Interpretations* 44
48. From the account of Edmond de Dynter, *Sources and Interpretations* 172. As the Duke of Brabant's secretary at the time he had very good reason to know what was in his personal correspondence.
49. Curry ... *The Archers' Story* 75

7 Agincourt: The Eve of Battle

1. Mortimer 413. De Heilly was subsequently to die at Agincourt. He in fact escaped twice from captivity, the second time from Wisbech at around the time that Henry was attacking Harfleur; Cooper 62.
2. See *Sources and Interpretations* 180
3. Curry ... *The Hundred Years' War* 84
4. Curry ... *A New History,* 180
5. From the chronicler known as the Religieux in *Sources and Interpretations* 102
6. From the Religieux in *Sources and Interpretations* 105
7. See Strickland/Hardy 202
8. Curry ... *A New History* 132
9. In Cooper 17
10. In Mortimer 416
11. *Gesta* 77
12. Walsingham 409
13. Mortimer 420
14. Curry ... *A New History* 161
15. *Gesta* 77–9
16. Prestwich 191
17. See Mortimer 423
18. Mortimer 425
19. From the Religieux, in *Sources and Interpretations* 104
20. In *Sources and Interpretations* 59
21. The account of Pierre de Fenin in *Sources and Interpretations* 117
22. From the chroniclers Le Fèvre and Waurin, see Curry ... *A New History* 155

23. *Gesta* 79
24. Shakespeare *King Henry V*, Scene 3 – Shakespeare though attributes comment of the missing 10,000 men to the Earl of Westmoreland rather than Hungerford. Elmham mentions the story but does not name the individual involved and talks of 1,000 men rather than 10,000.
25. Cooper 164
26. See Judges 7
27. *Gesta* 81; the biblical events referred to can be found in all four Gospels, for example in John 19:24. Classical scholars however prefer references to similar scenes found in accounts of the life of Caesar; see Curry ... *Sources and Interpretations* 20.
28. *Gesta* 81
29. Pseudo-Elmham in *Sources & Interpretations* 69
30. See http://eclipse.gsfc.nasa.gov/phase/phases1401.html
31. Walsingham 410
32. Ephesians 6:10–18
33. *Gesta* 79
34. In Barker 262
35. The Religieux in *Sources and Interpretations* 106
36. Walsingham 410

8 Agincourt: The False Start

1. Walsingham 410 quoting from Virgil's *Aeneid*.
2. The medieval religious day was divided into Prime (to coincide with daybreak), Terce (9 a.m.), Sext (about midday), nones (about 3 p.m.) and vespers (at sundown) followed by compline. Monks in monasteries would also hear night services, matins and lauds, normally combined. See Daniell 4.
3. From the slightly later *Brut* or *The Chronicles of England* quoted in Kerr 212
4. Deuteronomy 20:1
5. Curry ... *Sources and Interpretations* 46

6. In Keen 146
7. Ibid 209
8. Elmham in Curry ... *Sources and Interpretations* 46
9. Alexander was an inspiration for a number of subsequent military commanders both in classical and medieval times.
10. Pseudo-Elmham in *Sources and Interpretations* 70. Note that there is much debate about whether the device should refer to 'three leopards' or 'three lions'.
11. The size of the horse shows that it was not a warhorse, and the fact that the king was not wearing spurs suggests that he planned to fight on foot.
12. For example Pierre de Fenin in *Sources and Interpretations* 119
13. The Berry Herald in *Sources and Interpretations* 181
14. For example, from the *Chronique de Ruisseauville*
15. Le Fèvre and Waurin in *Sources and Interpretations* 159
16. Bennett in Curry ... *The Archers' Story* 32
17. Curry ... *The Archers' Story* 72
18. *Sources and Interpretations* 432
19. Strickland/Hardy 204
20. See Hitchin in Curry ... *The Archers' Story* 38
21. Prestwich 141
22. Hitchin in Curry ... *The Archers' Story* 42
23. Strickland/Hardy 405
24. See Bradbury *Medieval Warfare* 245
25. See Wylie Footnote 7, 153
26. First referred to in the Treaty of Arras of 1221; see Bradbury *Medieval Warfare* 246
27. In Strickland/Hardy 206
28. Ibid 199
29. Details from Hitchin in Curry ... *The Archers' Story* 40
30. Wylie 151
31. See Stirland 128
32. Further discussion can be found in Strickland/Hardy, see Chapter 1 for example.
33. The Duke of York's muster roll for the second quarter of the

expedition shows that most archers had one horse but men-at-arms had more than this; see for example Curry ... *A New History* 163

34. In Curry ... *The Archers' Story* 115
35. See Pseudo-Elmham in *Sources & Interpretations* 71
36. Walsingham 410
37. Reproduced in Bennett 64–6
38. In *Sources and Interpretations* 159
39. Ibid 106
40. Ibid 111
41. *Gesta* 81–3
42. Pseudo-Elmham in *Sources & Interpretations* 71. There is talk of the French ranks conversely being twenty ranks deep.
43. See Strickland/Hardy 214
44. See *Sources and Interpretations* 22
45. See Nicolle 183
46. See Strickland/Hardy 306 and following; the arguments presented there are to the author very convincing.
47. Strickland/Hardy incline to the view that the archers were interspersed with the men-at-arms and they are not alone; see also Jacob 155. I too subscribe to this view.
48. Strickland/Hardy 320
49. Ibid
50. Bennett 21
51. Rothero 24–6
52. Matthew Strickland in Strickland/Hardy 278
53. A great helm forms part of Henry V's funeral achievements in Westminster Abbey. There is a very old tradition that this was used by him at Agincourt, though this has not been definitively proven. See Rothero 3
54. Prestwich 23. Some writers have categorically stated that Henry would not have been wearing such a helmet at Agincourt; see for example Cooper 130
55. Bradbury *Medieval Warfare* 246
56. In *Sources & Interpretations* 105
57. Barber 149

58. Strickland/Hardy 331
59. In *Sources & Interpretations* 236
60. Strickland/Hardy 323
61. Wylie Footnote 4, 157
62. Nicolle 192
63. Wylie 107
64. In *Sources and Interpretations* 72
65. Walsingham 411
66. Quoted in Bennett 70
67. More classical allusions in Walsingham 411
68. Elizabeth Armstrong in Curry ...*The Archers' Story* 125

9 Agincourt: To Arms

1. Matthew Bennett in Curry ...*The Archers' Story* 25
2. Berry Herald in *Sources and Interpretations* 181
3. Wylie 141
4. Some accounts suggest that Erpingham shouted this some time before the arrow strike but it seems more likely, given the wording, that it was in fact the instruction to begin the battle.
5. Clifford J. Rogers in Keen 142
6. The wording of the *Gesta* chronicler infers that the French were advancing when the archers starting shooting. But French chroniclers like Monstrelet suggest that it was the English fire that prompted the French advance. The latter seems a most logical reaction for French soldiers who were suddenly faced with no real options than either to fight or retreat.
7. Strickland/Hardy 407
8. Ibid 272
9. Ibid 274
10. Ibid 313
11. The Religieux chronicler states that the crossbowmen were dismissed before the battle as it was felt that they were unneeded; see *Sources & Interpretations* 106.

12. In *Sources and Interpretations* 156
13. Strickland/Hardy 255
14. *Gesta* 87
15. The Tudor warship *Mary Rose*, which sank off Portsmouth in July 1545 was found to be carrying 200 stakes which it has been speculated were for use by the archers in any battle against the French. 172 longbows were also found on board. See Stirland 32. The Pseudo-Elmham chronicler is in a minority saying that the archers had left their stakes behind when they had advanced on Henry's orders; see Pseudo-Elmham in *Sources & Interpretations* 72.
16. Matthew Strickland in Curry ... *The Archers' Story* 119
17. From the account of the fifteen-year-old Frenchman Jean de Waurin who was present at the battle.
18. Oman 383
19. *Gesta* 87
20. Barker 295–6. In a strange coincidence that other, very different, memorable event in English history, the Charge of the Light Brigade, also took place on 25 October in 1854.
21. The Religieux in *Sources and Interpretations* 106
22. Walsingham 411
23. Ibid
24. *Ausblutung,* the mortal bleeding of the enemy in a battle of attrition, was the name given to the nihilistic strategy employed by the German army at Verdun in 1916, with the simple aim of killing more Frenchmen than they themselves lost.
25. The first known use of the SS collar is to be found on the tomb of Sir John Swynford, a prominent supporter of John of Gaunt, Duke of Lancaster, dated to 1371. In modern times for obvious reasons it has become more common to call it the Collar of Esses rather than the SS collar; however, the clear use of the S symbol in the collar seems to make this an unnecessary and unwarranted complication.
26. *Gesta* 89
27. Tito Livio in *Sources and Interpretations* 62
28. Walsingham 411

29. Ibid; the last quote sees the chronicler waxing lyrical again, quoting from the *Aeneid.*
30. It is interesting to note that tournaments at the time involved knights fighting with different weapons; first, while mounted, the lance, then, on foot, with a sword, an axe and a dagger. Barker 25.
31. In Curry ... *A New History* 210
32. See http://www.ruby-sapphire.com/black-princes-ruby.htm. The ruby is now part of the British Imperial State Crown.
33. From the account of the Berry Herald in *Sources and Interpretations* 184. His account also suggests that there were two other men in the English ranks dressed to look like the king, a ruse that had been used by his father on occasion in battle so not necessarily untrue.
34. Bennett in Curry ... *The Archers' Story* 35. Some historians, e.g. Barker 301, suggest that it was not the duke who attacked the king at all and that the story that he did was a later fabrication to boost family pride. The reference that it was him who attacked Henry is from Monstrelet, see *Sources & Interpretations* 168.
35. Reference at http://etext.library.adelaide.edu.au/b/borrow/george/wild/chapter79.html. The story of Gam and his deeds had found earlier sponsors who embellished his part in the battle; see for example the *History of Cambria* by David Powell which appeared in 1584.
36. As an example, a visit to Tretower Court and Castle, ancestral home of the Vaughans in Powys, in August 2014 highlighted the fact that the account continues to be presented as history, helping the story of Agincourt to live on.
37. Pseudo-Elmham in *Sources and Interpretations* 73
38. *Sources and Interpretations* 107
39. Walsingham 412
40. See http://fabpedigree.com/s062/f726700.htm. The line of descent for the British royal family is traced through Prince Albert, the husband of Queen Victoria.
41. *Sources and Interpretations* 73

10 Agincourt: The Massacre

1. A point made explicitly for example by the French chronicler the Religieux of St Denis.
2. In Strickland/Hardy 330
3. Nicolas cccxcviii. The family legends also suggest that he kept the Duke prisoner at his home in Groombridge, Kent, for the next twenty-four years until he was finally freed, though this is unlikely as he would probably have been moved around. See http://www.geni.com/people/ Sir-Richard-Waller-Sheriff-of-Kent/6000000009025672445
4. *Gesta* 91
5. Strickland/Hardy 284
6. From the *Chronique de Ruisseauville* in *Sources and Interpretations* 125
7. McGlynn 189
8. Ibid 37
9. Bennett in Curry ... *The Archers' Story* 36
10. Quoted in Prestwich 305
11. McGlynn 134
12. Elizabeth Armstrong in Curry ... *The Archers' Story* 124. It should be pointed out though that Monstrelet's account suggests that the Duke of Brabant was killed on the battlefield and not later. The version which has him killed as a prisoner comes from the account of the duke's secretary, Edmond de Dynter.
13. From the Religieux in *Sources and Interpretations* 109
14. Barker 371
15. From the chronicle known as the *Brut* in *Sources and Interpretations* 95. There are a number of versions of the *Brut* in existence, often including differences in the detail.
16. Pierre de Fenin in *Sources and Interpretations* 119
17. Act 4, Scene 7
18. Prestwich 230
19. See McGlynn 124
20. *Sources and Interpretations* 164
21. Ibid 62

22. Ibid 113
23. *Gesta* 93
24. Curry ...*The Archer's Story,* 16
25. See for example the *Daily Mail* 27 October 2008
26. Quoted in McGlynn 90
27. Strickland/Hardy 185
28. McGlynn 152
29. See for example Prestwich 219
30. Ibid 240
31. Ibid 11
32. McGlynn 15
33. Thomas Basin; see *Sources and Interpretations* 190
34. Although a number of historians refer to the Oriflamme being at the battle, if it was it is never recovered and although it was possibly lost in the detritus of battle it would certainly have been a prize trophy for the English to try and recover when the victory was won.
35. McGlynn 128
36. Ibid 133
37. Barber 329

11 Agincourt: The Final Reckoning

1. Tito Livio in *Sources and Interpretations* 62
2. In *Sources and Interpretations* 72
3. Henry Paston-Beningfield in Curry ... *The Archers' Story* 133
4. Cooper 10
5. *Henry V,* Act 4, Scene 8
6. Cooper 124
7. Thomas Elmham in *Sources & Interpretations* 47
8. Oman 386
9. In *Sources & Interpretations* 291
10. It was by now not unusual for a man to decree that he should have a humble funeral as a sign of humility. That said, £100 was still a

sizeable sum. The 'National Archives Currency Converter' equates this to a sum not far short of £50,000 in modern money equivalents.

11. Mortimer 333

12. See Pugh 44

13. Curry in ... *The Archers' Story* 75

14. See Kerr 217, note 27

15. Kerr 224

16. *Gesta* 93

17. Daniell 138

18. Footnote reference in *Gesta* 93 Footnote reference in *Gesta* 93

19. From the *Chronique de Ruisseauville* in *Sources and Interpretations* 127

20. *Gesta* 93

21. Ibid 99

22. Tito Livio in *Sources and Interpretations* 62

23. A banneret was a knight who was allowed to carry his own rectangular banner. He was often awarded the privilege in return for his services in battle. See Bradbury *Medieval Warfare* 273. A banneret was socially at a higher level than a 'mere' knight and required a good deal of money though by this period in history the importance of the position was diminishing. However the title would not disappear until the 1640s; Prestwich 15. A banneret was paid twice as much as an ordinary knight and effectively provided the majority of what might be termed the 'officer corps' of the cavalry.

24. *Gesta* 97. Walsingham, 112, gives a figure of 3,069 French knights dead – a surprisingly precise figure – and also states that an unrecorded number of ordinary soldiers were slain; their lives clearly had less importance in the grand scheme of things. The Religieux – in *Sources and Interpretations* 110 – quotes 4,000 French dead and 1,400 knights and esquires taken prisoner.

25. The Religieux in *Sources and Interpretations* 110.

26. Cooper 6–9. The traditional site has not been definitively disproved but neither has it been proved. The recent conclusion that the visitor centre built on the supposed site of the Battle of Bosworth had actually probably been erected several miles away from the right spot

is a salutary reminder that nothing can be taken for granted without definitive proof; see e.g. the *Daily Telegraph* of 29 October 2009. It is certainly true to say that battlefield archaeology has not told us much about Agincourt.

27. Footnote in *Gesta* 97.
28. Barker 344
29. Footnote in *Gesta* 96
30. *Gesta* 97
31. Walsingham 412
32. In Strickland/Hardy 186
33. A thesis that is admirably presented by Christopher Smith in Chapter 7 of Curry ... *The Archers' Story*
34. Strickland/Hardy 407
35. Cooper 2
36. *Gesta* 95
37. Walsingham 409. Monstrelet quotes the equally unbelievable figure of 150,000 men though of course he may just have been copying the numbers from other chroniclers writing in the immediate aftermath of the battle.
38. See especially Table 1 in Curry ... *Sources and Interpretations* 12.
39. In *Sources and Interpretations,* 169

12 Agincourt: After the Battle

1. According again to Monstrelet's account, for example
2. Elmham makes reference to St George fighting in the battle on behalf of the English.
3. Cooper 62
4. Elmham in *Sources and Interpretations* 47
5. *Henry V,* Act 4, Scene 8
6. From the *Chronique de Ruisseauville* in *Sources and Interpretations* 127
7. *Sources and Interpretations* 171
8. McGlynn 137

9. Pseudo-Elmham in *Sources and Interpretations* 74

10. See Barker 228 who quotes evidence that shows that the Duke of Clarence's retinue would return at the end of the campaign with 742 men and 1,225 horses and the Duke of York's with 283 men and 329 horses.

11. Barker 339

12. Curry ... *A New History* 228.

13. *Gesta* 101. The 'new born' reference is from Le Fèvre and Waurin in *Sources and Interpretations* 166

14. Waurin and Le Fèvre in *Sources and Interpretations* 167

15. *Gesta* 101

16. The issue of ransoms is discussed in more detail in Curry ... *A New History* 242–5

17. Tito Livio in *Sources and Interpretations* 63

18. Nicolas ccclxxiii

19. Agincourt: ... *A New History* 239

20. Matthew Strickland in Curry: ... *The Archers' Story* 119

21. Although Shakespeare died on St George's Day, his exact birthdate is not known. However his baptism on 26 April seems to make a birthdate of 23 April quite plausible.

22. See *Sources and Interpretations* 96

23. Cooper 85

24. Although this is the day most widely accepted for the entry to London, it should be noted that a possibly contemporary newsletter in the Wiltshire County Record Office clearly dates the entry into London of the king to 30 November. See *Sources & Interpretations* 263

25. Psalm 20

26. The quote is from *Gesta* 111. Much of the detail in this section is taken directly from the *Gesta,* pages 101 to 113, where the chronicler goes to great lengths to describe the ceremonies.

27. See Starkey, *Music and Monarchy*

28. Information on the MPs may be found in Roskell, *The House of Commons*

29. Myers 155

30. Ibid 120

31. Nicolas ccccxi.

32. The Berry Herald in *Sources and Interpretations* 185
33. See Kenyon
34. In *Sources and Interpretations* 449

Epilogue

1. *Gesta* 123
2. Myers 120
3. Ibid 122
4. *Henry V,* Act V, Scene 2
5. Ibid
6. A BBC article of 25 July 2014 stated emphatically that 'when Joan of Arc saved France, she ensured that Agincourt would not, in the long run, be decisive'; http://www.bbc.com/news/magazine-28484146
7. Freud letter to Einstein, September 1932
8. Prestwick 185
9. Myers 121
10. Ibid 126
11. From the Brut Chronicle in Curry ... *The Hundred Years' War* 26
12. *Sources and Interpretations* 113
13. There were also parallels from more ancient history too: Roman legionaries often carried two stakes with them on campaign so that temporary fortifications could quickly be constructed from them.
14. As a salutary reminder even as recently as the Second World War the phrase 'there are no atheists in foxholes' gained currency.
15. Prestwich 281
16. Nicolas ccccx and Barker 365. There is also a record that one Englishman with the odd name of 'Olandyne' was killed fighting on the 'wrong side' at Agincourt; see Cooper 44
17. Cooper 57
18. Nicolas cccciii
19. In Shakespeare's *Henry V,* Act 4 Scene 7, Gower mentions the famous Macedonian warrior father and son.
20. Myers 122

BIBLIOGRAPHY

Allmand, Christopher, *Henry V* (Berkeley and Los Angeles: University of California Press, 1992)

Armstrong, Peter, *Stirling Bridge & Falkirk 1297–98* (Oxford: Osprey, 2003)

Barber, Richard, *The Knight and Chivalry* (London: Cardinal, 1974)

Barker, Juliet, *Agincourt – The King, The Campaign, The Battle* (London: Abacus, 2005)

Bennett, Matthew, *Agincourt 1415 – Triumph Against the Odds* (Oxford: Osprey, 1991)

Bradbury, Jim, *The Medieval Siege* (Suffolk: Boydell, 1998)

Bradbury, Jim, *The Routledge Companion to Medieval Warfare* (London: Routledge, 2004)

Brown, Colin, *Glory and B*llocks – The Truth Behind 10 Defining Events in British History* (London: Oneworld Publications, 2013)

Cooper, Stephen, *Agincourt; Myth and Reality 1415–2015* (Barnsley: Pen & Sword, 2014)

Curry, Anne, *The Hundred Years' War* (Oxford: Osprey, 2002)

Curry, Anne, *Agincourt – A New History* (Stroud: Tempus, 2005)

Curry, Anne, 'The Battle Speeches of Henry V', *Reading Medieval Studies*, 34 (2008)

Curry, Anne, *Agincourt 1415 – The Archers' Story* (Stroud: Tempus, 2008)

Curry, Anne, *The Battle of Agincourt – Sources and Interpretations* (Woodbridge, Boydell and Brewer, 2009)

Daniell, Christopher, *Death and Burial in Medieval England* (London: Routledge, 1997)

Goodall, John, *Portchester Castle* (English Heritage, 2008)

Jacob, E. F., *The Oxford History of England* (Oxford: Clarendon Press, 1997 edn)

Keen, Maurice (ed.), *Medieval Warfare – A History* (Oxford University Press, 1999)

Kenyon, John R., *Raglan Castle* (Cadw, 2003 edn)

Kerr, Wilfred Brenton, 'The English Soldier in the Campaign of Agincourt', *The Journal of the American Military Institute*, 4(4) (winter 1940)

Machen, Arthur, *The Bowmen and Other Legends of the War* (London: Simpkin, Marshall, Hamilton, Kent & Co. Ltd, 1915)

McGlynn, Sean, *By Sword and Fire* (London: Weidenfeld & Nicolson, 2008)

Mortimer, Ian, *1415 – Henry V's Year of Glory* (London: Vintage, 2010)

Myers, A. R., *England in the Late Middle Ages* (Harmondsworth: Penguin, 1974 reprint)

Nicolas, Sir Nicholas Harris, *History of the Battle of Agincourt, and of the Expedition of Henry the Fifth into France in 1415* (Brooke Street, London: Johnson, 1827)

Nicolle, David, *Medieval Warfare Sourcebook* (London: BCA, 1995)

Oman, Sir Charles, *A History of the Art of War in the Middle Ages, Volume Two* (London: Greenhill Books, 1991 (originally published 1885))

Preest, David (trans.), *The Chronica Maiora of Thomas Walsingham (1376–1422)* (Woodbridge: The Boydell Press, 2005)

Prestwich, Michael, *Armies and Warfare in the Middle Ages – The English Experience* (New Haven and London: Yale, 1999)

Priestley, E. J., *The Battle of Shrewsbury 1403* (Shrewsbury and Atcham Borough Council, 1979)

Pugh, T. B., *Henry V and the Southampton Plot* (Stroud: Alan Sutton, 1988)

Roskell, J. S., *The House of Commons 1386–1421* (Stroud: Alan Sutton, 1992)

Rothero, Christopher, *The Armies of Agincourt* (Oxford: Osprey, 1981)

Scarisbrick, J. J., *Henry VIII* (London: Methuen, 1976)

Starkey, David, *Music and Monarchy* (Acorn Media, 2013)

Stirland, A. J., *The Men of the Mary Rose – Raising the Dead* (Stroud: Sutton Publishing, 2008)

Strickland, Matthew and Hardy, Robert, *The Great Warbow* (Stroud: Sutton Publishing, 2005)

Taylor, Frank and Roskell, John S. (trans), *Gesta Henrici Quinti – The Deeds of Henry the Fifth* (London: Oxford University Press, 1975)

The Complete Works of William Shakespeare (London: Murrays Sales and Services, 1977)

Tuchman, Barbara W., *A Distant Mirror: The Calamitous Fourteenth Century* (London: BCA, 1978)

Wylie, James Hamilton, *The Reign of Henry the Fifth Volume 2* (Cambridge University Press, 1919)

ACKNOWLEDGEMENTS

To all those who have helped in the research and preparation of this book, my sincere thanks and gratitude in particular to my wife Angela for driving hundreds of miles across the French countryside in search of the story while I was trying to read a map and to my daughter Deyna for her hard work and research in support of the book. Also to Jonathan Reeve and others at Amberley Publishing for their assistance in commissioning and finalising it.

And last but not least my thanks go to the outstanding historians past and present who have meticulously researched the fascinating history behind what happened on that epic day, 25 October 1415, on a quiet, unprepossessing field in north-western France. In particular, Professor Curry's encyclopedic *Sources and Interpretations* (as well as several other fine works she has written on the subject) forms a crucial starting point for any would-be student of Agincourt as it brings together in one convenient comprehensive volume all the key sources, both near-contemporary and later, that tell from many different perspectives what happened there.

LIST OF ILLUSTRATIONS

1. A statue of King Henry V (central figure) in York Minster. (Author's collection)
2. Housed in Winchester Cathedral is the tomb effigy of Cardinal Henry Beaufort, Henry's uncle and a crucial political figure behind the Agincourt campaign. (Author's collection)
3. The Battle of Shrewsbury, 21 July 1403. Henry V, then Prince of Wales, fought bravely at the battle although only sixteen years old. (Courtesy of Jonathan Reeve JR1817b90fp5c 14001500)
4. Wolvesey Castle in Winchester, where a French delegation made a futile last-ditch effort to stop Henry V's invasion of France. (Author's collection)
5. Looking over Portsmouth Harbour from Portchester Castle and the Solent beyond where the English armada assembled. (Author's collection)
6. Fifteenth-century archers. Detail from the *Pageant* of Richard Beauchamp, Earl of Warwick, Captain of Calais, 1414. (Courtesy of Jonathan Reeve JR1851b90fp80Lc 14001500)
7. The keep of Portchester Castle, where Henry V first learned of the Southampton plot to replace him. (Author's collection)
8. The Micklegate, York. The quartered royal arms of England and France can be clearly seen. The head of the executed Henry Scrope, Lord Masham, one of the Southampton plotters, was placed over the gate. (Author's collection)
9. Before the launch of the Agincourt campaign there was a flurry of diplomacy between Henry V and the King of France Charles VI.

Here, Henry V receives a letter from Charles. (Courtesy of Jonathan Reeve JR1727b90fp81 14001500)

10. The West Gate, Southampton. Many of the troops departing for France marched through the city walls on to the waiting ships. (Author's collection)

11. Thomas, Duke of Bedford, Henry V's eldest brother. Thomas was invalided back to England after the siege of Harfleur. (Courtesy of Jonathan Reeve JR783b57fp348 14001450)

12. Chateau Gaillard, Richard the Lionheart's famous castle, which by Henry V's time formed part of the French defences of the Seine guarding Paris. (Author's collection)

13. The formidable castle at Arques which fired on Henry's army as it passed by. (Author's collection)

14. Looking down on the town of Arques from the castle, showing the rolling country through which Henry would soon pass. (Author's collection)

15. The battlefield of Crecy. The achievements of Edward III were a source of significant inspiration for Henry V. (Author's collection)

16. The castle at Péronne, a major part of the French defences of the Somme. (Author's collection)

17. A fifteenth-century siege, manuscript illumination. (Courtesy of Jonathan Reeve JR1871b46fpvc 14001450)

18. The Somme at Bethencourt, one of the crossing points that Henry's army discovered which allowed them to ford the river. (Author's collection)

19. The church at Athies. The English army rested for a day here to recuperate after their long march. (Author's collection)

20. Dartmoor Cemetery near Albert. Henry V's army passed close to this spot, now the resting place of 760 First World War British and Commonwealth soldiers, including Private J. T. Bartlett. (Author's collection)

21. Frévent, where the Duke of York and the English vanguard stopped shortly before Agincourt was reached. (Author's collection)

22. The Ternoise near Blagny, where the English managed to fight their way across. (Author's collection)

36. The tomb of the Count of Eu in the family vault in the collegiate church in the town. The count spent many years after Agincourt as an English captive. (Author's collection)

37. The date '1838', scratched in the walls of Agincourt church, allegedly marks the spot where human remains unearthed by Lieutenant-Colonel John Woodford on the battlefield were reinterred. (Author's collection)

38. The battlefield memorial at Agincourt at the bottom of the road from Maisoncelle to Tramecourt. (Author's collection)

39. Tretower Castle in the Welsh Marches, ancestral home of the Vaughans, whose family members fought and died alongside Henry V at Agincourt. (Author's collection)

40. A statue of Joan of Arc from Winchester Cathedral. Her efforts helped to undo much of what had been achieved in France by Henry V. (Author's collection)

INDEX

Index

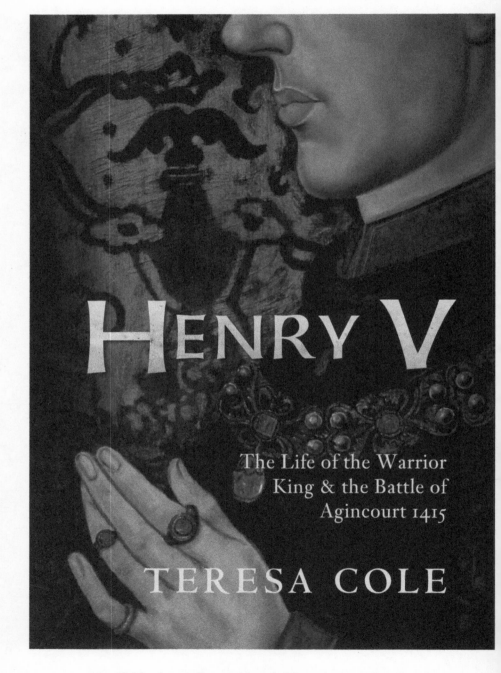